BTEC National MATHEMATICS for Technicians

3rd edition

3rd edition

BTEC National MATHEMATICS for Technicians

Graham Taylor
Alan Fuller
Alex Greer

Nelson Thornes
a Wolters Kluwer business

First published in 1982 by:
Stanley Thornes (Publishers) Ltd
Second edition 1994

Third edition published in 2004 by:
Nelson Thornes Ltd
Delta Place
27 Bath Road
CHELTENHAM
GL53 7TH
United Kingdom

08 / 10 9 8 7 6 5 4

A catalogue record for this book is available from the British Library

ISBN 978 0 7487 7949 9

Page make-up by Tech-Set Ltd, Gateshead, Tyne and Wear

Printed and bound in Spain by GraphyCems

Contents

About this Book

The Specifications

This book covers the core unit Mathematics for Technicians at BTEC National level. This unit, revised to cover the latest specifications, is used for electronics, construction, mechanical engineering and general basic science.

The book broadly follows the unit structure learning outcomes:

1. Algebra
2. Trigonometry and Graphs
3. Statistics
4. Calculus

Chapters on approximation and accuracy, the scientific calculator, units and graphs are included as we feel that a knowledge of these will help you in all your studies – not only in Mathematics.

Readers will also welcome extensive revision of basic algebraic techniques. In addition the treatment of trigonometry, statistics and calculus assumes no previous knowledge of these topics.

Assessment

BTEC qualifications are awarded in three grades:

Pass	This shows that you have a basic knowledge and understanding,
Merit	This shows that you have a sound knowledge and understanding,
Distinction	This requires that you have an in-depth knowledge and understanding.

Authors' note

We have tried to follow a sympathetic approach to basic maths as required by Engineers, together with application to real engineering problems.

We hope you will enjoy using this book, and find it a useful reference after you have finished your studies.

Approximation and Accuracy 1

Decimal place – significant figures – rounded numbers – accuracy in arithmetic operations – implied accuracy relevant to given data – truncation

In engineering the majority of numbers are not exact or discrete. An example of an exact number would be the thirteen persons employed by the local motor main agents. This number is exact or discrete, and therefore cannot be an approximation. It is often necessary to approximate any non-exact answers we calculate, to the level of precision required. This will depend on the particular application: for instance, if we are ordering raw materials it is likely that measurements to the nearest millimetre would be good enough. However, when manufacturing a component for a motor vehicle engine we may well be thinking in terms of thousandths of a millimetre.

ACCURACY OF NUMBERS

There are two principal methods of expressing the accuracy of a number. These are using either decimal places or significant figures, together with rounded numbers.

Decimal Places (abbreviated to 'd.p.')

These refer to the number of figures which follow (i.e. after or to the right of) the decimal point.

Thus: 35.1 has one d.p. and 2.402 has three d.p.

Significant Figures (abbreviated to 's.f.')

These are the number of figures, counted from the left to the right, starting with the first *non-zero* figure, unless stated otherwise.

Thus: 2700, 35.0, 0.89 and 0.0082 each have two s.f.

354, 7.21 and 0.000 234 each have three s.f.

5 782 100 and 0.537 91 each have five s.f.

Note that zero figures at the right hand end are not included in the count, as in 2700, 35.0 and 5 782 100 mentioned above.

ROUNDED NUMBERS

These are obtained by the process of 'rounding' or 'rounding off' and enable a degree of accuracy to be stated.

Thus: rounding 31.63 gives 31.6 correct to three s.f. and rounding 31.68 gives 31.7 correct to three s.f.

Rule for Rounding

Working from right to left figures are discarded in turn.

If the discarded figure is less than 5 the preceding figure is not altered – in the first example given above the 3 is discarded and the 6 is unaltered. If the discarded figure is greater than (or equal to) 5 then the preceding figure is increased by one – in the example given above the 8 is discarded and the preceding figure 6 is increased to 7.

Thus:	0.472	becomes	0.47	correct to 2 s.f.
		or	0.5	correct to 1 s.f
Also	24.0926	becomes	24.093	correct to 3 d.p.
		or	24.09	correct to 2 d.p.
		or	24.1	correct to 1 d.p.

An exception to the rule is shown below:

Now	0.008 246	
may be stated as	0.008 25	correct to 3 s.f.; alternatively to 5 d.p.
or	0.0082	correct to 2 s.f.; alternatively to 4 d.p.
or	0.008	correct to 1 s.f.; alternatively to 3 d.p.

Care must be taken to ensure that rounding is carried out directly from the original number – thus in the above case 0.008 246 rounds to 0.0082 correct to 2 s.f.

It would be wrong to round successively to 3 s.f. and then to 2 s.f.: the second rounding of 0.008 25 would give an incorrect 0.0083 !

Note: when rounding whole number amounts, 'discarded' figures preceding the decimal point must be replaced by zeros.

Thus:	1479	becomes	1480	(*not* 148) correct to 3 s.f.
		or	1500	(*not* 15) correct to 2 s.f.
		or	1000	(*not* 1) correct to 1 s.f.

Consider an attendance of 54 276 at a league soccer match. This is as precise as could have been obtained, no doubt from the turnstiles at entry.

Now 54 276 may be stated as	54 280	correct to 4 s.f.
or	54 300	correct to 3 s.f.
or	54 000	correct to 2 s.f.
or even	50 000	correct to 1 s.f.

As far as press reports are concerned, 54 000 may well be considered to be good enough. So when the papers state an attendance of 54 000 a 2 s.f. accuracy is implied (although it would not be mentioned!).

Exercise 1.1

Write down the following numbers correct to the number of significant figures stated:

1) 24.865 82	**a)** to 6	**b)** to 4	**c)** to 2
2) 0.008 3571	**a)** to 4	**b)** to 3	**c)** to 2
3) 4.978 48	**a)** to 5	**b)** to 3	**c)** to 1
4) 21.987 to 2			
5) 35.603 to 4			
6) 28.387 617	**a)** to 5	**b)** to 2	
7) 4.149 76	**a)** to 5	**b)** to 4	**c)** to 3
8) 9.2048 to 3			

Write down the following numbers correct to the number of decimal places stated:

9) 2.138 87	**a)** to 4	**b)** to 3	**c)** to 2
10) 25.165	**a)** to 2	**b)** to 1	
11) 0.003 988	**a)** to 5	**b)** to 4	**c)** to 3
12) 7.2039	**a)** to 3	**b)** to 2	**c)** to 1
13) 0.7259	**a)** to 3	**b)** to 2	

ERRORS IN NUMBERS

In technology it is important that we know, and are able to state clearly, the exact accuracy of a value. A convenient way is to state the amount of allowable error in a measurement.

A typical, non-exact, measurement is a person's height of 117.8 cm (an approximation to 4 s.f., or to the nearest $\frac{1}{10}$ cm).

Now consider an electrical resistance measured as 52 ohm, to the nearest ohm, and considered correct to 2 s.f. The number 52 could have been obtained by rounding any number between the lowest value of 51.5 and up to the highest value of 52.5. These extremes are $52 - 0.5$ and $52 + 0.5$ and the value of the resistance would be stated as 52 ± 0.5 ohm. This shows, at a glance, the maximum possible error is 0.5 greater, or 0.5 smaller, than 52. This does not mean that the error is bound to be as great at 0.5 ohm – it may be considerably less, but it certainly cannot be any more.

Similarly, 7.49 gram is considered accurate to 3 s.f., or to $\frac{1}{100}$ gram: this would come from rounding a number between the extremes of 7.485 and 7.495 and would be given as 7.49 ± 0.005 gram.

Also 0.1370 mV given accurate to the nearest $\frac{1}{10\,000}$ mV is also considered accurate to 4 s.f. You should note how the extra zero is included to indicate accuracy greater than would be implied by 0.137 mV which is only correct to $\frac{1}{1000}$ mV and only accurate to 3 s.f. Now 0.1370 mV would come from rounding between the extremes of 0.136 95 mV and 0.137 05 mV and would be stated as $0.1370 \pm 0.000\,05$ mV.

ABSOLUTE AND RELATIVE ACCURACY

Suppose we are told that a spring balance has an error of 1 kg. This is an actual or true error value and is known as the absolute error.

How important is this? Well, this will depend on the mass being measured. It is unlikely that anyone would be bothered when the balance was used for 50 kg of potatoes, but when used for 2 kg of tomatoes such an error would not be acceptable.

In each case, we are comparing the absolute error value with another measured value. We are, in fact, considering the error relative to the mass measured. You will now see the importance of a relative value.

Absolute Accuracy

Absolute accuracy refers to the maximum absolute errors of a number. Thus for the 52 ohm mentioned earlier, which if written in full is 52 ± 0.5 ohm, the maximum absolute error is 0.5 ohm. Thus, the absolute accuracy of 52 ohm is 0.5 ohm.

Relative Accuracy

The word relative means that the absolute error of a number must be compared with the number itself. This is usually given as a percentage using the expression:

$$\text{relative error} = \frac{\text{absolute error}}{\text{number}} \times 100$$

Relative accuracy is the phrase we use for the maximum relative error of a number.

So referring to the 52 ohm and the 0.5 ohm maximum absolute error:

$$\text{maximum relative error} = \frac{0.5}{52} \times 100$$
$$= 0.96\% \text{ correct to 2 d.p.}$$

Thus, the relative accuracy of 52 ohm to the nearest ohm is 0.96% correct to 2 d.p.

Accuracy in Addition and Subtraction

A contractor has five vehicles. If he sells two he is left with three. So in this case of $5 - 2 = 3$ the answer 3 is exact, and there is no error since the numbers 5 and 2 are discrete.

However, let us consider the result of adding electrical resistances of 52 ± 0.5 ohm and 36 ± 0.5 ohm.

We may state this problem as $(52 \pm 0.5) + (36 \pm 0.5)$

$$\begin{aligned}\text{Now the greatest answer} &= \text{the greatest value of } 52 \pm 0.5 \\ &\quad + \text{the greatest value of } 36 \pm 0.5 \\ &= (52 + 0.5) + (36 + 0.5) \\ &= (52 + 36) + (0.5 + 0.5) \\ &= (88 + 1.0) \text{ or } 89\end{aligned}$$

$$\text{Similarly the smallest answer} = (88 - 1.0) \text{ or } 87$$

So the final result of adding the resistances lies between 87 and 89 ohm, and would be given as 88 ± 1.0 ohm, which has a maximum absolute error of 1.0 ohm.

> In general, when adding and subtracting numbers the maximum absolute error of the results may be found by adding the maximum absolute errors of the original numbers

$$\begin{aligned}\text{Thus } 623 + 56.3 \text{ implies} &\quad (623 \pm 0.5) + (56.3 \pm 0.05) \\ \text{giving a result} &\quad (623 + 56.3) \pm (0.5 + 0.05) \\ \text{or} &\quad 679.3 \pm 0.55\end{aligned}$$

$$\begin{aligned}\text{Now } 27.24 - 9.3 \text{ implies} &\quad (27.24 \pm 0.005) - (9.3 \pm 0.05) \\ \text{giving a result} &\quad (27.24 - 9.3) \pm (0.005 + 0.05) \\ \text{or} &\quad 17.94 \pm 0.055\end{aligned}$$

Note that even when the original numbers are being *subtracted* the maximum absolute error (0.055 in the above example) is still obtained by *adding* the given individual maximum absolute errors.

Accuracy in Multiplication and Division

Consider finding the area of a rectangle with sides measured as 67 mm and 62 mm. Each of the numbers will be considered accurate to two significant figures and so the problem may be stated as:

$$\begin{aligned}
\text{Area} &= (67 \pm 0.5) \times (62 \pm 0.5) \\
\text{Now the greatest area} &= (\text{the greatest value of } 67 \pm 0.5) \\
&\quad \times (\text{the greatest value of } 62 \pm 0.5) \\
&= 67.5 \times 62.5 \\
&= 4218.75 \\
\text{And the smallest area} &= (\text{the smallest value of } 67 \pm 0.5) \\
&\quad \times (\text{the smallest value of } 62 \pm 0.5) \\
&= 66.5 \times 61.5 \\
&= 4089.75
\end{aligned}$$

If we examine these two extremes, we see that only the four thousand figure is guaranteed in the value of the area.

Now it is generally accepted that:

> When multiplying and dividing numbers the answer should not be given to an accuracy greater than the least accurate of the given numbers

If we simply calculate 67×62 we get 4154.

Here both the given lengths are to the same accuracy, so in this particular case either may be taken to be the least accurate, namely to two significant figures. Thus, after rounding, we have the area as 4200 mm^2, which would be an acceptable result.

You will possibly grumble at this answer and point out that even this is not strictly correct – and you would be right! Anyway, you now realise how wrong it is to give results to an accuracy which cannot be justified by the given data: we are all guilty of this from time to time so beware!

Consider also $\dfrac{5.73 \times 21}{0.6243}$ the result of which is 192.743 87 from a calculator.

The least accurate of the three given numbers is 21 which has a two significant figure accuracy. Hence, the answer must not be stated any more accurately than this: namely 190 obtained by rounding 192.743 87 correct to two significant figures.

Implied Accuracy

Suppose we decided to check graphically, by counting the squares, the area of the rectangle in the preceding section. Sides of 67 mm and 62 mm would be measured out, possibly with a rule, on squared paper. It is likely that we should try for, and achieve, a measuring accuracy to one tenth of a millimetre – thus the area we would be checking would be 67.0 mm by 62.0 mm. Now, since the calculated result of 67×62 is 4154, the area being checked would be 4150 mm^2 after rounding to three significant figures, which is the accuracy of 67.0 mm and 62.0 mm.

With this in mind, unless there is a very good reason otherwise, a three significant figure accuracy is generally accepted on this type of data. We are really covering up for our inability to state the original data to its correct accuracy e.g. 67 mm which we should have given as 67.0 mm.

Consider, also, the problem of calculating the angles of a triangle with the sides given as 6, 8 and 9 m respectively. An accuracy of one significant figure (to which these dimensions are given) would only allow us to give the calculated angles such as 10°, 20°, 30°, ... etc. Again, we would assume the dimensions should have been given as 6.00 m, 8.00 m and 9.00 m, and thus give the results to a three significant figure accuracy.

Truncation or Cutting Off

Some calculators 'truncate' or 'cut-off' figures in their displays after computation. For instance, in an eight-figure display, the result of 5 divided by 3 would be shown as 1.666 666 666 (most modern calculators would round the result to show 1.666 666 667). If truncation does occur each time successive computations are performed then an accumulating error may be introduced.

Exercise 1.2

In the questions below relative accuracies should be given to 3 s.f.

What are the greatest and least values, and also the relative accuracy, of:

1) 64 ± 0.5

2) 2469 ± 5

3) 3.07 ± 0.005

4) 0.6 ± 0.05

What are the greatest and least values, and the absolute accuracy of the results, of:

5) $(26 \pm 0.5) + (3.4 \pm 0.05)$

6) $(0.56 \pm 0.005) + (0.7 \pm 0.05)$

7) $(5.6 \pm 0.05) - (2.9 \pm 0.05)$

8) $(0.78 \pm 0.005) - (0.034 \pm 0.0005)$

9) A measurement has been taken of 39.07 km to the nearest $\frac{1}{100}$ km. State this in conventional form together with the absolute and relative accuracies.

10) A rectangle has sides of length 0.372 m and 1.238 m both measured to the nearest millimetre. State both these measurements in conventional form. Find also the maximum and minimum values of the perimeter of the rectangle, together with the absolute and relative accuracies of its nominal value.

11) Find the absolute and relative accuracies of the result of $(2.3 \pm 0.05) - (0.76 \pm 0.003) + (64 \pm 0.5)$.

12) A current has been measured correct to $\frac{1}{100}$ A but has been listed incorrectly as 7 A. How should it have been listed, and what is the maximum absolute error and the relative accuracy?

13) Careless recording gave the lengths of the sides of the triangle as 3 mm, 4 mm and 5 mm when in actual fact they had been measured to the nearest $\frac{1}{100}$ mm. What are the greatest and least values of the perimeter of the triangle? Also, what are the absolute and relative accuracies of the perimeter value?

The Scientific Calculator 2

Roughs checks – keyboard layout and operation – display – calculation sequence – memories – numbers in standard form – worked examples involving square root, 'pi', power keys – modes – trigonometrical functions – nesting a polynomial

The calculator is an important tool for engineers and so it is important that we are familiar with its use. It enables us to complete numerical calculations quickly, accurately and reliably. However, we all make mistakes and we should therefore be able to recognise a blatantly wrong answer. How? By getting into the habit of doing a rough check first so you will have some idea of the result.

ROUGH CHECKS

When using a calculator it is essential for you to do a rough check in order to obtain an approximate result. Any error, however small it may seem, in carrying out a sequence of operations will result in a wrong answer.

Suppose, for instance, that you had £1000 in the bank and then withdrew £97.82. The bank staff then used a calculator to find how much money you had left in your account – they calculated that £1000 less £978.2 left only £21.80 credited to you. You would be extremely annoyed and probably point out to them that a rough check of £1000 less £100 would leave £900, and that if this had been done much embarrassment would have been avoided.

The 'small' mistake was to get the decimal point in the wrong place when recording the money withdrawn, which is typical of errors we all make from time to time. You should get in the habit of doing a **rough check** on any calculation **before using your machine**. The advantage of a rough check answer before the actual calculation avoids the possibility of forgetting to do it in the excitement of obtaining a machine result. Also your rough check will not be influenced by the result obtained on your calculator.

KEYBOARD LAYOUT AND OPERATION

There are many different calculators on the market but they all have similar functions. This section will look at the common features which apply to most scientific calculators. However, each calculator is supplied with its own instructions and you should refer to these as you work through the examples in this chapter.

Don't be put off by complicated instructions, perhaps under a heading like 'Before getting started' which may include notes on Modes, Input capacity, Corrections, Replays and Error locators. These may be important to you as you use the machine for more complicated work, but to start with just go ahead and follow through this chapter. Note: Some operations may differ slightly from those shown here, but a typical keyboard layout is shown in Fig. 2.1.

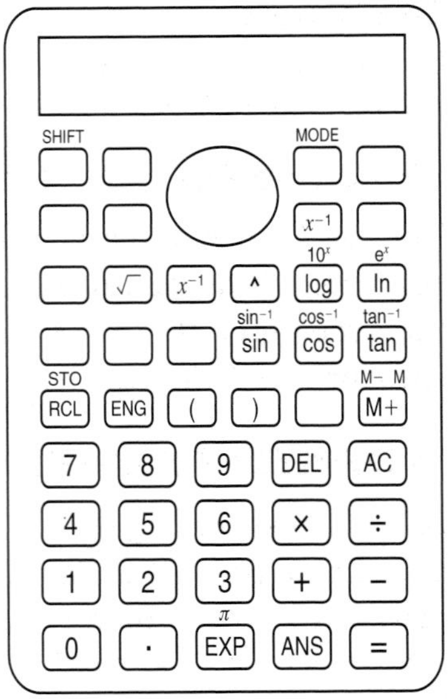

Fig. 2.1

The following are the figure keys:

[1] [2] [3] [4] [5] [6] [7] [8] [9] [0]

The other more common keys are summarised as follows:

[·] decimal point key.

[EXP] exponential key – allows entry of numbers in standard form (e.g. 1.46×10^3).

[DEL] clear key – enables an incorrect entry to be deleted (either a figure or an operation) if pressed immediately afterwards.

[AC] all clear key – clears machine of all numbers – except memory contents.

[+] [–] [×] [÷] [=] arithmetical operation keys.

[STO] memory in key – enters a number on display into the memory, erasing any number previously in the memory.

[M+] or [M–] adds to, or subtracts from, the previous content of memory.

[RCL] memory recall key – enables content of memory to be shown on display.

[x^{-1}] pressed after a number gives its reciprocal (e.g. $\frac{1}{2}$ to 2, or 4 to 0.25).

[x^2] pressed after a number squares it.

[√] pressed before a number gives its square root.

[∧] power key: typical use is $x \wedge y$ giving a value of x to index y (i.e. x^y).

[π] 'pi' key - gives the numerical value of π.

[sin] [cos] [tan] trigonometric function keys pressed before an angle value gives the sine, cosine or tangent.

[SHIFT] or [INV] is pressed before another key in order to obtain the function written (usually in orange or red) above that key.

Displays

Some calculators have a two-line display. The first line shows the problem as you have entered it and the second line gives the result.

How the Machine Tackles a Calculation Sequence

The machine will carry out operations strictly in the order Brackets, Divide, Multiply, Add and Subtract. (See 'BODMAS' in Chapter 4.) So if you enter $9 - 6 \div 3$ the correct answer will be 7 and **not** 1 !
Also for $7 + 5\,(3 - 1)$ the correct answer, from $7 + 5 \times 2$, is 17 (**not** 24).

WORKED EXAMPLES

After first switching on the calculator, or commencing a fresh problem, you should press the [AC] key. This ensures that all figures entered previously have been erased, except in the memories, and will not interfere with new data to be entered.

The memories are automatically cleared when new numbers are entered using the [STO] key.
Numbers are entered one digit at a time. So strictly 32.963 should be shown on the entry sequence as [3] [2] [·] [9] [6] [3]
However, for convenience, we shall show this entry as [32.963]

EXAMPLE 2.1

Find the value of $\dfrac{34.7 - 28.8}{6.4}$

A rough check gives $\dfrac{35 - 30}{6} \approx \dfrac{5}{6} \approx 1$

We must not enter $34.7 - 28.8 \div 6.4$ because the machine will do the division first.

One way is to do the calculation in two stages:–

[AC] [34.7] [−] [28.8] [=] [÷] [6.4] [=] and the display shows 0.921 875

Strictly the answer should not be given to an accuracy greater than the least accurate of the given numbers, here 6.4 which has two significant figures.

Thus the result is 0.92 correct to two significant figures, which is in the vicinity of our rough check.

However in most engineering problems you will not often be wrong if you give answers to three significant figures – this is consistent with the accuracy of much of the data (such as ultimate tensile strengths of materials). There are exceptions, of course, such as certain machine shop problems which may require a much greater degree of accuracy.

Another way to enter the problem is to use brackets to 'tell' the machine to do the sum inside the brackets first, giving the same result.

[AC] [(] [34.7] [−] [28.8] [)] [÷] [6.4] [=]

MEMORIES

MEMORIES are 'pigeon holes' where numbers may be stored and used when needed. Some machines only have one memory M whilst others have several. The instructions will tell you how to access these – a typical instruction is [51.9] [SHIFT] [STO] [B] which will store 51.9 in memory 'B', first clearing out any other figures which may have been there – rather like a cookoo does when putting its egg into another bird's nest.

[M+] adds to, and [M−] subtracts from, a number in a memory,

whilst [RCL] [M] reads the contents of a memory.

EXAMPLE 2.2

Evaluate $$(6.1 + 1.72)^2 + \frac{1}{0.1375} - \frac{11.36}{-3.2}$$

A rough check gives $$(6 + 2)^2 + \frac{1}{0.1} - \frac{12}{-3} \approx 64 + 10 + 4 \approx 78$$

We will only use one memory, [M] and [M+] to store a number. Thus our sequence of operations is

[AC] [(] [6.1] [+] [1.72] [)] [x^2] [Min] [0.1375] [x^{-1}] [M+] [11.36] [÷] [−]

[3.2] [M−] [RCL] [M]

The display gives: 71.975 127 and so a reasonable answer is 72.0 correct to three significant figures.

Note the rough check shows that the answer is reasonable, being of the correct order.

NUMBERS IN STANDARD FORM

If we have a very large or very small number, it can be difficult to deal with for a number of reasons. First, if it has more than eight digits (often mostly zeros) it may not be possible to enter it directly into a calculator. Then, the greater the number of digits, the more likely it is that errors will be made in manipulating the figures. So we show numbers like this in standard form. This means they are all displayed in the same way: a single digit 1 to 9 followed by the decimal places which are then multiplied by a power of ten.

Let us consider $589\,000\,000\,000 = 5.89 \times 100\,000\,000\,000$
$= 5.89 \times 10^{11}$ in standard form

This tells us that the original number is 5.89 with the decimal point moved eleven places to the right.

Another example is $0.000\,001\,2763 = 1.2763 \div 1\,000\,000$
$= 1.2763 \div 10^6$
$= 1.2763 \times 10^{-6}$

Here the index is negative, and so we must move the decimal point six places to the left to make 1.2763 smaller.

EXAMPLE 2.3

Find the value of $6\,857\,000 \times 0.001\,19 \times 85.3$

For the rough check, numbers which contain as many figures as these are better considered in standard form (remembering that 10 is the same as 10^1):

$(6.857 \times 10^6) \times (1.19 \times 10^{-3}) \times (8.53 \times 10)$

or approximately $(7 \times 10^6) \times (1 \times 10^{-3}) \times (10 \times 10^1) \approx 7 \times 1 \times 10 \times 10^{6-3+1}$
$\approx 70 \times 10^4$
$\approx 7 \times 10^5$

The sequence of operations is:

[AC] [6857000] [×] [0.00119] [×] [85.3] [=]

The display will show 696 033.499. The least accurate of the given numbers has 3 s.f. Thus, the answer is 696 000 or 6.96×10^5 correct to 3 s.f.

An alternative is to enter the numbers in standard form using the exponent key [EXP] in the sequence:

[AC] [6.857] [EXP] [6] [×] [1.19] [EXP] [−] [3] [×] [8.53] [EXP] [1] [=]

giving the same result – check this for yourself.

The sequence used in a problem such as this would be personal choice, but if the problem includes numbers with powers of 10 the latter sequence is usually better.

Exercise 2.1

Evaluate the following; take care to give the answers to an accuracy determined by the given data.

1) $45.6 + 3.5 - 21.4 - 14.6$

2) $-23.94 - 6.93 + 1.92 + 17.60$

3) $\dfrac{40.72 \times 3.86}{5.73}$

4) $\dfrac{4.86 \times 0.008\,34 \times 0.640}{0.860 \times 0.934 \times 21.7}$

5) $\dfrac{57.3 \times 64.29 \times 3.17}{64.2}$

6) $\dfrac{32.2}{6.45 + 7.29 - 21.3}$

7) $\dfrac{1}{\frac{1}{3} + \frac{1}{4} + \frac{1}{5}}$ to 2 d.p.

8) $\dfrac{3.76 + 42.2}{1.60 + 0.86}$

9) $\dfrac{4.82 + 7.93}{-0.730 \times 6.92}$

10) $9.38(4.86 + 7.60 \times 1.89^3)$

11) $4.93^2 - 6.86^2$

12) $(4.93 + 6.86)(4.93 - 6.86)$

13) $\dfrac{1}{6.3^2 + 9.6^2}$

14) $\dfrac{3.864^2 + 9.62}{3.74 - 8.62^2}$

15) $\dfrac{9.5}{(6.4 \times 3.2) - (6.7 \times 0.9)}$

16) $1 - \dfrac{5.0}{3.6 + 7.49}$

17) $\dfrac{1}{6} - \dfrac{1}{5}(4.6)^2$

18) $\dfrac{6.4}{20.2}\left(3.94^2 - \dfrac{5.7 + 4.9}{6.7 - 3.2}\right)$

19) $\dfrac{3.64^3 + 5.6^2 - (1/0.085)}{9.76 + 3.4 - 2.9}$

20) $\dfrac{6.54(7.69 \times 10^{-5})}{0.643^2 - 79.3(3.21 \times 10^{-4})}$

EXAMPLES INVOLVING SQUARE ROOT, 'PI' , AND POWER KEYS

EXAMPLE 2.4

The period, T seconds (the time for a complete swing), of a simple pendulum is given by the formula $T = 2\pi\sqrt{\dfrac{l}{g}}$ where l m is its length and g m/s^2 is the acceleration due to gravity.

Find the value of T if $l = 1.37$ m and $g = 9.81$ m/s^2.

Substituting the given values into the formula we have $T = 2\pi\sqrt{\dfrac{1.37}{9.81}}$

The rough check gives: $T \approx 2 \times 3\sqrt{\dfrac{1}{9}} \approx 2 \times 3 \times \dfrac{1}{3} \approx 2$ s

The square root key [√] will only work on the number which follows immediately, 1.37 in this case. Thus we use brackets so that the square root will work on the result of $(1.37 \div 9.81)$. Hence the sequence of operations:

[AC] [2] [×] [π] [×] [√] [(] [1.37] [÷] [9.81] [)] [=] giving 2.348 04

Thus the value of T is 2.35 seconds, correct to 3 s.f.

Alternatively try using the sequence for $T = 2\pi\dfrac{\sqrt{1.37}}{\sqrt{9.81}}$ (gives same result)

EXAMPLE 2.5

The relationship between the luminosity I of a metal filament lamp and the voltage V is given by the equation $I = aV^4$ where a is a constant. Find the value of I if $a = 9 \times 10^{-7}$ and $V = 60$.

Substituting the given values into the equation we have $I = (9 \times 10^{-7})60^4$

The rough check gives

$I \approx (10 \times 10^{-7})(6 \times 10)^4 \approx 10^{-6} \times 6^4 \times 10^4 \approx 10^{-2} \times 36 \times 36$

and if we approximate by putting 30×40 instead of 36×36 then

$I \approx 10^{-2} \times 30 \times 40 \approx 10^{-2} \times 1200 \approx 12$

The sequence of operations:

[AC] [(] [9] [EXP] [−] [7] [)] [×] [(] [60] [^] [4] [)] [=] gives 11.664

Thus the value of I is 11.7 correct to 3 s.f.

It is possible for one make of calculator to complete the calculation successfully without putting in any brackets at all. But be careful and if you are not fully familiar with your machine take a few more steps.

EXAMPLE 2.6

The law of expansion of a gas is given by the expression $pV^{1.2} = k$ where p is the pressure, V is the volume, and k is a constant. Find the value of k if $p = 0.8 \times 10^6$ and $V = 0.2$.

Substituting the given values into the formula, then $k = (0.8 \times 10^6) \times 0.2^{1.2}$

The rough check gives

$$k \approx 1 \times 10^6 \times \left(\frac{2}{10}\right)^{1.2} \approx 10^6 \times \frac{2^{1.2}}{10^{1.2}} \approx 10^6 \times \frac{3}{30} \approx 1 \times 10^5$$

Since it is difficult to assess the approximate value of a decimal number to an index, it becomes simpler to express the decimal number as a fraction using whole numbers. In this case it is convenient to express 0.2 as $\frac{2}{10}$. We guess the rough value of $2^{1.2}$, since we know that $2^1 = 2$ and $2^2 = 4$. Similarly, we judge the value of $10^{1.2}$ as being between $10^1 = 10$ and $10^2 = 100$. The more practice you have in doing calculations of this type, the more accurate your guess will be.

The sequence of operations:

[AC] [(] [0.8] [EXP] [6] [)] [×] [(] [0.2] [^] [1.2] [)] [=] gives 115 964.7

Thus the value of k is 116 000 or 1.16×10^5 correct to 3 s.f.

MODES

In computer work the word default means the 'fall-back' condition, position, number or instruction which will automatically be used unless an order is given to over-ride it.

The basic set-up for normal calculations uses default modes. These are present each time the machine is switched on.

Special mode positions must be set for more unusual work e.g. using grades for angles instead of the usual degrees; or for doing statistical calculations rather than ordinary arithmetic.

Each machine will have instructions telling you what to do.

EXAMPLES INVOLVING TRIGONOMETRICAL FUNCTIONS

EXAMPLE 2.7

Find angle A if $$\sin A = \frac{3.68 \sin 42^\circ}{5.26}$$

Rough check: It is always difficult to find an approximate answer for a calculation involving trigonometrical functions. However, we may use a 'backwards substitution' method which is carried out after an answer has been obtained.

On most calculators there is a mode selection which for angles may be set at either DEG (degrees), RAD (radians), or GRAD (grades – a grade being one-hundredth of a right angle, used more on the continent). In this example the angles are in degrees and so we may wish to check that the mode is set to the DEG position. Most machines have DEG as the default for angles.

Thus to find the value of the right hand side (RHS) a sequence is:

[AC] [3.68] [×] [sin] [42] [÷] [5.26] [=] giving 0.4681, the value of $\sin A$

Hence A is the angle whose sine is 0.4681 and is written as either

$$A = \text{inv}\sin 0.4681 \qquad \text{or} \qquad A = \sin^{-1} 0.4681$$

Both notations are commonly used and will depend on the calculator.

So we may use either the sequence [INV] [sin] [0.4681] [=]

or alternatively [SHIFT] [sin] [0.4681] [=]

both giving 27.911. Thus angle $A = 27.9^\circ$ correct to 3 s.f.

Answer check: From our calculations we have $\sin 27.9^\circ = \dfrac{3.68 \sin 42^\circ}{5.26}$

Now we may rearrange this expression to give $\sin 42^\circ = \dfrac{5.26 \sin 27.9^\circ}{3.68}$

Thus if we find the value of the right hand side of this new expression, it should give the value of sin 42° if the value of angle $A = 27.9^\circ$ is correct.

The sequence of operations is similar to that given for the original calculation. Do it for yourself and check the result.

NESTING (OR STACKING) A POLYNOMIAL

A polynomial in x is an expression containing a sum of terms, each term being a power of x.

A typical polynomial is $ax^4 + bx^3 + cx^2 + dx + e$

where a, b, c, d and e are constants.

The polynomial may be factorised successively as follows:

$$\begin{aligned} ax^4 + bx^3 + cx^2 + dx + e &= (ax + b)x^3 + cx^2 + dx + e \\ &= \{(ax + b)x + c\}x^2 + dx + e \\ &= [\{(ax + b)x + c\}x + d]x + e \end{aligned}$$

The opening bracket symbols [{(are usually omitted and all the remaining closure brackets are shown in the same form. Thus the polynomial looks like:

$$ax + b)x + c)x + d)x + e$$

This is called the nested (or stacked) form of the polynomial. When evaluating its value **we must always work from *left* to *right*.**

EXAMPLE 2.8

Find the value of $y = 5x^3 - 7x^2 + 8x - 5$ when $x = 3.32$

The nested form gives $y = 5x - 7)x + 8)x - 5$

When $x = 3.32$ then $y = 5 \times 3.32 - 7)3.32 + 8)3.32 - 5$

Working from *left* to *right* a sequence of operation is :

[AC] [3.32] [Min] [×] [5] [−] [7] [=] [×] [RCL] [M] [+] [8] [=]
[×] [RCL] [M] [−] [5] [=] giving 127.37504

Thus $y = 127$ correct to 3 s.f.

Note that if the polynomial is not nested it would be necessary to evaluate

$$5(3.32)^3 - 7(3.32)^2 + 8(3.32) - 5$$

Try this for yourself and you will appreciate the advantage of nesting.

Exercise 2.2

Remember the accuracy to which you give an answer will depend on the given figures in each set of data.

1) Evaluate $4\pi r^2$ when $r = 6.1$.

2) Evaluate $5\pi(R^2 - r^2)$ when $R = 1.32$ and $r = 1.24$.

3) The total iron P watts loss in a transformer is given by the equation $P = 0.1f + 0.006f^2$. If the frequency of the current is 50 Hz find the total iron loss.

4) The length L of a wire stretched tightly between two supports in the same horizontal line is given by $L = S + \dfrac{8D^2}{3S}$ where S is the span, and D is the (small) sag. If $S = 149.55$ and $D = 4.97$ find the length of wire.

5) The volume of the frustum of a cone is given by the formula $V = \frac{1}{3}\pi h(R^2 + rR + r^2)$ where h is the height of the frustum and R and r are the radii at the large and small ends respectively. If $h = 90$ mm, $R = 40$ mm and $r = 28.75$ mm find the volume.

6) In a beam the stress, σ, due to bending is given by the expression $\sigma = \dfrac{My}{I}$. Find σ if $M = 12 \times 10^6$, $y = 60$ and $I = 11.5 \times 10^6$.

7) The polar second moment of area J of a hollow shaft is given by the equation $J = \dfrac{\pi}{32}(D^4 - d^4)$. Find J if $D = 220$ and $d = 140$.

8) The velocity v of a body performing simple harmonic motion is given by the expression $v = \omega\sqrt{A^2 - x^2}$.
Find v if $\omega = 20.9$, $A = 0.060$, and $x = 0.020$.

9) The natural frequency of oscillation, f, of a mass, m, supported by a spring of stiffness, λ, is given by the formula $f = \dfrac{1}{2\pi}\sqrt{\dfrac{\lambda}{m}}$.
Find f if $\lambda = 5000$ and $m = 1.5$

10) Find the value of a if $a = \dfrac{80.6 \sin 55°}{\sin 70°}$

11) If $\cos C = \dfrac{a^2 + b^2 - c^2}{2ab}$, find the value of the angle C when $a = 19.37$ mm, $b = 26.42$ mm and $c = 22.31$ mm.

12) In a test circuit the current i is given by $i = 200 \sin (20t - 0.3)$. When the time t is 0.034 find the value of the current. [Hint – the angle will be in radians.]

13) In a particular circuit the voltage v is given by $v = 50 \cos (0.05 - 2\pi t)$. When the time t is 0.003 find the value of v.

14) If $v = 40 \cos (100\pi t)$ find a value of time t when $v = 31.5$.

15) In electrical circuits the total capacitance C in a circuit containing several capacitances C_1, C_2, C_3 .... is given by the equation

$$\frac{1}{C} = \frac{1}{C_1} + \frac{1}{C_2} + \frac{1}{C_3} + \ldots\ldots .$$

Find C if $C_1 = 20.8 \times 10^{-6}$, $C_2 = 31.3 \times 10^{-6}$ and $C_3 = 13.7 \times 10^{-6}$.

16) The root mean square (rms) value of an alternating current is given by the expression $\sqrt{\dfrac{I_1^2 + I_2^2 + I_3^2 + \ldots\ldots + I_n^2}{n}}$ where $I_1, I_2, I_3 \ldots\ldots I_n$ are mid-ordinates of the current waveform. Find the rms value if there are eight mid-ordinates having values 1.17, 3.33, 4.99, 5.88, 5.88, 4.99, 3.33 and 1.17 amperes.

17) The impedance of a circuit is given by $Z = \sqrt{\{R^2 + (X_L - X_C)^2\}}$ Find Z if $R = 2.31$, $X_L = 1.39$ and $X_C = 0.84$.

18) Use the method of nesting to evaluate the following:

a) $5x^2 + 4x - 15$ when $x = 3.8$ correct to 1 d.p.

b) $7x^3 + 3x^2 - 7x + 5$ when $x = 0.35$ correct to 2 d.p.

c) $x^4 + 3x^3 - 8x^2 + x - 3$ when $x = 3.75$ correct to 3 s.f.

d) $x^3 + 5x^2 - 6x + 9$ when $x = 1.2$ correct to 1 d.p.

3 Units

SI base units – multiples and submultiples – preferred units – length – area – volume – mass – density – velocity – acceleration – force – weight – pressure – energy – power – electrical charge and resistance – Imperial units – conversion to SI units

Here we look at the different units of measure used in industry. First, we cover the standard units, and then the way they are modified for use with very large or very small quantities. We must also be able to convert from units of one system to those of another, for example, from inches to millimetres.

There are two main unit systems in engineering. They are:

a) The Système International d'Unités (the international system of units), which is usually abbreviated to SI and is similar to the metric system (using metres etc.)
b) The old British 'imperial' system (using feet and inches etc.).

SI UNITS

Base Units

We will look now at the six fundamental (or base) units, so called because they are fundamental to the whole system of measurement:

	Base unit	Abbreviation
Length	metre	m
Mass	kilogram	kg
Time	second	s
Electric current	ampere	A
Luminous intensity	candela	cd
Temperature	kelvin	K

Multiples and Submultiples

Sometimes in engineering measurements are too big or too small to be measured using the base unit, so we use multiples and submultiples of 10

(10 being the number base of SI). These are known as prefixes and are shown in front of the base unit, and are given special names as follows:

Multiplication Factor		Prefix	Symbol
1 000 000 000 000	$= 10^{12}$	tera	T
1 000 000 000	$= 10^{9}$	giga	G
1 000 000	$= 10^{6}$	Mega	M
1 000	$= 10^{3}$	kilo	k
100	$= 10^{2}$	hecto	h
10	$= 10^{1}$	deca	da
0.1	$= 10^{-1}$	deci	d
0.01	$= 10^{-2}$	centi	c
0.001	$= 10^{-3}$	milli	m
0.000 001	$= 10^{-6}$	micro	μ
0.000 000 001	$= 10^{-9}$	nano	n
0.000 000 000 001	$= 10^{-12}$	pico	p
0.000 000 000 000 001	$= 10^{-15}$	femto	f
0.000 000 000 000 000 001	$= 10^{-18}$	atto	a

The choice of which unit to use will often be yours, but there are some other guidelines – for example, distances between towns on a road map are in kilometres.

Preferred Units

Preferred units are those which have the multiplication factors:

10^{12}, 10^{9}, 10^{6}, 10^{3}, 10^{-3}, 10^{-6}, 10^{-9}, 10^{-12}, 10^{-15} and 10^{-18}

together with the base unit.

Thus, 5000 metres should be written as 5 kilometres, i.e. 5 km which is 5×10^{3} metres, and NOT as 50 hectometres (50 hm) which is 50×10^{2} metres.

Length (Symbol *l*)

The SI base unit of length is the metre, which is suitable for work-shop or plan sites, but too large for plate thickness and too small for geographical distances, so the use of multiples and submultiples is needed.

For **large distances**,	the kilometre	1 km	$= 10^3$ m
small lengths,	the millimetre	1 mm	$= 10^{-3}$ m
tiny lengths,	the micrometre (or micron)	1 μm	$= 10^{-6}$ m

The above are a selection of preferred units – one non-preferred unit in common use for small distances is the centimetre: 1 cm = 10 mm = 10^{-2} m.

EXAMPLE 3.1

The shortest (great circle) distance between Cape Town and New York is 12 551 000 metres. Express this measurement in suitable preferred units.

$$\text{Now } 12\,551\,000\text{ m} = 12\,551 \times 10^3\text{ m} = 12\,551 \text{ kilometres (km)}$$
$$= 12.551 \times 10^6\text{ m} = 12.551 \text{ megametres (Mm)}$$

EXAMPLE 3.2

An extremely small aperture has width 0.000 000 82 metres. Express this measurement in suitable preferred units.

$$\text{Now } 0.000\,000\,82\text{ m} = 0.000\,82 \times 10^{-3}\text{ m} = 0.000\,82 \text{ millimetres (mm)}$$
$$= 0.82 \times 10^{-6}\text{ m} = 0.82 \text{ microns } (\mu\text{m})$$
$$= 820 \times 10^{-9}\text{ m} = 820 \text{ nanometres (nm)}$$

Area (Symbol *A*)

The basic unit of area is: the square metre (m^2).

For **large areas**:	the square kilometre	$1\text{ km}^2 = 10^6\text{ m}^2$
field areas:	the square hectometre (or hectare)	1 hm^2 (or 1 ha) $= 10^4\text{ m}^2$
lesser areas:	the square decametre (or are)	1 dam^2 (or 1 a) $= 10^2\text{ m}^2$
small areas:	the square centimetre	$1\text{ cm}^2 = 10^{-4}\text{ m}^2$
tiny areas:	the square millimetre	$1\text{ mm}^2 = 10^{-6}\text{ m}^2$

Although non-preferred, the units hectare, are, and square centimetre are all in common use.

EXAMPLE 3.3

Find, in square metres, the area of a rectangular metal sheet measuring 1840 mm by 730 mm.

Now $1840\text{ mm} = 1.84 \times 10^3\text{ mm}$ and $730\text{ mm} = 0.73 \times 10^3\text{ mm}$

$$\text{Thus sheet area} = (1.84 \times 10^3) \times (0.73 \times 10^3)\text{ mm}^2$$
$$= (1.84 \times 0.73) \times 10^{3+3}\text{ mm}^2$$
$$= 1.34 \times 10^6\text{ mm}^2$$
$$= 1.34\text{ m}^2 \quad \text{correct to 3 s.f.}$$

Volume (or Capacity) (Symbol V)

The basic unit of volume is: the cubic metre (m^3) – this is suitable for most large volumes. For smaller volumes we use:

everyday measure,
the litre* (or cubic decimetre) $1\,\ell$ (or $1\,dm^3$) $= 10^{-3}\,m^3$

small measure,
the millilitre* (or cubic centimetre) $1\,m\ell$ (or $1\,cm^3$) $= 10^{-6}\,m^3$

tiny volumes,
the cubic millimetre $1\,mm^3 = 10^{-9}\,m^3$

*The litre (ℓ) has become the common unit for liquid measure, and to four-figure accuracy may be treated as $1\,dm^3$, but for any precise calculation the relationship between the litre and cubic decimetre is: 1 litre $= 1.000\,028\,dm^3$.

EXAMPLE 3.4

A large tool-box measures 1330 mm by 650 mm by 550 mm. Find its volume in cubic metres.

$$\begin{aligned}\text{Now box volume} &= (1.33 \times 10^3) \times (0.65 \times 10^3) \times (0.55 \times 10^3)\,mm^3 \\ &= (1.33 \times 0.65 \times 0.55) \times 10^{3+3+3}\,mm^3 \\ &= 0.475 \times 10^9\,mm^3 \\ &= 0.475\,m^3 \quad \text{correct to 3 s.f.}\end{aligned}$$

Mass (Symbol m)

The SI base unit of mass is the kilogram, suitable for everyday use.

For **large mass,** the tonne (the metric ton) $1\,t = 10^3\,kg$
small mass, the gram $1\,g = 10^{-3}\,kg$
tiny mass, the milligram $1\,mg = 10^{-3}\,g = 10^{-6}\,kg$
minute mass, the microgram $1\,\mu g = 10^{-6}\,g = 10^{-9}\,kg$

The tonne (metric ton) is very nearly equal to an imperial ton (1 imperial ton = 1.016 tonne). The symbol, t, is used only for the tonne: the imperial ton should be written in full.

Exercise 3.1

Express more briefly each of the following with a suitable preferred unit.

1) 8000 m **2)** 15 000 kg **3)** 3800 km

4) 1 800 000 kg **5)** 0.007 m **6)** 0.000 0013 m

7) 0.028 kg **8)** 0.000 36 km **9)** 0.000 064 kg

10) 0.0036 A

Density (Symbol ρ)

Density is defined as mass per unit volume. Since 'per' means 'divided by' we have:

$$\text{Density} = \frac{\text{mass}}{\text{volume}} \quad \text{kilograms per cubic metre}$$

$$\text{or} \quad \rho = \frac{m}{V} \quad \text{kg/m}^3 \text{ or kg m}^{-3}$$

Density of water

From the original metric definition:

$$1\text{ cm}^3 \quad \text{of water has a mass of} \quad 1\text{ g}$$

$$\text{so} \quad 1000\text{ cm}^3 = 1\ \ell \quad \text{of water has a mass of} \quad 1000\text{ g} = 1\text{ kg}$$

$$\text{or} \quad 1000\ \ell = 1\text{ m}^3 \quad \text{of water has a mass of} \quad 1000\text{ kg} = 1\text{ t}$$

A litre of water has a mass of one kilogram
A cubic metre of water has a mass of one tonne

Density of common materials

The densities of common materials may be found in engineering tables. A selection is given here:

Material	**Density** (kg/m^3)	**Material**	**Density** (kg/m^3)
Aluminium	2700	Mercury	13 600
Concrete	2200	Oak	700
Copper	8800	Oil (heavy)	900
Ice	900	Petrol	720
Iron (cast)	7200	Steel	7900
Lead	11 400	Water	1000

EXAMPLE 3.5

Find the mass of a concrete floor 5 m by 6 m by 50 mm thick, if the density of concrete is 2200 kg/m^3.

Now we know
$$m = \rho V$$
$$= 2200 \times \left(5 \times 6 \times \frac{50}{1000}\right) \frac{\text{kg}}{\cancel{\text{m}^3}} \times \cancel{\text{m}^3}$$
$$= 3300\text{ kg}$$

Velocity (Symbol *v*)

Velocity is 'the rate of change of distance with respect to time'.

It has a derived unit: metres per second (m/s or $\frac{\text{m}}{\text{s}}$ or m s^{-1})

Another common unit: kilometres per hour (km/h or $\frac{\text{km}}{\text{h}}$ or km h^{-1})

EXAMPLE 3.6

Find the value of 20 m/s in km/h.

Our problem is to express $20\frac{\text{m}}{\text{s}}$ as $?\frac{\text{km}}{\text{h}}$

Now 1000 m = 1 km so $\left(\frac{1\text{ km}}{1000\text{ m}}\right) = 1$ and $\left(\frac{60 \times 60\text{ s}}{1\text{ h}}\right) = 1$

If we multiply anything by 1 it will remain unchanged in value, so:

$$20\frac{\text{m}}{\text{s}} = 20\frac{\cancel{\text{m}}}{\cancel{\text{s}}} \times \left(\frac{1\text{ km}}{1000\,\cancel{\text{m}}}\right) \times \left(\frac{60 \times 60\,\cancel{\text{s}}}{1\text{ h}}\right)$$

$$= \frac{20 \times 60 \times 60}{1000}\,\frac{\text{km}}{\text{h}}$$

thus 20 m/s = 72 km/h

Note how, by careful choice of the unity brackets, we arranged for the 'm' units on the top line to be cancelled out and replaced by 'km' units. Similarly, the 's' units on the bottom line to be replaced by 'h' units. This choice is not luck or magic but something you will learn to do with practice.

Acceleration (Symbol *a*)

Acceleration is 'the rate of change of velocity with respect to time'.

Its units are: metres per second per second (m/s/s or $\frac{\text{m}}{\text{s}^2}$ or m s^{-2}).

EXAMPLE 3.7

A vehicle increases speed, at a uniform rate, from 30 km/h to 60 km/h in a time of 8 seconds. Find the vehicle's acceleration.

Now, because the increase in velocity is uniform, the acceleration is constant.

Thus constant acceleration $= \dfrac{\text{change in velocity}}{\text{time}}$

$$= \frac{\text{final velocity} - \text{initial velocity}}{\text{time}}$$

or in symbols $a = \dfrac{v - u}{t}$

Now we need to change the velocity units from km/h to m/s.

Thus $$u = 30\frac{\text{km}}{\text{h}} = \frac{30\,\cancel{\text{km}}}{\cancel{\text{h}}} \times \frac{1000\text{ m}}{1\,\cancel{\text{km}}} \times \frac{1\,\cancel{\text{h}}}{3600\text{ s}} = 8.33\text{ m/s}$$

Also since v was given as twice u,

then $$v = 2 \times 8.33 = 16.66\text{ m/s}$$

hence $$a = \frac{16.66 - 8.33}{8}\frac{\text{m/s}}{\text{s}}$$

therefore $$a = 1.04\text{ m/s/s} \quad \text{or} \quad \text{m/s}^2 \quad \text{or} \quad \text{m s}^{-2}$$

Force (Symbol *F*)

Newton's second law of motion, providing we have a coherent system of units, such as SI, may be simplified to:

$$\text{Force} = \text{mass} \times \text{acceleration}$$

Now in SI the unit of force is: the newton (N) derived from the statement:

1 N is the force which will accelerate 1 kg mass at a rate of 1 m/s^2

or in symbols $$F(N) = m\text{ (kg)} \times a\text{ (m/s}^2\text{)}$$

So, just looking at the units

$$1\text{ N} = 1\text{ kg} \times 1\text{ m/s}^2$$

or $$1\text{ N} = 1\frac{\text{kg m}}{\text{s}^2}$$

So N units may be replaced by $\frac{\text{kg m}}{\text{s}^2}$ or kg m/s^2 or kg m s^{-2} units and vice versa.

EXAMPLE 3.8

Find the force needed to give a mass of 600 kg an acceleration of 5 m/s

Now $$\begin{aligned} F &= m \times a \\ &= 600\text{ kg} \times 5\text{ m/s}^2 \\ &= 600 \times 5\text{ kg m/s}^2 \\ &= 3000\text{ N} \end{aligned}$$

Weight (Symbol *W*)

Weight is simply the force of gravity acting on a body. On earth, it attracts the body towards the centre of the earth; on the moon, it attracts the body towards the centre of the moon, but to a lesser extent (gravity on the moon is approximately one sixth of that on earth).

So using Force $=$ mass $\times$ acceleration

then Weight $=$ mass $\times$ (acceleration of a free falling body)

or, in symbols $W\,(\mathrm{N}) = m\,(\mathrm{kg}) \times g\,(\mathrm{m/s^2})$

On earth the average value of g is $9.81\,\mathrm{m/s^2}$ (often taken as $10\,\mathrm{m/s^2}$ without too much error).

Thus, on earth, 1 kg weighs 9.81 newtons

SI calculations use mass in kilograms almost exclusively. Weight in newtons is only needed when, for example, calculating stresses in a weight carrying structure, or determining the lift required from an aircraft.

The general public, unaware of any difference between the two, will continue wrongly to refer to mass as weight, in phrases like ‘my luggage weighs 20 kilograms’. So, probably, will the engineer, except when he or she has to design a luggage rack! Then he or she will recall that it is the mass which is 20 kilograms; its weight is 20×9.81 or 196 newtons.

EXAMPLE 3.9

What is the mass of a vehicle which weighs 9500 N?

From Force $=$ mass $\times$ acceleration

then $W = m \times g$

$$\therefore \quad m = \frac{W}{g} = \frac{9500}{9.81} = 968\,\mathrm{kg}$$

Pressure (Symbol *p*)

$$\text{Pressure (or stress)} = \frac{\text{force}}{\text{area on which it acts}}$$

or in symbols $p = \dfrac{F}{A}$

The SI unit of pressure is the: newton per square metre ($\mathrm{N/m^2}$ or $\mathrm{N\,m^{-2}}$) and is sometimes called the: pascal (Pa).

A more useful unit is the bar, since atmospheric pressure is almost exactly equal to 1 bar (or 1.013 25 bar exactly, international standard).

Thus 1 bar $=$ 1 atmosphere $=$ 100 000 or $10^5\ \mathrm{N/m^2}$

EXAMPLE 3.10

Find the force on a rectangular sheet of plastic 200 mm by 300 mm if a pressure of 0.9 kN/m^2 is applied.

$$\text{Now} \qquad \text{pressure} = \frac{\text{force}}{\text{area}}$$

$$\text{Thus} \qquad \text{force} = \text{pressure} \times \text{area}$$

Converting to basic SI units: $0.9\,\text{kN/m}^2 = 0.9 \times 1000\,\text{N/m}^2$,

$$\text{So} \qquad \text{force} = (0.9 \times 1000) \times \left(\frac{200}{1000} \times \frac{300}{1000}\right)$$

$$= 54\,\text{N}$$

Energy

Energy is measured in joules, and 1 joule is the work done when a force of 1 newton acts through a distance of 1 metre. Assuming no losses, this amount of work would be capable of generating 1 watt of electricity for 1 second. Thus:

$$1\,\text{joule} = 1\,\text{watt second} = 1\,\text{newton metre}$$

or

$$1\,\text{J} = 1\,\text{W s} = 1\,\text{N m}$$

The joule is also the unit of heat and the unit of electrical energy.

Power (Mechanical)

$$\text{Power is the rate of doing work} \qquad \text{or} \qquad \frac{\text{work done}}{\text{time}}$$

The SI unit of power is the: watt (W).

A mechanical power of 1 watt is a rate of working of 1 joule per second.

$$1\,\text{W} = 1\frac{\text{J}}{\text{s}} = 1\frac{\text{N m}}{\text{s}}$$

EXAMPLE 3.11

In a belt drive the belt velocity is 740 metres per minute and the power transmitted is 64 kW. Find the difference in tension between the tight and slack sides of the belt.

$$\text{Now} \qquad \text{power} = \frac{\text{work done}}{\text{time}} = \frac{\text{force} \times \text{distance}}{\text{time}} = \text{force} \times \frac{\text{distance}}{\text{time}}$$

$$\text{or} \qquad \text{power} = \text{force} \times \text{velocity}$$

$$\text{thus} \qquad \text{force} = \frac{\text{power}}{\text{velocity}} = \frac{64 \times 1000}{740/60}\ \frac{\text{W}}{\text{m/s}} = 5190\,\text{N}$$

So the difference in tension is 5190 N since all data was in basic SI units.

Power (Electrical)

In SI the unit of electrical power and the unit of mechanical power are one and the same: the watt. Thus, if there were no losses in the conversion from one form to the other, the work input to a dynamo at the rate of 1 newton metre per second would generate 1 watt of electricity. Similarly, an input to an electric motor of 1 watt of electricity would cause it to do work at a rate of 1 Nm/s or 1 J/s.

In direct current circuits (or alternating circuits where the voltage and current are in phase):

$$\text{Power (watts)} = \text{current (amperes)} \times \text{voltage (volts)}$$

EXAMPLE 3.12

An electric motor has an efficiency of 90% and gives an output of 12 kW when connected to a 240 V supply. Calculate

a) the current taken, and

b) the energy over a three hour run.

a) Now
$$\text{efficiency} = \frac{\text{output}}{\text{input}} \times 100\%$$

so
$$\text{input power} = \frac{\text{output power}}{\text{efficiency}} \times 100\%$$

$$= \frac{12 \times 1000}{90} \times 100 = 13\,333\ \text{W}$$

also
$$\text{power} = \text{current} \times \text{voltage}$$

so
$$\text{input current} = \frac{\text{input power}}{\text{voltage}} = \frac{13\,333}{240}$$

$$= 55.6\ \text{A}$$

b) Now
$$\text{Energy (joules)} = \text{power (watts)} \times \text{time (seconds)}$$

so
$$\text{energy input for 3 hours} = 13\,333 \times (3 \times 60 \times 60)\ \text{J}$$

$$= 1.44 \times 10^8\ \text{J}$$

$$= 144\ \text{MJ}$$

Electric Charge (Symbol Q)

$$\text{Now} \qquad \text{charge} = \text{current} \times \text{time}$$

$$\text{or in symbols} \qquad Q = I \times t$$

The unit of charge is the coulomb (C) and is defined as the quantity of electricity which flows past a certain point in an electrical circuit when a current of 1 ampere is maintained for 1 second.

Electrical Resistance (Symbol R)

The resistance in an electrical circuit is its opposition to the flow of electrical current.

The unit of resistance is the: ohm (Ω), which is the resistance between two points of a conductor when a potential difference of 1 volt applied between these points produces a current of 1 ampere.

$$\text{Ohm's law gives} \qquad \text{current (A)} = \frac{\text{voltage (V)}}{\text{resistance } (\Omega)}$$

$$\text{So} \qquad V = IR \quad \text{or} \quad R = \frac{V}{I}$$

EXAMPLE 3.13

a) What is the voltage difference across an $8\,\text{k}\Omega$ resistor when a current of $80\,\mu\text{A}$ is flowing?

b) What charge is transferred if the current flows for 14 hours?

a) Ohm's law says $V = IR$

so, in basic SI units $8\,\text{k}\Omega = 8 \times 10^3\,\Omega$ and $80\,\mu\text{A} = 80 \times 10^{-6}\,\text{A}$

gives
$$V = (80 \times 10^{-6}) \times (8 \times 10^3)\,\text{V}$$
$$= 640 \times 10^{-3}\,\text{V}$$
$$= 0.64\,\text{V}$$

b) Now we know $Q = It$

so, working in basic SI units of amperes and seconds

then, $Q = (80 \times 10^{-6}) \times (14 \times 60 \times 60) = 4.032\,\text{C}$

Thus the transferred charge is 4.03 coulombs.

Exercise 3.2

1) Electric voltage V (units V, volts), current I (units A, amperes) and resistance R (units Ω, ohms) are connected by the expression $V = IR$. Find the voltage if $I = 15\,\mu\text{A}$ and $R = 30\,\text{k}\Omega$.

2) The equation $F = ma$ relates force F (units N, newtons), mass m (units kg, kilograms) and acceleration a (units m s^{-2}, metres per second per second).

(a) If a 1 tonne vehicle accelerates at $2\,\text{m s}^{-2}$ find the force required.

(b) A motor-car weighing 8000 N slows down due to an average braking force of 3.2 kN. Find the deceleration of the vehicle.

3) The work done by a force F (units N, newtons) moving through a distance s (units m, metres) is given by Fs (units J, joules). Find the work done in kJ if a force of 300 N moves through a distance of 0.1 km.

4) Power, in mechanics, is the rate of doing work and is given by $\dfrac{\text{work done}}{\text{time}}$ or in symbols $\dfrac{Fs}{t}$ or $F \times \dfrac{s}{t}$ which is Fv, where v is the velocity in units m s^{-1}. Using standard basic SI units, power is measured in units W watts.

Find the power in kW when a driving force of 5 kN (being the difference in tensions between the tight and slack sides of a belt drive) is moving with a belt speed of $12\,\text{m s}^{-1}$.

5) Electrical power is also measured in W watts and can be found by multiplying current I amperes by voltage V volts, or using symbols $W = IV$. Find the power of an electric fire which takes a current of 8 A from a 250 V mains supply.

6) Kinetic energy is the energy due to the motion of a mass and is given by $\frac{1}{2}mv^2$ J where mass m kg has velocity $v\,\text{m s}^{-1}$. What is the kinetic energy in MJ units possessed by a motor-car which has a mass of 0.8 tonne, when travelling at a speed of $60\,\text{km h}^{-1}$?

7) Calculate the work done, in kJ, in raising a 500 kg rolled steel joist, by a crane from ground level, to the top floor of a building, 30 m above. Also, what is the power needed if this takes place in 30 seconds?

IMPERIAL SYSTEM OF UNITS

This system still exists for a number of reasons:

1) It has been in place throughout the development of engineering in Great Britain,

2) People have resisted, and found difficulty in accepting, a new system,

3) The cost of replacing equipment and machinery is large, and

4) There is a need to produce imperial components for existing plant.

Conversions to SI Units

We must be able to convert units from one system to the other, and so conversion factors are listed below for the more common imperial units.

Length	12 inches (in) = 1 foot 3 feet (ft) = 1 yard (yd) 1760 yards (yd) = 1 mile	1 in = 25.4 mm 1 ft = 0.305 m 1 mile = 1.61 km
Area	1 acre = 4840 yd^2	1 acre = 0.405 ha
Volume (capacity)	8 pints = 1 gallon (gal)	1 gal = 4.55 ℓ
Mass	16 ounces (oz) = 1 pound (lb) 112 pounds (lb) = 1 hundredweight (cwt) 20 cwt = 1 ton	1 lb = 0.454 kg 1 ton = 1020 kg or 1 ton ≈ 1000 kg ≈ 1 tonne (t)

EXAMPLE 3.14

Express 5.24 yards in metres.

Since 3 ft = 1 yd and 0.305 m = 1 ft

then
$$5.24\,\text{yd} = 5.24\,\cancel{\text{yd}} \times \left(\frac{3\,\cancel{\text{ft}}}{1\,\cancel{\text{yd}}}\right) \times \left(\frac{0.305\,\text{m}}{1\,\cancel{\text{ft}}}\right)$$
$$= 4.79\,\text{m} \text{ correct to 3 s.f.}$$

EXAMPLE 3.15

Change 72 kilograms into hundredweight.

Since $1\,\text{lb} = 0.454\,\text{kg}$ and $1\,\text{cwt} = 112\,\text{lb}$

then
$$72\,\text{kg} = 72\,\cancel{\text{kg}} \times \left(\frac{1\,\cancel{\text{lb}}}{0.454\,\cancel{\text{kg}}}\right) \times \left(\frac{1\,\text{cwt}}{112\,\cancel{\text{lb}}}\right)$$
$$= 1.42\,\text{cwt} \quad \text{correct to 3 s.f.}$$

EXAMPLE 3.16

What is a pint of beer measured in litres? Also, how many pints would I get if I ordered a litre of beer?

Since $1\,\text{gal} = 8\,\text{pt}$ and $4.55\,\ell = 1\,\text{gal}$

then
$$1\,\text{pt} = 1\,\cancel{\text{pt}} \times \left(\frac{1\,\cancel{\text{gal}}}{8\,\cancel{\text{pt}}}\right) \times \left(\frac{4.55\,\ell}{1\,\cancel{\text{gal}}}\right)$$
$$= 0.57\,\text{litres} \quad \text{correct to 2 s.f.}$$

Now using this result we get $1\,\ell = \frac{1}{0.57}\,\text{pt}$ or $1.75\,\text{pt}$, but a word of warning before we tell everyone that one litre is 1.75 pints. This implies an accuracy correct to 3 s.f. However, 0.57 was rounded correct to only 2 s.f. Thus we must either content ourselves by saying that 1 litre is either 1.7 or 1.8 pints, or start afresh with more accurate conversion factors.

Exercise 3.3

Give the answers to 3 s.f. unless there is a good reason for doing otherwise.

1) The dimensions of a factory workshop are being converted from imperial to SI units. One of these measurements is 880 yards and its equivalent in metre units is needed.

2) Slip gauges are required for a measurement of 2.16 inches. As only metric ones are available, what is this dimension in millimetres?

3) A component has a surface area of 4.2 square feet. Since painting costs are quoted per square metre, how many square metres are there?

4) A spherical gas container has a volume of $8\,\text{ft}^3$. A customer wishes to know its capacity in m^3.

5) A milk marketing company wishes to know how many pints of milk can be transported in a container, that we manufacture, which has a nominal capacity of 25 litres.

6) A motor van has a mass of 25 cwt. What figures should be used for the vehicle mass on a registration form stating kilogram units?

7) A development department wishes to know how many mℓ of an extremely high grade and expensive oil are required to fill a reservoir for a bearing of a heavy machine. Its capacity, etched on the side of the reservoir, is $3\ \text{in}^3$.

8) A drawing dimension is given as 0.906 ± 0.0012 inches. Convert to mm.

9) Three important dimensions of a 6 BA thread are: diameter 2.8 mm, pitch 0.53 mm, and depth of thread 0.0125 mm. Convert these to inches.

10) A tank is to hold 150 gallons.

a) Find its volume in ft^3.

b) How many litres does the tank hold?

c) What is the volume in m^3?

11) How much must be ground off a plug gauge 1.625 inches in diameter so that it can be used for checking a hole of 41 mm diameter? Give your answer to the nearest 0.001 in.

12) Express a speed of 60 mile/hour as:

a) ft/s **b)** m/s **c)** km/h.

13) A vehicle travels 30 miles to the gallon of petrol. How many kilometres will it travel on 4 litres of petrol?

Basic Operations 4

Operations on algebraic terms – brackets – binomial expressions – HCF – factorisation – LCM – algebraic fractions – partial fractions

DOWN TO EARTH!

Most of us tend to think that messing about with algebraic terms requires some sort of magic. To avoid this fear all you have to do is to remember that in algebra letters replace the numbers used in arithmetic – all the rules that apply in arithmetic also apply in algebra and with practice we need have no worries.

This chapter covers the ways in which we approach and handle expressions arising from the application of algebra to engineering problems. Situations are often modelled as algebraic expressions and it is essential that these can be simplified into a form suitable for finding a solution

POSITIVE AND NEGATIVE NUMBERS

We are all familiar with a Celsius thermometer; Fig. 4.1 shows part of one. The freezing point of water is 0°C (zero degrees Celsius). Temperatures above and below freezing may be read directly off the scale.

We now have to decide on a method for showing whether a temperature is above or below zero. We may say that a temperature is 5 degrees above zero or 6 degrees below zero, but these statements are not compact enough for calculations.

So, we write them as +5°C and −6°C, and we have examples of a positive and a negative number.

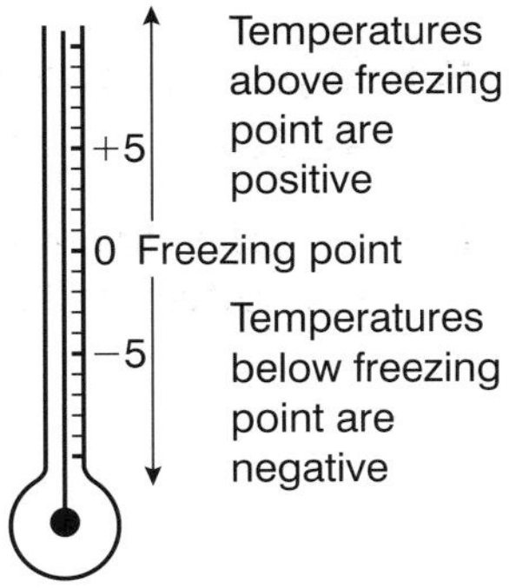

Fig. 4.1

When multiplying or dividing positive and negative numbers we use the rules:

Two numbers with	*like*	signs give a positive result
Two numbers with	*unlike*	signs give a negative result

As usual, we are lazy, and the + sign is usually omitted, so +12 is written simply as 12.

Some typical examples of the above rules are:

$7 \times 4 = 28$ $7 \times (-4) = -28$		$(-7) \times (4) = -28$ $(-7) \times (-4) = 28$	
$\frac{20}{4} = 5$	$\frac{20}{-4} = -5$	$\frac{-20}{4} = -5$	$\frac{-20}{-4} = 5$

THE MODULUS OF A NUMBER

Sometimes we are only interested in the size (or magnitude) of a number irrespective of whether it is positive or negative. This magnitude is called the modulus, and if x is the number then it is written as

$|x|$ and pronounced 'mod x'

Such an occasion is finding the size of a square of area 4 square units. The length of the side is given by a square root value, namely $\sqrt{4}$. We are only interested in the magnitude, 2, of the number, although strictly $\sqrt{4} = +2$ or -2 since $(+2)^2 = 4$ and $(-2)^2 = 4$.

OPERATIONS ON ALGEBRAIC QUANTITIES

Multiplication and Division

The rules are exactly the same as those used with numbers:

The product of two expressions with like signs is positive

$$(+x)(+y) = +(xy) = +xy = xy$$
$$5x \times 3y = 5 \times 3 \times x \times y = 15xy$$
$$(-3a)(-2b) = +(3a)(2b) = 6ab$$

The product of two expressions with unlike signs is negative

$$(-4x)(2y) = -(4x)(2y) = -8xy$$
$$(5p)(-6q) = -(5p)(6q) = -30pq$$

The result of dividing two expressions with like signs is positive

$$\frac{+2c}{+d} = +\frac{2c}{d} = \frac{2c}{d} \quad \text{or} \quad \frac{-3m}{-9n} = +\frac{3m}{9n} = \frac{m}{3n}$$

The result of dividing two expressions with unlike signs is negative

$$\frac{-5x}{2y} = -\frac{5x}{2y} \qquad \text{or} \qquad \frac{4r}{-s} = -\frac{4r}{s}$$

When *multiplying* expressions containing the same symbols, indices are used:

$$m \times m = m^2$$
$$3m \times 5m = 3 \times m \times 5 \times m = 15m^2$$
$$(-m) \times m^2 = (-m) \times m \times m = -m^3$$
$$5m^2n \times 3mn^3 = 5 \times m \times m \times n \times 3 \times m \times n \times n \times n = 15m^3n^4$$
$$3mn \times (-2n^2) = 3 \times m \times n \times (-2) \times n \times n = -6mn^3$$

When *dividing* algebraic expressions, cancellation between numerator and denominator is often possible. Cancelling is equivalent to dividing both numerator and denominator by the same quantity:

Thus $$\frac{pq}{p} = \frac{\not{p} \times q}{\not{p}} = q$$

or $$\frac{3p^2q}{6pq^2} = \frac{3 \times \not{p} \times p \times \not{q}}{6 \times \not{p} \times q \times \not{q}} = \frac{3p}{6q} = \frac{p}{2q}$$

or $$\frac{18x^2y^2z}{6xyz} = \frac{18 \times \not{x} \times x \times \not{y} \times y \times \not{z}}{6 \times \not{x} \times \not{y} \times \not{z}} = 3xy$$

Sequence of Mixed Operations

Algebraic quantities contain symbols (or letters) which represent numbers. Thus the sequence of operations, namely:

Brackets, Of, Divide, Multiply, Add, Subtract

when simplifying algebraic expressions is exactly the same as used for number expressions.

Remember the mnemonic **'BODMAS'** which gives the initial letters in the correct order.

Thus:

$$\begin{aligned} 2x^2 + (12x^4 - 3x^4) \div 3x^2 - x^2 &= 2x^2 + 9x^4 \div 3x^2 - x^2 \\ &= 2x^2 + 3x^2 - x^2 \\ &= 5x^2 - x^2 \\ &= 4x^2 \end{aligned}$$

Brackets

Brackets are used for convenience in grouping terms together. When removing brackets each *term* within the bracket is multiplied by the quantity outside the bracket:

$$3(x+y) = 3x + 3y$$
$$5(2x+3y) = 5 \times 2x + 5 \times 3y = 10x + 15y$$
$$4(a-2b) = 4 \times a - 4 \times 2b = 4a - 8b$$
$$m(a+b) = ma + mb$$
$$3x(2p+3q) = 3x \times 2p + 3x \times 3q = 6px + 9qx$$
$$4a(2a+b) = 4a \times 2a + 4a \times b = 8a^2 + 4ab$$

When a bracket has a minus sign in front of it, the signs of all the terms inside the bracket are changed when the bracket is removed. The reason for this rule may be seen from the following examples:

$$-3(2x-5y) = (-3) \times 2x + (-3) \times (-5y) = -6x + 15y$$
$$-(m+n) = -m - n$$
$$-(p-q) = -p + q$$
$$-2(p+3q) = -2p - 6q$$

When simplifying expressions containing brackets first remove the brackets and then add the like terms together:

$$(3x+7y) - (4x+3y) = 3x + 7y - 4x - 3y = -x + 4y$$
$$3(2x+3y) - (x+5y) = 6x + 9y - x - 5y = 5x + 4y$$
$$x(a+b) - x(a+3b) = ax + bx - ax - 3bx = -2bx$$
$$2(5a+3b) + 3(a-2b) = 10a + 6b + 3a - 6b = 13a$$

Exercise 4.1

Remove the brackets and simplify the following:

1) $3(3x+2y)$

2) $5(2p-3q)$

3) $-(a-2b)$

4) $-4(x+3)$

5) $2k(k-5)$

6) $-3y(3x+4)$

7) $a(p-q-r)$

8) $4xy(ab-ac+d)$

9) $3x^2(x^2-2x+y^2)$

10) $-7P(2P^2-P+1)$

11) $-2m(-1+3m-2n)$

12) $3(x+4)-(2x+5)$

13) $4(1-2x)-3(3x-4)$

14) $5(2x-y)-3(x+2y)$

15) $\frac{1}{2}(y-1)+\frac{1}{3}(2y-3)$

16) $-(4a+5b-3c)-2(2a+3b-4c)$

17) $3(a-b)-2(2a-3b)+4(a-3b)$

18) $3x(x^2+7x+1)-2x(2x^2+3)-3(x^2+5)$

BINOMIAL EXPRESSIONS

A binomial expression consists of two terms. Thus $3x + 5$, $a + b$, $2x + 37$ and $4p - q$ are all binomial expressions.

The Product of Two Binomial Expressions

To find the product $(a + b)(c + d)$ consider the diagram below:

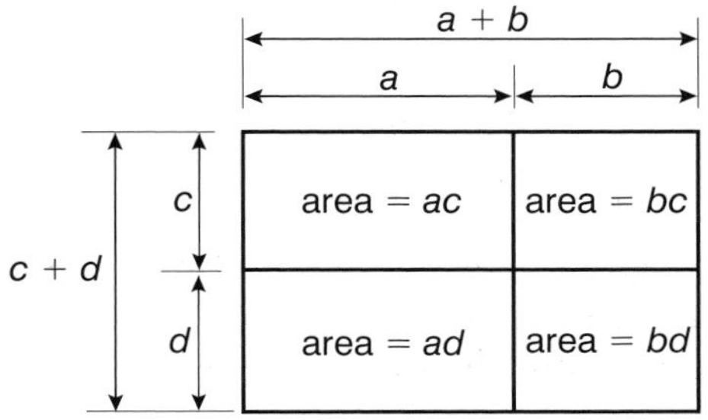

For the rectangles shown in the figure:

$$\text{Outer area} = \text{sum of the four smaller areas}$$

i.e. $$(a + b)(c + d) = ac + ad + bc + bd$$

It will be noticed that the expression on the right hand side is obtained by multiplying each term in the one bracket by each term in the other bracket.

The process is illustrated below:

$$\begin{aligned}(a + b)(c + d) &= a(c + d) + b(c + d) \\ &= ac + ad + bc + bd\end{aligned}$$

EXAMPLE 4.1

a) $$\begin{aligned}(3x + 2)(4x + 5) &= 3x \times 4x + 3x \times 5 + 2 \times 4x + 2 \times 5 \\ &= 12x^2 + 15x + 8x + 10 \\ &= 12x^2 + 23x + 10\end{aligned}$$

b) $$\begin{aligned}(2p - 3)(4p + 7) &= 2p \times 4p + 2p \times 7 - 3 \times 4p - 3 \times 7 \\ &= 8p^2 + 14p - 12p - 21 \\ &= 8p^2 + 2p - 21\end{aligned}$$

c) $$\begin{aligned}(z - 5)(3z - 2) &= z \times 3z + z \times (-2) - 5 \times 3z - 5 \times (-2) \\ &= 3z^2 - 2z - 15z + 10 \\ &= 3z^2 - 17z + 10\end{aligned}$$

d) $$\begin{aligned}(2x + 3y)(3x - 2y) &= 2x \times 3x + 2x \times (-2y) + 3y \times 3x + 3y \times (-2y) \\ &= 6x^2 - 4xy + 9xy - 6y^2 \\ &= 6x^2 + 5xy - 6y^2\end{aligned}$$

The Square of a Binomial Expression

$$(a+b)^2 = (a+b)(a+b) = a^2+ab+ab+b^2 = a^2+2ab+b^2$$

$$\therefore \quad (a+b)^2 = a^2+2ab+b^2$$

$$(a-b)^2 = (a-b)(a-b) = a^2-ab-ab+b^2 = a^2-2ab+b^2$$

$$\therefore \quad (a-b)^2 = a^2-2ab+b^2$$

EXAMPLE 4.2

a) $$(2x+5)^2 = (2x)^2 + 2\times 2x\times 5 + 5^2 = 4x^2+20x+25$$

b) $$(3x-2)^2 = (3x)^2 + 2\times 3x\times(-2) + (-2)^2 = 9x^2-12x+4$$

c) $$(2x+3y)^2 = (2x)^2 + 2\times 2x\times 3y + (3y)^2 = 4x^2+12xy+9y^2$$

The Product of the Sum and Difference of Two Terms

$$(a+b)(a-b) = a^2-ab+ab-b^2$$

$$(a+b)(a-b) = a^2-b^2$$

The result is the difference of the squares of the two terms

EXAMPLE 4.3

a) $$(8x+3)(8x-3) = (8x)^2-3^2 = 64x^2-9$$

b) $$(2x+5y)(2x-5y) = (2x)^2-(5y)^2 = 4x^2-25y^2$$

SIMPLIFYING THREE BRACKETS

If you are happy multiplying out two brackets, then this will seem easy!

Consider $\quad (x-2)(x+3)(2x+7)$

First, we simplify two of the brackets. So choosing the last two and multiplying out

$$\begin{aligned}(x+3)(2x+7) &= x(2x+7)+3(2x+7)\\ &= x\times 2x + x\times 7 + 3\times 2x + 3\times 7\\ &= 2x^2+7x+6x+21\\ &= 2x^2+13x+21\end{aligned}$$

The problem is now reduced to

$(x-2)(2x^2+13x+21)$ and if we multiply out as before

then

$$\begin{aligned}(x-2)(2x^2+13x+21) &= x(2x^2+13x+21)-2(2x^2+13x+21)\\ &= x\times 2x^2 + x\times 13x + x\times 21 - 2\times 2x^2\\ &\qquad - 2\times 13x - 2\times 21\\ &= 2x^3+13x^2+21x-4x^2-26x-42\\ &= 2x^3+9x^2-5x-42\end{aligned}$$

Exercise 4.2

Find the products of the following:

1) $(x+4)(x+5)$

2) $(2x+5)(x+3)$

3) $(2x+4)(3x+2)$

4) $(5x+1)(2x+3)$

5) $(7x+2)(3x+5)$

6) $(x-1)(x-3)$

7) $(x+3)(x-1)$

8) $(x-2)(x+7)$

9) $(x-5)(x+3)$

10) $(2x+5)(x-2)$

11) $(3x+5)(2x-3)$

12) $(6x-7)(2x+3)$

13) $(2p-q)(p-3q)$

14) $(3v+2u)(2v-3u)$

15) $(2a+b)(3a-b)$

16) $(x+1)^2$

17) $(2x+3)^2$

18) $(3x+7)^2$

19) $(x-1)^2$

20) $(2x-3)^2$

21) $(x+y)^2$

22) $(P+3Q)^2$

23) $(3x-4y)^2$

24) $(2x+y)(2x-y)$

25) $(2m-3n)(2m+3n)$

26) $(x^2+y)(x^2-y)$

27) $(x+1)(x-2)(x+3)$

28) $(2x-1)(x+2)(x-3)$

29) $(x+1)^2(x-2)$

30) $(x+1)(x-1)(x^2+1)$

31) $(x+a)(x+b)(x+c)$

Highest Common Factor (HCF)

The HCF of a set of algebraic expressions is the highest expression which is a factor of each of the given expressions.
The method used is similar to that for finding the HCF of a set of numbers.

EXAMPLE 4.4

Find the HCF of ab^2c^5, $a^2b^3c^3$ and $a^2b^4c^4$.

We express each expression as the product of its factors.

Thus $ab^2c^5 = a \times b \times b \times c \times c \times c \times c \times c$

and $a^2b^3c^3 = a \times a \times b \times b \times b \times c \times c \times c$

and $a^2b^4c^4 = a \times a \times b \times b \times b \times b \times c \times c \times c \times c$

We now note the factors which are common to each of the lines. Factor a is common once, factor b twice, and factor c three times. The product of these factors gives the required HCF.

Thus HCF $= a \times b \times b \times c \times c \times c$

$= ab^2c^3$

EXAMPLE 4.5

Find the HCF of $\dfrac{x^3y}{m^2n^4}$, $\dfrac{x^2y^3}{m^2n^2}$ and $\dfrac{x^4y^2}{mn^3}$.

Now $\dfrac{x^3y}{m^2n^4} = x \times x \times x \times y \times \dfrac{1}{m} \times \dfrac{1}{m} \times \dfrac{1}{n} \times \dfrac{1}{n} \times \dfrac{1}{n} \times \dfrac{1}{n}$

and $\dfrac{x^2y^3}{m^2n^2} = x \times x \times y \times y \times y \times \dfrac{1}{m} \times \dfrac{1}{m} \times \dfrac{1}{n} \times \dfrac{1}{n}$

and $\dfrac{x^4y^2}{mn^3} = x \times x \times x \times x \times y \times y \times \dfrac{1}{m} \times \dfrac{1}{n} \times \dfrac{1}{n} \times \dfrac{1}{n}$

Factor x is common twice, factor y is common once, factor $\dfrac{1}{m}$ once and factor $\dfrac{1}{n}$ twice.

Thus HCF $= x \times x \times y \times \dfrac{1}{m} \times \dfrac{1}{n} \times \dfrac{1}{n}$

$= \dfrac{x^2y}{mn^2}$

An alternative method is to select the lowest power of each of the quantities which occur in all of the expressions, and then multiply them together.

EXAMPLE 4.6

Find the HCF of $3m^2np^3$, $6m^3n^2p^2$ and $24m^3p^4$.

Dealing with the numerical coefficients 3, 6 and 24 we note that 3 is a factor of each of them. The quantities m and p occur in all three expressions, their lowest powers being m^2 and p^2. Hence,

$$\text{HCF} = 3m^2p^2$$

(Note that n does not occur in each of the three expressions and hence it does **not** appear in the HCF.)

Factorising

A factor is a common part of two or more terms which make up an algebraic expression. Thus, the expression $3x + 3y$ has two terms which have the number 3 common to both of them. Thus $3x + 3y = 3(x + y)$. We say that 3 and $(x + y)$ are the factors of $3x + 3y$. To factorise algebraic expressions of this kind, we first find the HCF of all the terms making up the expression. The HCF then appears outside the bracket. To find the terms inside the bracket divide each of the terms making up the expression by the HCF. With practice you will be able to factorise by just inspecting all the terms.

EXAMPLE 4.7

a) Find the factors of $ax + bx$.

The HCF of ax and bx is x.

$$\therefore \quad ax + bx = x(a + b) \quad \text{since} \quad \frac{ax}{x} = a \quad \text{and} \quad \frac{bx}{x} = b$$

b) Find the factors of $m^2n - 2mn^2$.

The HCF of m^2n and $2mn^2$ is mn.

$$\therefore \quad m^2n - 2mn^2 = mn(m - 2n) \quad \text{since} \quad \frac{m^2n}{mn} = m \quad \text{and} \quad \frac{2mn^2}{mn} = 2n$$

c) Find the factors of $3x^4y + 9x^3y^2 - 6x^2y^3$.

The HCF of $3x^4y$, $9x^3y^2$ and $6x^2y^3$ is $3x^2y$

$$\therefore \quad 3x^4y + 9x^3y^2 - 6x^2y^3 = 3x^2y(x^2 + 3xy - 2y^2)$$

$$\text{since} \quad \frac{3x^4y}{3x^2y} = x^2, \quad \frac{9x^3y^2}{3x^2y} = 3xy \quad \text{and} \quad \frac{6x^2y^3}{3x^2y} = 2y^2$$

d) Find the factors of $\dfrac{ac}{x}+\dfrac{bc}{x^2}+\dfrac{cd}{x^3}$.

The HCF of $\dfrac{ac}{x}$, $\dfrac{bc}{x^2}$ and $\dfrac{cd}{x^3}$ is $\dfrac{c}{x}$.

$$\therefore \quad \frac{ac}{x}+\frac{bc}{x^2}+\frac{cd}{x^3} = \frac{c}{x}\left(a+\frac{b}{x}+\frac{d}{x^2}\right)$$

since $\dfrac{ac}{x}\div\dfrac{c}{x}=a$, $\dfrac{bc}{x^2}\div\dfrac{c}{x}=\dfrac{b}{x}$ and $\dfrac{cd}{x^3}\div\dfrac{c}{x}=\dfrac{d}{x^2}$

Exercise 4.3

Find the HCF of the following:

1) $p^3q^2,\ p^2q^3,\ p^2q$

2) $a^2b^3c^3,\ a^3b^3,\ ab^2c^2$

3) $3mn^2,\ 6mnp,\ 12m^2np^2$

4) $2ab,\ 5b,\ 7ab^2$

5) $3x^2yz,\ 12x^2yz,\ 6xy^2z^3,\ 3xyz^2$

Factorise the following:

6) $2x+6$

7) $4x-4y$

8) $5x-5$

9) $4x-8xy$

10) $mx-my$

11) $ax+bx+cx$

12) $\dfrac{x}{2}-\dfrac{y}{8}$

13) $5a-10b+15c$

14) ax^2+ax

15) $2\pi r^2+\pi rh$

16) $3y-9y^2$

17) ab^3+a^2b

18) $x^2y^2-axy+bxy^2$

19) $5x^3-10x^2y+15xy^2$

20) $9x^3y-6x^2y^2+3xy^5$

21) $I_0+I_0\alpha t$

22) $\dfrac{x}{3}-\dfrac{y}{6}+\dfrac{z}{9}$

23) $2a^2-3ab+b^2$

24) x^3-x^2+7x

25) $\dfrac{m^2}{pn}-\dfrac{m^3}{pn^2}+\dfrac{m^4}{p^2n^2}$

Factorising by Grouping

To factorise the expression $ax+ay+bx+by$ first, group the terms in pairs so that each pair of terms has a common factor. Thus,

$$ax+ay+bx+by = (ax+ay)+(bx+by) = a(x+y)+b(x+y)$$

Now notice that in the two terms $a(x+y)$ and $b(x+y)$, a common factor is $(x+y)$.

$$
\begin{aligned}
\text{Hence,}\quad a(x+y)+b(x+y) &= (x+y)(a+b)\\
\therefore\quad ax+ay+bx+by &= (a+b)(x+y)
\end{aligned}
$$

$$
\begin{aligned}
\text{Similarly,}\quad np+mp-qn-qm &= (np+mp)-(qn+qm)\\
&= p(n+m)-q(n+m)\\
&= (p-q)(n+m)
\end{aligned}
$$

Exercise 4.4

Factorise the following:

1) $ax+by+bx+ay$

2) $mp+np-mq-nq$

3) $a^2c^2+acd+acd+d^2$

4) $2pr-4ps+qr-2qs$

5) $4ax+6ay-4bx-6by$

6) $ab(x^2+y^2)-cd(x^2+y^2)$

7) $mn(3x-1)-pq(3x-1)$

8) $k^2l^2-mnl-k^2l+mn$

Factorising Quadratic Expressions

A quadratic expression is one in which the highest power of the symbol used is the square. Typical examples are x^2-5x+3 or $3x^2-9$ in which there is no power of x greater than x^2.

You will see, from the work in the previous section, that when two binomial expressions are multiplied together the result is always a quadratic expression.

It is often necessary to try and reverse this procedure. This means that we start with a quadratic expression and wish to express this as the product of two binomial expressions – this is not always possible. For example the expressions x^2+1 or a^2+b^2 cannot be factorised. You may check this for yourself after following the next section of this chapter.

$$
\begin{aligned}
\text{Consider}\quad (7x+4)(2x+3) &= 14x^2+21x+8x+12\\
&= 14x^2+29x+12
\end{aligned}
$$

The following points should be noted:

1) The first terms in each bracket when multiplied together give the first term of the quadratic expression.

2) The middle term of the quadratic expression is formed by multiplying together the terms connected by a line (see the above equation) and then adding them together.

3) The last terms in each bracket when multiplied together give the last term of the quadratic expression.

In most cases, when factorising a quadratic expression, we find all the possible factors of the first and last terms. Then, by trying various combinations, the combination which gives the correct middle term may be found.

EXAMPLE 4.8

Factorise $2x^2 + 5x - 3$

Factors of $2x^2$		Factors of -3	
$2x$	x	$+1$	-3
		-1	$+3$

Combinations of these factors are:

$$(2x-3)(x+1) = 2x^2 - x - 3 \quad \text{which is incorrect,}$$
$$(2x+1)(x-3) = 2x^2 - 5x - 3 \quad \text{which is incorrect,}$$
$$(2x+3)(x-1) = 2x^2 + x - 3 \quad \text{which is incorrect,}$$
$$(2x-1)(x+3) = 2x^2 + 5x - 3 \quad \text{which is correct.}$$

Hence $\quad 2x^2 + 5x - 3 = (2x-1)(x+3)$

EXAMPLE 4.9

Factorise $12x^2 - 35x + 8$

Factors of $12x^2$		Factors of 8	
$12x$	x	1	8
$6x$	$2x$	8	1
$3x$	$4x$	-1	-8
		-8	-1
		2	4
		4	2
		-2	-4
		-4	-2

By trying each combination in turn the only one which will produce the correct middle term of $-35x$ is found to be $(3x-8)(4x-1)$.

$\therefore \quad 12x^2 - 35x + 8 = (3x-8)(4x-1)$

Where the Factors Form a Perfect Square

A quadratic expression, which factorises into the product of two identical brackets resulting in a perfect square, may be factorised by the method used previously. However, if you can recognise that the result will be a perfect square then the problem becomes easier.

It has been shown that

$$(a+b)^2 = a^2+2ab+b^2 \quad \text{and} \quad (a-b)^2 = a^2-2ab+b^2$$

The square of a binomial expression consists of:
(Square of 1st term) + (Twice the product of terms) + (Square of 2nd term)

EXAMPLE 4.10

Factorise $9a^2+12ab+4b^2$

Now $9a^2=(3a)^2$, $4b^2 = (2b)^2$ and $12ab = 2\times 3a\times 2b$

$$\therefore \quad 9a^2+12ab+4b^2 = (3a+2b)^2$$

EXAMPLE 4.11

Factorise $16m^2-40m+25$

Now $16m^2 = (4m)^2$, $25=(-5)^2$ and $-40m = 2\times 4m\times(-5)$

$$\therefore \quad 16m^2-40m+25 = (4m-5)^2$$

The Factors of the Difference of Two Squares

It has previously been shown that

$$(a+b)(a-b) = a^2-b^2$$

The factors of the difference of two squares are the sum and the difference of the square roots of each of the given terms.

EXAMPLE 4.12

Factorise $9m^2-4n^2$

Now $9m^2 = (3m)^2$ and $4n^2 = (2n)^2$

$$\therefore \quad 9m^2-4n^2 = (3m+2n)(3m-2n)$$

EXAMPLE 4.19

Simplify: **a)** $\dfrac{\frac{1}{x}+x}{\frac{1}{x}}$ **b)** $\dfrac{1}{\frac{1}{c}-\frac{1}{d}}$

a)

$$\frac{\frac{1}{x}+x}{\frac{1}{x}} = \left(\frac{1}{x}+x\right) \div \frac{1}{x}$$

$$= \left(\frac{1}{x}+\frac{x^2}{x}\right) \times \frac{x}{1}$$ we are making each term inside the brackets have a common denominator, namely, x

$$= \left(\frac{1+x^2}{\cancel{x}}\right) \times \cancel{x}$$ making use of the common denominator

$$= (1+x^2) \quad \text{or} \quad 1+x^2$$

b)

$$\frac{1}{\frac{1}{c}-\frac{1}{d}} = 1 \div \left(\frac{1}{c}-\frac{1}{d}\right)$$

$$= 1 \div \left(\frac{d}{cd}-\frac{c}{cd}\right)$$ again we are making each term inside the bracket have a common denominator – here cd

$$= 1 \div \left(\frac{d-c}{cd}\right)$$ making use of the common denominator

$$= 1 \times \left(\frac{cd}{d-c}\right)$$

$$= \frac{cd}{d-c}$$ and we cannot simplify any more

Exercise 4.9

Simplify:

1) $\dfrac{1}{1+\frac{1}{x}}$

2) $\dfrac{x-\frac{1}{x}}{\frac{1}{x}}$

3) $\dfrac{\frac{1}{a}}{a-\frac{1}{a}}$

4) $\dfrac{1}{\frac{1}{u}-1}$

5) $\dfrac{\frac{1}{x}+\frac{1}{y}}{\frac{1}{xy}}$

6) $\dfrac{1}{\frac{1}{R_1}+\frac{1}{R_2}}$

Where the Factors Form a Perfect Square

A quadratic expression, which factorises into the product of two identical brackets resulting in a perfect square, may be factorised by the method used previously. However, if you can recognise that the result will be a perfect square then the problem becomes easier.

It has been shown that

$$(a+b)^2 = a^2+2ab+b^2 \quad \text{and} \quad (a-b)^2 = a^2-2ab+b^2$$

The square of a binomial expression consists of:
(Square of 1st term) + (Twice the product of terms) + (Square of 2nd term)

EXAMPLE 4.10

Factorise $9a^2 + 12ab + 4b^2$

Now $9a^2 = (3a)^2$, $4b^2 = (2b)^2$ and $12ab = 2 \times 3a \times 2b$

$\therefore \quad 9a^2 + 12ab + 4b^2 = (3a + 2b)^2$

EXAMPLE 4.11

Factorise $16m^2 - 40m + 25$

Now $16m^2 = (4m)^2$, $25 = (-5)^2$ and $-40m = 2 \times 4m \times (-5)$

$\therefore \quad 16m^2 - 40m + 25 = (4m - 5)^2$

The Factors of the Difference of Two Squares

It has previously been shown that

$$(a+b)(a-b) = a^2 - b^2$$

The factors of the difference of two squares are the sum and the difference of the square roots of each of the given terms.

EXAMPLE 4.12

Factorise $9m^2 - 4n^2$

Now $9m^2 = (3m)^2$ and $4n^2 = (2n)^2$

$\therefore \quad 9m^2 - 4n^2 = (3m + 2n)(3m - 2n)$

EXAMPLE 4.13

Factorise $4x^2 - 9$

Now $4x^2 = (2x)^2$ and $9 = (3)^2$

$\therefore \quad 4x^2 - 9 = (2x + 3)(2x - 3)$

Exercise 4.5

Factorise:

1) $x^2 + 4x + 3$

2) $x^2 + 6x + 8$

3) $x^2 - 3x + 2$

4) $x^2 + 2x - 15$

5) $x^2 + 6x - 7$

6) $x^2 - 5x - 14$

7) $x^2 - 2xy - 3y^2$

8) $2x^2 + 13x + 15$

9) $3p^2 + p - 2$

10) $4x^2 - 10x - 6$

11) $3m^2 - 8m - 28$

12) $21x^2 + 37x + 10$

13) $10a^2 + 19a - 15$

14) $6x^2 + x - 35$

15) $6p^2 + 7pq - 3q^2$

16) $12x^2 - 5xy - 2y^2$

17) $x^2 + 2xy + y^2$

18) $4x^2 + 12x + 9$

19) $p^2 + 4pq + 4q^2$

20) $9x^2 + 6x + 1$

21) $m^2 - 2mn + n^2$

22) $25x^2 - 20x + 4$

23) $x^2 - 4x + 4$

24) $m^2 - n^2$

25) $4x^2 - y^2$

26) $9p^2 - 4q^2$

27) $x^2 - 1/9$

28) $1 - b^2$

29) $1/x^2 - 1/y^2$

30) $121p^2 - 64q^2$

Lowest Common Multiple (LCM)

The LCM of a set of algebraic terms is the simplest expression having each of the given terms as a factor.

The method used is similar to that for finding the LCM of a set of numbers.

EXAMPLE 4.14

Find the LCM of $2a$, $3ab$ and a^2b.

We express each term as a product of its factors.

Thus $\quad 2a = 2 \times a$

and $\quad 3ab = 3 \times a \times b$

and $\quad a^2b = a \times a \times b$

We now note the greatest number of times each factor occurs in any one particular line.

Now factor 2 occurs once in the line for $2a$,
and factor 3 occurs once in the line for $3ab$,
and factor a occurs twice in the line for a^2b,
and factor b occurs once in either of the lines for $3ab$ or a^2b

The product of these factors gives the required LCM.

Thus
$$\text{LCM} = 2 \times 3 \times a \times a \times b$$
$$= 6a^2b$$

EXAMPLE 4.15

Find the LCM of $4x$, $8yz$, $2x^2y$ and yz^2.

With practice the LCM may be found by inspection, by finding the product of the highest powers of *all* factors which occur in any of the terms.

Thus
$$\text{LCM} = 8 \times x^2 \times y \times z^2$$
$$= 8x^2yz^2$$

EXAMPLE 4.16

Find the LCM of $(a - 1)$, $n(m + n)$, and $(m + n)^2$.

Brackets must be treated as single factors – not the individual terms inside each bracket.

Hence
$$\text{LCM} = (a - 1) \times n \times (m + n)^2$$
$$= n(a - 1)(m + n)^2$$

Exercise 4.6

Find the LCM for the terms in each of the following examples:

1) $2a,\ 3a^2,\ a,\ a^2$

2) $xy,\ x^2y,\ 2x,\ 2y$

2) $m^2n,\ mn^2,\ mn,\ m^2n^2$

4) $2ab,\ abc,\ bc^2$

3) $2(x+1),\ (x+1)$

6) $(a+b),\ x(a+b)^2,\ x^2$

4) $(a+b),\ (a-b)$

8) $x,\ (1-x),\ (x+1)$

Algebraic Fractions

Since algebraic expressions contain symbols (or letters), which represent numbers, all the rules of operations with numbers also apply to algebraic terms, including fractions.

Thus $$\frac{1}{\frac{1}{a}} = 1 \div \frac{1}{a} = 1 \times \frac{a}{1} = \frac{1 \times a}{1} = a$$

and $$\frac{\frac{a}{b}}{\frac{c}{d}} = \frac{a}{b} \div \frac{c}{d} = \frac{a}{b} \times \frac{d}{c} = \frac{a \times d}{b \times c} = \frac{ad}{bc}$$

and $$\frac{x+y}{\frac{1}{x-y}} = \frac{(x+y)}{\frac{1}{(x-y)}} = (x+y) \div \frac{1}{(x-y)} = (x+y) \times \frac{(x-y)}{1}$$

$$= (x+y)(x-y)$$

You should note in the last example how we put brackets round the $(x+y)$ and $(x-y)$ to remind us that they must be treated as single expressions – otherwise we may have been tempted to handle the terms x and y on their own.

Adding and Subtracting Algebraic Fractions

Consider the expression $\frac{a}{b} + \frac{c}{d}$ which is the addition of two fractional terms.

These are called partial fractions.

If we wish to express the sum of these partial fractions as one single fraction then we proceed as follows. (The method is similar to that used when adding or subtracting number fractions.)

First find the lowest common denominator. This is the LCM of b and d which is bd. Each fraction is then expressed with bd as the denominator.

Now $\dfrac{a}{b} = \dfrac{a \times d}{b \times d} = \dfrac{ad}{bd}$ and $\dfrac{c}{d} = \dfrac{c \times b}{d \times b} = \dfrac{cb}{bd}$

and adding these new fractions we have:

$$\frac{a}{b} + \frac{c}{d} = \frac{ad}{bd} + \frac{cb}{bd} = \frac{ad + cb}{bd}$$

EXAMPLE 4.17

Express each of the following as a single fraction:

a) $\dfrac{1}{x} - \dfrac{1}{y}$ **b)** $a - \dfrac{1}{b}$ **c)** $\dfrac{1}{m} + n - \dfrac{a}{b}$

d) $\dfrac{a}{b^2} - \dfrac{1}{bc}$ **e)** $\dfrac{2}{x} + \dfrac{3}{x-1}$

a) $\dfrac{1}{x} - \dfrac{1}{y} = \dfrac{y}{xy} - \dfrac{x}{xy}$ since LCM of denominator is xy

$= \dfrac{y - x}{xy}$

b) $a - \dfrac{1}{b} = \dfrac{a}{1} - \dfrac{1}{b}$

$= \dfrac{ab}{b} - \dfrac{1}{b}$ since LCM of denominator is b

$= \dfrac{ab - 1}{b}$

c) $\dfrac{1}{m} + n - \dfrac{a}{b} = \dfrac{1}{m} + \dfrac{n}{1} - \dfrac{a}{b}$

$= \dfrac{b}{mb} + \dfrac{nmb}{mb} - \dfrac{am}{mb}$ since LCM of denominator is mb

$= \dfrac{b + nmb - am}{mb}$

d) $\dfrac{a}{b^2} - \dfrac{1}{bc} = \dfrac{ac}{b^2c} - \dfrac{b}{b^2c}$ since LCM of denominator is b^2c

$= \dfrac{ac - b}{b^2c}$

e) $$\frac{2}{x}+\frac{3}{x-1}=\frac{2(x-1)}{x(x-1)}+\frac{3x}{x(x-1)}$$ since LCM of denominator is $x(x-1)$

$$=\frac{2(x-1)+3x}{x(x-1)}$$

$$=\frac{2x-2+3x}{x(x-1)}$$

$$=\frac{5x-2}{x(x-1)}$$

Exercise 4.7

Rearrange the following and thus express in a simplified form:

1) $\dfrac{1}{\frac{b}{a}}$ 2) $\dfrac{\frac{1}{a}}{\frac{1}{b}}$ 3) $\dfrac{\frac{x}{y}}{\frac{y}{x}}$ 4) $\dfrac{1}{\frac{2}{xy}}$

5) $\dfrac{\frac{a}{b}}{a^2}$ 6) $\dfrac{(a+b)}{\frac{1}{c}}$ 7) $\dfrac{1-x}{\frac{1}{1+x}}$ 8) $\dfrac{\frac{1}{a-b}}{\frac{a-b}{c}}$

Express with a common denominator:

9) $\dfrac{1}{x}+\dfrac{1}{y}$

10) $1+\dfrac{1}{a}$

11) $\dfrac{m}{n}-1$

12) $\dfrac{b}{c}-c$

13) $\dfrac{a}{b}-\dfrac{c}{d}$

14) $\dfrac{a}{b}-\dfrac{1}{bc}$

15) $\dfrac{1}{xy}+\dfrac{1}{x}+1$

16) $\dfrac{3}{x}+\dfrac{x}{4}$

17) $\dfrac{3}{c}+\dfrac{2}{d}-\dfrac{5}{e}$

18) $\dfrac{a}{b}+\dfrac{c}{d}+1$

19) $\dfrac{1}{3fg}-\dfrac{5}{6gh}-\dfrac{1}{2fh}$

20) $\dfrac{2}{x}-\dfrac{4}{x+2}$

21) $1-\dfrac{x}{x-2}$

Expressing a Single Fraction as Partial Fractions

Here we are starting with a single fraction and then splitting it up into partial fractions – in fact it is the exact reverse of adding and subtracting fractions.

The procedure is to take each individual term of the numerator in turn, divide it by the denominator, and then write it on its own.

The following examples use this method.

EXAMPLE 4.18

Express as partial fractions: **a)** $\dfrac{ab + bc - 1}{abc}$ **b)** $\dfrac{(x-1)+y}{a(x-1)}$

a)

$$\frac{ab + bc - 1}{abc} = \frac{\cancel{ab}}{\cancel{ab}c} + \frac{\cancel{bc}}{a\cancel{bc}} - \frac{1}{abc}$$

$$= \frac{1}{c} + \frac{1}{a} - \frac{1}{abc}$$

b)

$$\frac{(x-1)+y}{a(x-1)} = \frac{\cancel{(x-1)}}{a\cancel{(x-1)}} + \frac{y}{a(x-1)}$$

$$= \frac{1}{a} + \frac{y}{a(x-1)}$$

Exercise 4.8

Express as partial fractions:

1) $\dfrac{a+b}{a}$ **2)** $\dfrac{a-b}{ab}$

3) $\dfrac{1+c}{c}$ **4)** $\dfrac{x^2+y}{2x}$

5) $\dfrac{a^2 - ab + ac}{abc}$ **6)** $\dfrac{x+(x-y)}{x(x-y)}$

Mixed Operations with Algebraic Fractions

We will now combine all the ideas already used. It helps to work methodically and to avoid taking short cuts by leaving out stages of simplification.

EXAMPLE 4.19

Simplify: **a)** $\dfrac{\frac{1}{x}+x}{\frac{1}{x}}$ **b)** $\dfrac{1}{\frac{1}{c}-\frac{1}{d}}$

a)

$$\frac{\frac{1}{x}+x}{\frac{1}{x}} = \left(\frac{1}{x}+x\right) \div \frac{1}{x}$$

$$= \left(\frac{1}{x}+\frac{x^2}{x}\right) \times \frac{x}{1}$$ we are making each term inside the brackets have a common denominator, namely, x

$$= \left(\frac{1+x^2}{\not{x}}\right) \times \not{x}$$ making use of the common denominator

$$= (1+x^2) \quad \text{or} \quad 1+x^2$$

b)

$$\frac{1}{\frac{1}{c}-\frac{1}{d}} = 1 \div \left(\frac{1}{c}-\frac{1}{d}\right)$$

$$= 1 \div \left(\frac{d}{cd}-\frac{c}{cd}\right)$$ again we are making each term inside the bracket have a common denominator – here cd

$$= 1 \div \left(\frac{d-c}{cd}\right)$$ making use of the common denominator

$$= 1 \times \left(\frac{cd}{d-c}\right)$$

$$= \frac{cd}{d-c}$$ and we cannot simplify any more

Exercise 4.9

Simplify:

1) $\dfrac{1}{1+\frac{1}{x}}$

2) $\dfrac{x-\frac{1}{x}}{\frac{1}{x}}$

3) $\dfrac{\frac{1}{a}}{a-\frac{1}{a}}$

4) $\dfrac{1}{\frac{1}{u}-1}$

5) $\dfrac{\frac{1}{x}+\frac{1}{y}}{\frac{1}{xy}}$

6) $\dfrac{1}{\frac{1}{R_1}+\frac{1}{R_2}}$

Solving Linear Equations 5

Equality of both sides – solve for one unknown – answer checks – simultaneous linear equations

LINEAR EQUATIONS

Linear equations occur more frequently than most other types; they are equations in which the variable is no higher than the first power, e.g. x or p. Equations arise from the modelling of engineering situations and so we must be able to solve them and find numerical solutions.

Linear equations contain only the first power of the unknown quantity.

Remember the first power of anything is written as itself, e.g. $a^1 = a$

So $\quad x + 7 = 10, \quad 6t = 4t + 9 \quad$ and $\quad \dfrac{5p}{3} = \dfrac{2p + 6}{2}$

are all examples of linear equations.

Solving Equations

The statement 'a number plus 7 equals 10'

may be written as an equation $x + 7 = 10$

We can see that there is only one value of x, namely 3, which will **'satisfy'** the equation, or make the left hand side (LHS) equal to the right hand side (RHS). The process of finding $x = 3$ is called **'solving'** the equation, and the value 3 is known as the **'solution'** or **'root'** of the equation.

When handling equations *balance* must be maintained between the LHS and the RHS.

Consider the pair of scales in balance.

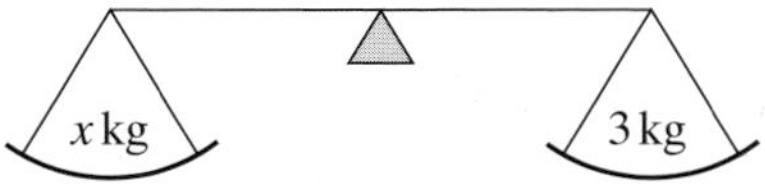

A mathematical model of this arrangement is the equation $\quad x = 3 \quad$ [1]

Now whatever changes we make to the left hand and right hand sides of an equation, *balance* must be maintained.

This new loading still keeps the balance.

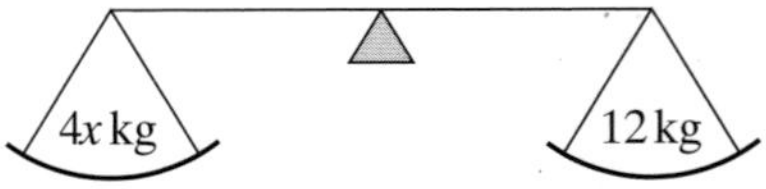

Now multiplying both sides of equation [1] by 4, then $\quad 4x = 4 \times 3$

giving $\quad 4x = 12$

Remember that when 'manipulating' an equation, whatever you do to one side of an equation you must do the same to the other.

For example if we add 7 to both sides of equation [1] $\quad x + 7 = 3 + 7$

giving $\quad x + 7 = 10$

Or if we divide both sides of equation [1] by 5 then $\quad \dfrac{x}{5} = \dfrac{3}{5}$

We may even become ambitious and square both sides of equation [1] $\quad x^2 = 3^2$

giving $\quad x^2 = 9$

Now let us use this idea of 'doing the same thing to both sides' to solve some equations.

EXAMPLE 5.1

Solve $\quad 7x = 5x + 18$

We shall group all the terms containing the unknown, here x, on one side (the LHS of the given equation), and the remainder on the other.

So if we subtract $5x$ from both sides, then $\quad 7x - 5x = \cancel{5x} + 18 - \cancel{5x}$

giving $\quad 2x = 18$

or dividing both sides by 2 $\quad \dfrac{\cancel{2}x}{\cancel{2}} = \dfrac{18}{2}$

giving $\quad x = 9$

We must now check to see if this value is correct. We shall substitute the value into both sides of the original equation.

Check: When then $x = 9$ then LHS $= 7 \times 9 = 63$, RHS $= 5 \times 9 + 18 = 63$. Thus, the value obtained is correct.

We say that $x = 9$ is the solution, or root, of the given equation – or we may say that $x = 9$ satisfies the given equation.

EXAMPLE 5.2

Solve $2(4y + 3) = 3y + 8$

Removing the bracket gives $8y + 6 = 3y + 8$

Subtracting $3y$ and 6 from both sides, then $8y + \not{6} - 3y - \not{6} = \not{3y} + 8 - \not{3y} - 6$

giving $5y = 2$

Dividing both sides by 5, then $\frac{\not{5}y}{\not{5}} = \frac{2}{5}$

from which $y = \frac{2}{5}$ or 0.4

Check: When $x = 0.4$

LHS $= 2(4 \times 0.4 + 3) = 9.2$
RHS $= 3 \times 0.4 + 8 = 9.2$ } Hence the solution is correct.

Equations Containing Fractions

Consider $\frac{2t}{5} + \frac{3}{2} = \frac{3t}{4} + 6$ and $\frac{1}{x-2} = \frac{2}{x} - 7$

Both are equations which contain fractions. They are not the 'flat line type' of equation with which we are familiar.

The method we use on these is to eliminate the fractions as a first step. This is achieved by multiplying through (i.e. multiplying both sides of the equation) by the LCM of the denominators.

You should remember that any individual term is a fraction if it has a top and bottom line; so both $\frac{3}{2}$ and $\frac{1}{x-2}$ are fractions and we must give them similar treatment.

EXAMPLE 5.3

Solve the equation $\frac{2t}{5} + \frac{3}{2} = \frac{3t}{4} + 6$

The LCM of the denominators 5, 2 and 4 is 20, since 20 is the lowest whole number into which 5, 2 and 4 will divide easily.

So multiplying both sides by 20, we have $\left(\frac{2t}{5} + \frac{3}{2}\right) \times 20 = \left(\frac{3t}{4} + 6\right) \times 20$

and removing brackets $\quad \dfrac{2t \times 20}{5} + \dfrac{3 \times 20}{2} = \dfrac{3t \times 20}{4} + 6 \times 20$

giving $\quad 8t + 30 = 15t + 120$

Subtracting $15t$ and 30 from both sides, then $\quad 8t + \cancel{30} - 15t - \cancel{30} = \cancel{15t} + 120 - \cancel{15t} - 30$

giving $\quad -7t = 90$

Dividing both sides by -7, then $\quad \dfrac{\cancel{-7}t}{\cancel{-7}} = \dfrac{90}{-7}$

or $\quad t = -12.9$ correct to 3 s.f.

Check: When $t = -12.9$ then LHS $= \frac{2}{5}(-12.9) + \frac{3}{2} = -3.66$

and RHS $= \frac{3}{4}(-12.9) + 6 = -3.68$

Bearing in mind the answer was rounded to 3 s.f. we may say that the LHS = RHS, and hence that the solution is correct.

EXAMPLE 5.4

Solve $\quad \dfrac{z-4}{3} - \dfrac{2z-1}{2} = 4$

The LCM of the denominators 3 and 2 is 6.

Multiplying through by 6 $\quad \dfrac{(z-4)}{3} \times 6 - \dfrac{(2z-1)}{2} \times 6 = 4 \times 6$

giving $\quad 2(z-4) - 3(2z-1) = 24$

Removing the brackets $\quad 2z - 8 - 6z + 3 = 24$

giving $\quad -4z - 5 = 24$

Adding 5 to both sides $\quad -4z - \cancel{5} + \cancel{5} = 24 + 5$

giving $\quad -4z = 29$

Dividing both sides by -4, then $\quad \dfrac{-\cancel{4}z}{-\cancel{4}} = \dfrac{29}{-4}$

giving $\quad z = -\dfrac{29}{4}$ or -7.25

Check this value for yourself to see if it is correct.

EXAMPLE 5.5

Solve the equation $\dfrac{3}{m+4} = \dfrac{7}{m}$

In order to bring the unknowns m to 'the top line' we will multiply both sides of the equation by the LCM of the denominators $m(m+4)$.

Multiplying both sides by $m(m+4)$, then $\quad \dfrac{3}{(m+4)} \times m(m+4) = \dfrac{7}{m} \times m(m+4)$

giving $\quad 3m = 7(m+4)$

$\therefore \quad 3m = 7m + 28$

Subtracting $7m$ from both sides, then $\quad 3m - 7m = 7m + 28 - 7m$

giving $\quad -4m = 28$

Dividing both sides by -4 $\quad \dfrac{-4m}{-4} = \dfrac{28}{-4}$

from which $\quad m = -7$

Again we will leave you to check if this answer is correct.

Exercise 5.1

1) $6m + 11 = 25 - m$

2) $1.2x - 0.8 = 0.8x + 1.2$

3) $5(m-2) = 15$

4) $3(x-1) - 4(2x+3) = 14$

5) $4(x-5) = 7 - 5(3-2x)$

6) $3x = 5(9-x)$

7) $\dfrac{x}{5} - \dfrac{x}{3} = 2$

8) $3m + \dfrac{3}{4} = 2 + \dfrac{2m}{3}$

9) $\dfrac{4}{t} = \dfrac{2}{3}$

10) $\dfrac{4}{7}y - \dfrac{3}{5}y = 2$

11) $\dfrac{1}{3x} + \dfrac{1}{4x} = \dfrac{7}{20}$

12) $\dfrac{x+3}{4} - \dfrac{x-3}{5} = 2$

13) $\dfrac{3-u}{4} = \dfrac{u}{3}$

14) $\dfrac{x-2}{x-3} = 3$

15) $\dfrac{3}{v-2} = \dfrac{4}{v+4}$

16) $\dfrac{x}{3} - \dfrac{3x-7}{5} = \dfrac{x-2}{6}$

17) Kirchhoff's laws in an electric circuit show that currents, i_1, i_2 and i_3 are connected by the equation $2i_1 + 3i_2 + i_3 = 5(i_2 - i_1)$.

If $i_2 = 7\,\text{A}$ and $i_3 = 5\,\text{A}$, find the value of current i_1.

18) If the sides of a sheet metal template which is triangular in shape have lengths of l, $(l+2)$ and $(2l+3)$, and the perimeter is 200 mm, find the length of the shortest side.

19) An inspection hatch covers an aperture which is rectangular in shape. If the depth, d, of the aperture is one half of the width, and the perimeter is 1.8 metres find the depth in millimetres.

20) Current division in an electric circuit is given by $i_2 = \left(\dfrac{R_2}{R_1+R_2}\right)i$.

Find resistance R_2 if $R_1 = 3$ ohms, $i_1 = 6$ amps and $i = 9$ amps.

21) In a particular fine measurement we have two lengths x and $(x+2)$. If the ratio of these lengths is $2:3$, what is the value of x?

22) For resistances in parallel the effective resistance R is given by the expression $R = \dfrac{R_1 R_2}{R_1+R_2}$.

Find the value of R_1, if $R = 1.8$ ohms and $R_2 = 4.9$ ohms.

SIMULTANEOUS EQUATIONS

Simultaneous equations result from a problem containing sets of data which must be taken together when solving. For instance the use of Kirchhoff's law at junctions in an electric circuit network may result in relationships which are completely different equations, each containing the same unknown currents.

Solution of Simultaneous Linear Equations

Remember that linear equations are those which contain only the first power of the unknown quantities. Two such equations may be obtained by applying Kirchhoff's laws to two junctions in an electric circuit network. These equations both contain unknown currents i_1 and i_2 and have to be solved 'together' or **'simultaneously'** as we say.

EXAMPLE 5.6

Two equations for currents i_1 and i_2 obtained as explained above are $5i_1 + 3i_2 = 19$ and $3i_1 + 2i_2 = 12$. Solve these equations simultaneously and hence find i_1 and i_2.

We have $\quad 5i_1 + 3i_2 = 19 \quad$ [1]

and $\quad 3i_1 + 2i_2 = 12 \quad$ [2]

Now if we multiply equation [1] by 3, and equation [2] by 5, then the coefficient of i_1 will be the same in both equations.

Thus $$15i_1 + 9i_2 = 57 \qquad [3]$$

and $$15i_1 + 10i_2 = 60 \qquad [4]$$

We may now eliminate i_1 by subtracting equation [3] from equation [4],

giving $$10i_2 - 9i_2 = 60 - 57$$

or $$i_2 = 3$$

To find the other unknown i_1 we may substitute in either of the original equations. So substituting $i_2 = 3$ into equation [1],

then $$5i_1 + 3 \times 3 = 19$$

giving $$5i_1 = 19 - 9$$

and hence $$i_1 = 2$$

Thus the two currents are $i_1 = 2$ and $i_2 = 3$.

We must now check these results. We know that the values satisfy equation [1] since it was used in the solution, so we should try the values in equation [2].

Thus for equation [2] $$\text{LHS} = 3 \times 2 + 2 \times 3$$
$$= 12 = \text{RHS}$$

So the values $i_1 = 2$ and $i_2 = 3$ also satisfy equation [2], and therefore may be considered to be correct.

Exercise 5.2

1) $3x + 2y = 7$
$x + y = 3$

2) $4x - 3y = 1$
$x + 3y = 19$

3) $x + 3y = 7$
$2x - 2y = 6$

4) $7x - 4y = 37$
$6x + 3y = 51$

5) $4x - 6y = -2.5$
$7x - 5y = -0.25$

6) $x + y = 17$
$\frac{x}{5} - \frac{y}{7} = 1$

7) $\frac{3x}{2} - 2y = \frac{1}{2}$
$x + \frac{3y}{2} = 6$

8) $2x + \frac{y}{2} = 11$
$\frac{3x}{5} + 3y = 9$

Problems Involving Simultaneous Equations

In problems, which involve two unknowns, it is necessary to form two separate equations from the given data and then to solve these simultaneously.

EXAMPLE 5.7

In a certain lifting machine, it is found from a test that the effort E and the load W, which is being raised, are connected by the equation $E = aW + b$. An effort of 3.7 N raises a load of 10 N whilst an effort of 7.2 N raises a load of 20 N. Find the values of the constants a and b and hence find the effort needed to lift a load of 12 N.

Substituting $E = 3.7$ and $W = 10$ into the given equation we have

$$3.7 = 10a + b \qquad [1]$$

Substituting $E = 7.2$ and $W = 20$ into the given equation we have

$$7.2 = 20a + b \qquad [2]$$

Subtracting equation [1] from equation [2] gives

$$3.5 = 10a$$

from which $a = 0.35$

Substituting for a in equation [1] gives

$$3.7 = 10 \times 0.35 + b$$

giving $3.7 = 3.5 + b$

or $b = 3.7 - 3.5 = 0.2$

The given equation therefore becomes:

$$E = 0.35W + 0.2$$

We leave you to check if these answers are correct.

When $W = 12$ $\quad E = 0.35 \times 12 + 0.2 = 4.2 + 0.2 = 4.4$

Hence an effort of 4.4 N is needed to raise a load of 12 N.

EXAMPLE 5.8

A heating installation for one house consists of 5 radiators and 4 convector heaters and the cost of the installation is £1130. In a second house 6 radiators and 7 convector heaters are used, the cost of this installation being £1740. The labour costs are £400 and £600 respectively. Find the cost of a radiator and the cost of a convector heater.

For the first house the cost of the heaters is

$$£1130 - £400 = £730$$

For the second house the cost of the heaters is

$$£1470 - £600 = £1140$$

Let $£x$ be the cost of a radiator and $£y$ be the cost of a convector heater.

For the first house, $5x + 4y = 730$ [1]

For the second house, $6x + 7y = 1140$ [2]

Multiplying [1] by 6 gives $30x + 24y = 4380$ [3]

Multiplying [2] by 5 $30x + 35y = 5700$ [4]

Subtracting equation [3] from equation [4] gives

$$11y = 1320$$

giving $y = 120$

Substituting for y in equation [1] gives

$$5x + 4 \times 120 = 730$$

or $5x = 250$

thus $x = 50$

Therefore the cost of a radiator is £50 and the cost of a convector heater is £120.

You should check these results as before.

Exercise 5.3

1) In an experiment to find the friction force F between two metallic surfaces when the load is W, the two quantities were connected by a law of the type $F = mW + b$. When $F = 2.5$, $W = 6$ and when $F = 3.1$, $W = 9$. Find the values of m and b. Hence find the value of F when $W = 12$.

2) A foreman and seven men together earn £1400 per week whilst two foremen and 17 men together earn £3304 per week. Find the earnings for a foreman and for a man.

3) For one installation 6 ceiling roses and 8 plugs are required, the total cost of these items being £16. For a second installation 5 ceiling roses and 12 plugs are used, the cost being £17.60. Find the cost of a ceiling rose and a plug.

4) In a certain lifting machine it is found that the effort E and the load W are connected by the equation $E = aW + b$. An effort of 2.6 raises a load of 8, whilst an effort of 3.8 raises a load of 12. Find the values of the constants a and b and determine the effort required to raise a load of 15.

5) If 100 m of wire and 8 plugs cost £62, whilst 150 m of wire and 10 plugs cost £90, find the cost of 1 m of wire and the cost of a plug.

6) An alloy containing 8 cm^3 of copper and 7 cm^3 of tin has a mass of 121 g. A second alloy containing 9 cm^3 of copper and 11 cm^3 of tin has a mass of 158 g. Find the densities of copper and tin in units g/cm^3.

7) An equation of motion for a motor vehicle is $s = ut + \frac{1}{2}at^2$ where s m is the distance travelled at time t s, the initial velocity is u m s^{-1} and the constant acceleration is a m s^{-2}.

Test measurements give $s = 32$ m when $t = 1.5$ s
and $s = 71$ m when $t = 3$ s

Find the values of the initial velocity and of the constant acceleration.

8) Applying Kirchhoff's laws to an electric circuit gives the following two relationships for currents i_1 and i_2:

$$6 - 0.3i_1 = 2(i_1 - i_2)$$

and

$$12 - 3.4i_2 = 3(i_2 - i_1)$$

Find the values of i_1 and i_2.

9) The relationship $R = R_0(1 + \alpha t)$ shows how a resistance R ohms varies with temperature t°C. R_0 is the value of the resistance at 0°C, and α is called the temperature coefficient of resistance. If $R = 28$ ohms at 40°C, and $R = 34$ ohms at 100°C, find the values of R_0 and α.

(Hint: Rearrange the equations, after putting in the given values, and form two simultaneous equations for $\dfrac{1}{R_0}$ and α.)

Transposition of Formulae 6

Equality of both sides – transposition where subject is contained in more than one term – formulae containing roots and powers

WHY TRANSPOSE FORMULAE?

We have an expression, often called a formula, which enables temperature in degrees Celsius to be calculated if we know the temperature in degrees Fahrenheit. Suppose, however, that we need a formula to give 'Fahrenheit' in terms of 'Celsius' – we now have to transpose the original expression.

When solving a linear equation we grouped all the terms containing the unknown, say x, on one side (usually the LHS) and the remainder on the other. We simplified the equation as we went along until a value was obtained for x. This rearrangement could have been called a transposition for x.

However, many equations, or formulae as they are often known, contain several symbols representing unknown quantities, and possibly numbers (called constants) as well.

Such an equation, containing three unknowns but no constants, is $W = IV$. This is a formula in which W is called the subject and is given in terms of I and V. We may wish to transpose this equation for V, which is the same as making V the subject, or rearranging for V in terms of I and W.

MAINTAINING EQUALITY OF BOTH SIDES OF AN EQUATION

As you will see from the worked examples which follow, we use the same rules for maintaining the balance between both sides of an equation as were used previously. The principal object is to group all the terms containing the subject on one side (usually the LHS) and the remainder on the other.

EXAMPLE 6.1

Power W, current I and voltage V, are connected by the formula $W = IV$. Transpose to make V the subject.

Divide both sides by I: $\qquad \dfrac{W}{I} = \dfrac{\cancel{I}V}{\cancel{I}}$

$$\therefore \qquad \frac{W}{I} = V$$

$$\text{or} \qquad V = \frac{W}{I}$$

Check: It is possible to check whether the transposition has been made correctly by substituting numerical values.

$$\text{Putting} \quad \left.\begin{aligned} I &= 6 \\ V &= 4 \end{aligned}\right\} \quad \text{into} \quad W = IV$$

$$\text{we get} \quad W = 6 \times 4 = 24$$

Now if we use the transposed form of the given equation,

$$\text{Putting} \quad \left.\begin{aligned} W &= 24 \\ I &= 6 \end{aligned}\right\} \quad \text{into} \quad V = \frac{W}{I}$$

$$\text{we get} \quad V = \frac{24}{6} = 4$$

and this verifies the correctness of the transposition.

You may say this was unnecessary as it was obvious the transposition was correct – but this is only because the original equation was comparatively simple. Just accept that this is the procedure and use it for the more difficult formulae.

EXAMPLE 6.2

Heat energy, H, is given by $H = I^2Rt$ where I is current, R is resistance and t is time. Make R the subject of the equation.

Divide both sides by I^2 and t $\qquad \dfrac{H}{I^2t} = \dfrac{\cancel{I^2}R\cancel{t}}{\cancel{I^2}\cancel{t}}$

$$\therefore \qquad \frac{H}{I^2t} = R$$

$$\text{or} \qquad R = \frac{H}{I^2t}$$

Check: Put $I = 3$, $R = 2$ and $t = 7$ and use the method given in the previous example.

EXAMPLE 6.3

The expression $R = \frac{V}{I}$ relates resistance R, voltage V, and current I. Express V in terms of R and I.

Multiply both sides by I $\quad R \times I = \frac{V}{\not{I}} \times \not{I}$

$\therefore \quad RI = V$

or $\quad V = RI$

Check this result for yourself.

EXAMPLE 6.4

The tension T in a cord which is whirling a mass m round in a circular path of radius r and tangential velocity v is given by $T = \frac{mv^2}{r}$.

Transpose for radius r.

Multiply both sides by r $\quad T \times r = \frac{mv^2}{\not{r}} \times \not{r}$

$\therefore \quad Tr = mv^2$

Divide both sides by T $\quad \frac{\not{T}r}{\not{T}} = \frac{mv^2}{T}$

$\therefore \quad r = \frac{mv^2}{T}$

Again, you may check this for yourself.

EXAMPLE 6.5

Temperature t on the Celsius scale, and temperature T on the Absolute scale are related by $T = t + 273$. Make t the subject.

Subtract 273 from both sides $\quad T - 273 = t + \not{273} - \not{273}$

giving $\quad T - 273 = t$

or $\quad t = T - 273$

Check this result for yourself.

EXAMPLE 6.6

Pressure p at a depth h in a fluid of density ρ is given by $p = p_a + \rho gh$ where p_a is atmospheric pressure and g is the gravitational constant. Express h in terms of the other symbols.

Subtract p_a from both sides $\quad p - p_a = \cancel{p_a} + \rho gh - \cancel{p_a}$

giving $\quad p - p_a = \rho gh$

Divide both sides by ρg $\quad \dfrac{p - p_a}{\rho g} = \dfrac{\cancel{\rho g}h}{\cancel{\rho g}}$

or $\quad h = \dfrac{p - p_a}{\rho g}$

Check this result for yourself.

EXAMPLE 6.7

F_1 and F_2 are the tensions in the tight and slack sides of a belt drive over a pulley wheel. The velocity v of the belt is given by $v = \dfrac{P}{F_1 - F_2}$ where P is the power transmitted. Make F_2 the subject of this formula.

Multiply both sides by $(F_1 - F_2)$ $\quad v(F_1 - F_2) = \dfrac{P}{\cancel{(F_1 - F_2)}} \times \cancel{(F_1 - F_2)}$

giving $\quad v(F_1 - F_2) = P$

Divide both sides by v $\quad \dfrac{\cancel{v}(F_1 - F_2)}{\cancel{v}} = \dfrac{P}{v}$

giving $\quad (F_1 - F_2) = \dfrac{P}{v}$

Subtract F_1 from both sides $\quad \cancel{F_1} - F_2 - \cancel{F_1} = \dfrac{P}{v} - F_1$

giving $\quad -F_2 = \dfrac{P}{v} - F_1$

Multiply both sides by (-1) $\quad -F_2(-1) = \left(\dfrac{P}{v} - F_1\right)(-1)$

giving $\quad F_2 = \dfrac{P}{v}(-1) - F_1(-1)$

or $\quad F_2 = F_1 - \dfrac{P}{v}$

Check: Let us use $F_1 = 3$, $F_2 = 1$ and $P = 8$ in the given equation

then $$v = \frac{8}{3-1} = 4$$

and putting $F_1 = 3$, $P = 8$ and $v = 4$ into the transposed form,

then: $$F_2 = 3 - \frac{8}{4} = 1$$

and this verifies the transposition.

EXAMPLE 6.8

The resistance R of a wire after a temperature rise t is given by $R = R_0(1 + \alpha t)$ where R_0 is the resistance at zero temperature and α is the temperature coefficient of resistance. Transpose for t.

We may approach this problem in two ways:

Either (a) Divide both sides by R_0 $$\frac{R}{R_0} = \frac{\cancel{R_0}(1 + \alpha t)}{\cancel{R_0}}$$

giving $$\frac{R}{R_0} = (1 + \alpha t)$$

Subtract 1 from both sides $$\frac{R}{R_0} - 1 = \cancel{1} + \alpha t - \cancel{1}$$

giving $$\alpha t = \frac{R}{R_0} - 1$$

Divide both sides by α $$\frac{\cancel{\alpha} t}{\cancel{\alpha}} = \frac{(R/R_0 - 1)}{\alpha}$$

So the first solution $$t = \frac{1}{\alpha}\left(\frac{R}{R_0} - 1\right)$$

or (b) Remove the bracket $$R = R_0 + R_0\alpha t$$

Subtract R_0 from both sides $$R - R_0 = R_0\alpha t$$

Divide both sides by $R_0\alpha$ $$\frac{R - R_0}{R_0\alpha} = \frac{\cancel{R_0\alpha} t}{\cancel{R_0\alpha}}$$

Thus the second solution $$t = \frac{R - R_0}{R_0\alpha}$$

We will leave you to verify that the two solutions are both versions of the same result.

TRANSPOSITION WITH SUBJECT IN MORE THAN ONE TERM

EXAMPLE 6.9

The percentage profit P made in a transaction, where the selling price is s and the buying price was b, is given by

$$P = \frac{s-b}{b} \times 100$$

Make b the subject of this equation.

Multiply both sides by b $\quad P \times b = \frac{(s-b)}{\cancel{b}} \times 100 \times \cancel{b}$

Removing the brackets $\quad Pb = 100s - 100b$

Add $100b$ to both sides $\quad Pb + 100b = 100s - \cancel{100b} + \cancel{100b}$

Factorising the LHS $\quad b(P + 100) = 100s$

Divide both sides by $(P + 100)$ $\quad \frac{b\cancel{(P+100)}}{\cancel{(P+100)}} = \frac{100s}{(P+100)}$

giving $\quad b = \frac{100s}{(P+100)}$

Check this transposition for yourself.

EXAMPLE 6.10

A formula for resistances connected in parallel in an electrical circuit is

$R = \frac{R_1 R_2}{R_1 + R_2}$. Transpose for R_1.

The LCM of the RHS is $(R_1 + R_2)$ so we

Multiply both sides of the given equation by $(R_1 + R_2)$ $\quad R(R_1 + R_2) = \frac{R_1 R_2}{\cancel{(R_1 + R_2)}} \times \cancel{(R_1 + R_2)}$

Remove brackets $\quad RR_1 + RR_2 = R_1 R_2$

and taking RR_1 from both sides $\quad \cancel{RR_1} + RR_2 - \cancel{RR_1} = R_1 R_2 - RR_1$

from which $\quad R_1 R_2 - RR_1 = RR_2$

Factorise the LHS $\quad R_1(R_2 - R) = RR_2$

Divide through by $(R_2 - R)$ $\qquad \dfrac{R_1(R_2 - R)}{(R_2 - R)} = \dfrac{RR_2}{(R_2 - R)}$

thus $\qquad R_1 = \dfrac{RR_2}{(R_2 - R)}$

We leave you to verify the result.

Exercise 6.1

1) In thermodynamics the characteristic gas equation is $pV = nRT$ which connects pressure p, volume V and temperature T. Make T the subject of this formula.

2) A large cone has radius R and height H. A small cone has radius r and height h. These dimensions are related by $\dfrac{R}{r} = \dfrac{H}{h}$. Rearrange this equation for h.

3) The equation of motion $v = u + at$ is for movement with constant acceleration a. The initial velocity is u and the final velocity is v arrived at after time t. Make u the subject of the equation.

4) Using $v = u + at$ again, transpose for t.

5) Temperature in degrees Fahrenheit F and in degrees Celsius C are related by $F = \dfrac{9}{5}C + 32$. Rearrange this formula for C.

6) The standard equation of a straight line is $y = mx + c$ in coordinate geometry. Rearrange to make x the subject of the equation.

7) Provided r is less than 1, the sum to infinity, S, of a geometric progression is given by the expression $S = \dfrac{a}{1 - r}$ where a is the first term and r is the common ratio. Transpose to make r the subject.

8) The current I and the voltage V in a circuit containing two resistances R and r in series are connected by the formula $I = \dfrac{V}{R + \mathrm{r}}$. Transpose for R.

9) The surface area S of a cone having height h and base radius r is given by $S = \pi r(r + h)$. Find h in terms of π, r and S.

10) The expression $H = \omega s(T - t)$ is used in finding total heat H. Rearrange to make T the subject of the formula.

11) The length l of a metal bar varies with the temperature t according to the relationship $l = l_0(1 + \alpha t)$ where l_0 is the initial length and α is the coefficient of linear expansion. Transpose the equation for t expressing the RHS as a single fraction.

12) The common difference d of an arithmetic progression whose sum S to n terms is given by $d = \dfrac{2(S - an)}{n(n - 1)}$ where the first term is a.

Transpose this formula: **a)** for S and **b)** for a.

13) The expression $R = \dfrac{1}{1/R_1 + 1/R_2}$ is for resistances in parallel in an electrical circuit. Transpose for R_1.

14) Another form of the expression for parallel resistances in an electrical circuit is $R = \dfrac{R_1 R_2}{R_1 + R_2}$. Make R_2 the subject of this equation.

TRANSPOSITION OF FORMULAE CONTAINING ROOTS AND POWERS

The same basic principles of transposition apply here. In Example 6.11 the new subject, albeit squared, has been isolated on the LHS – thus to obtain u we take the square root of both sides, so maintaining the balance of the equation.

In Example 6.12 the new subject is 'inside the square root'. If we square both sides of the equation we can get rid of the square root and then carry on the transposition as usual.

EXAMPLE 6.11

An equation of motion for constant acceleration a is $v^2 = u^2 + 2as$ where the initial velocity u is changed to the final velocity v after travelling a distance s. Make u the subject of the equation.

Subtract $2as$ from both sides $\qquad v^2 - 2as = u^2 + \cancel{2as} - \cancel{2as}$

giving $\qquad u^2 = v^2 - 2as$

Taking the square root of both sides $\qquad \sqrt{u^2} = \sqrt{v^2 - 2as}$

giving $\qquad u = \sqrt{v^2 - 2as}$

Check this result for yourself.

EXAMPLE 6.12

The period t of a simple pendulum of length l is given by $t = 2\pi\sqrt{\dfrac{l}{g}}$ where g is the gravitational constant. Transpose this equation for l.

Divide both sides by 2π $$\frac{t}{2\pi} = \sqrt{\frac{l}{g}}$$

Square both sides $$\left(\frac{t}{2\pi}\right)^2 = \left(\sqrt{\frac{l}{g}}\right)^2$$

or $$\frac{t^2}{4\pi^2} = \frac{l}{g}$$

Multiply both sides by g $$l = \frac{t^2 g}{4\pi^2}$$

Again we leave the checking to you.

Exercise 6.2

1) The velocity v of a jet of water is given by the expression $v = \sqrt{2gh}$. Transpose this for head of water h.

2) The formula $A = \pi r^2$ gives the area A of a circle in terms of its radius r. Find r in terms of π and A.

3) The kinetic energy E of a mass m travelling at velocity v is given by $E = \frac{1}{2}mv^2$. Make v the subject of this expression.

4) The diameter d of a circle of area A is given by $d = 2\sqrt{\dfrac{A}{\pi}}$. Find A in terms of π and d.

5) The strain energy U of a material under stress is given by $U = \dfrac{f^2V}{2E}$. Rearrange this for f.

6) In a right-angled triangle $b = \sqrt{a^2 - c^2}$. Transpose for c.

7) The frequency f of a simple pendulum is given by $f = \dfrac{1}{2\pi}\sqrt{\dfrac{g}{l}}$. Make l the subject of this expression.

8) A shaft is acted on by a bending moment M and a torque T. The equivalent torque T_e is given by $T_e^2 = M^2 + T^2$. Transpose this for M.

9) The crippling load on a strut, according to the Euler theory, is given by $P = \dfrac{\pi^2 EI}{(CL)^2}$. Make C the subject of this equation.

10) The total energy E_t of a mass m at a height h above a given datum and travelling with a velocity v is given by the equation $E_t = mgh + \frac{1}{2}mv^2$. Find an expression for velocity v.

11) A property of a solid rectangular block, called the radius of gyration, is given by $k = \sqrt{\dfrac{a^2 + b^2}{12}}$. Rearrange this equation for b.

12) A property of a solid cylinder, called the radius of gyration k, is given by $k = \sqrt{\dfrac{L^2}{12} + \dfrac{R^2}{4}}$. Make L the subject of this equation.

13) A formula connected with stress in cylinders is $\dfrac{D}{d} = \sqrt{\dfrac{f+p}{f-p}}$. Transpose this for f.

14) A formula for equivalent shear load in the design of a bolt is $Q_e = \frac{1}{2}\sqrt{P^2 + Q^2}$. Rearrange this to make an equation for P.

15) A formula for the equivalent tensile load P_e in the design of a bolt is $P_e = \frac{1}{2}(P + \sqrt{P^2 + 4Q^2})$. Transpose for Q.

Quadratic Equations

7

Recognition – roots – solution by factors – solution by formula – problems involving quadratics

WHAT IS A QUADRATIC EQUATION?

Just as we have been able to solve simple equations, we may well have to cope with more difficult arrangements. Consider a square whose side is x units long and whose area is 4 square units – to find the area we use the equation $x^2 = 4$. This is an example of a quadratic equation – this one is simple but they can be more extensive.

An equation of the type $ax^2 + bx + c = 0$, involving x in the second degree and containing no higher power of x, is called a quadratic equation. The constants a, b and c have any numerical values. Thus:

$$x^2 - 9 = 0 \quad \text{where} \quad a = 1,\ b = 0 \quad \text{and} \quad c = -9$$

$$x^2 - 2x - 8 = 0 \quad \text{where} \quad a = 1,\ b = -2 \quad \text{and} \quad c = -8$$

$$2.5x^2 - 3.1x - 2 = 0 \quad \text{where} \quad a = 2.5,\ b = -3.1 \quad \text{and} \quad c = -2$$

are all examples of quadratic equations. A quadratic equation may contain only the square of the unknown quantity, as in the first of the above equations, or it may contain both the square and the first power as in the other two.

There are two commonly used methods of solution:

1) by factorisation, and

2) by use of a formula.

1) *Factorisation* is the reverse of multiplying two brackets together. On seeing a quadratic equation our first thoughts are usually 'can we factorise it easily?' If we can, it provides a quick and neat method, but if there is any difficulty go immediately to method 2):

2) *Use of a formula* which, although more tedious, can be used for solving any quadratic equation.

ROOTS OF AN EQUATION

Before we commence solving equations it is instructive to work backwards from knowing the solutions or roots, and then constructing the quadratic equation which they satisfy.

If either of two factors has zero value, then their product is zero.

Thus if either $M = 0$ or $N = 0$ then $M \times N = 0$

Now suppose that either $x = 1$ or $x = 2$

$\therefore$ rearranging gives either $x - 1 = 0$ or $x - 2 = 0$

Hence $(x - 1)(x - 2) = 0$

since either of the factors has zero value.

If we now multiply out the brackets of this equation we have.

$$x^2 - 3x + 2 = 0$$

and we know that $x = 1$ and $x = 2$ are values of x which satisfy this equation. The values 1 and 2 are called the solutions or roots of the equation $x^2 - 3x + 2 = 0$

EXAMPLE 7.1

Find the equation whose roots are -2 and 4.

From the values given either $x = -2$ or $x = 4$

$\therefore$ either $x + 2 = 0$ or $x - 4 = 0$

Hence $(x + 2)(x - 4) = 0$

since either of the factors is zero

$\therefore$ multiplying out gives $x^2 - 2x - 8 = 0$

EXAMPLE 7.2

Find the equation whose roots are 3 and -3.

From the values given either $x = 3$ or $x = -3$

$\therefore$ either $x - 3 = 0$ or $x + 3 = 0$

Hence $(x - 3)(x + 3) = 0$

since either of the factors is zero

$\therefore$ multiplying out gives $x^2 - 9 = 0$

EXAMPLE 7.3

Find the equation whose roots are 5 and 0.

From the values given either $x = 5$ or $x = 0$

$\therefore$ either $x - 5 = 0$ or $x = 0$

Hence $x(x-5) = 0$

since either of the factors is zero

And multiplying out gives $x^2 - 5x = 0$

Exercise 7.1

Find the equations whose roots are:

1) 3, 1

2) 2, −4

3) −1, −2

4) 1.6, 0.7

5) 2.73, −1.66

6) −4.76, −2.56

7) 0, 1.4

8) −4.36, 0

9) −3.5, +3.5

10) repeated, each = 4

SOLUTION BY FACTORS

This method is the reverse of the procedure used to find an equation when given the two roots. We shall now start with the equation and proceed to solve the equation and find the roots.

We shall again use the fact that if the product of two factors is zero then one factor or the other must be zero.

Thus if $M \times N = 0$ then either $M = 0$ or $N = 0$

When the factors are easy to find, the factor method is very quick and simple. However do not spend too long trying to find factors: if they are not readily found use the formula given in the next method to solve the equation.

EXAMPLE 7.4

Solve the equation $(2x+3)(x-5) = 0$

Since the product of the two factors $2x + 3$ and $x - 5$ is zero then

either $2x + 3 = 0$ or $x - 5 = 0$

Hence $x = -\dfrac{3}{2}$ or $x = 5$

EXAMPLE 7.5

Solve the equation $6x^2 + x - 15 = 0.$

Factorising gives $(2x - 3)(3x + 5) = 0$

either $2x - 3 = 0$ or $3x + 5 = 0$

Hence $x = \frac{3}{2}$ or $x = -\frac{5}{3}$

EXAMPLE 7.6

Solve the equation $14x^2 = 29x - 12.$

Bring all the terms to the left-hand side $14x^2 - 29x + 12 = 0$

Factorising gives $(7x - 4)(2x - 3) = 0$

$\therefore$ either $7x - 4 = 0$ or $2x - 3 = 0$

Hence $x = \frac{4}{7}$ or $x = \frac{3}{2}$

EXAMPLE 7.7

Find the roots of the equation $x^2 - 16 = 0.$

Factorising gives $(x - 4)(x + 4) = 0$

$\therefore$ either $x - 4 = 0$ or $x + 4 = 0$

Hence $x = 4$ or $x = -4$

In this case an alternative method may be used: rearranging the given equation gives $x^2 = 16$ and taking the square root of both sides $x = \sqrt{16} = \pm 4.$ Remember that when we take a square root we must insert the $\pm$ sign, because $(+4)^2 = 16$ and $(-4)^2 = 16.$

EXAMPLE 7.8

Solve the equation $x^2 - 2x = 0.$

Factorising gives $x(x - 2) = 0$

$\therefore$ either $x = 0$ or $x - 2 = 0$

Hence $x = 0$ or $x = 2$

Note: The solution $x = 0$ must not be omitted as it is a solution in the same way as $x = 2$ is a solution. Equations should not be divided through by variables, such as x, and then mindlessly discarded since this removes a root of the equation.

EXAMPLE 7.9

Solve the equation $x^2 - 6x + 9 = 0$.

Factorising gives $(x - 3)(x - 3) = 0$

$\therefore$ either $x - 3 = 0$ or $x - 3 = 0$

Hence $x = 3$ or $x = 3$

In this case there is only one arithmetical value for the solution. Technically, however, there are two roots and when they have the same numerical value they are said to be repeated roots.

SOLUTION BY FORMULA

In general quadratic expressions do not factorise easily and so some other method of solving quadratic equations must be used.

The standard form of the quadratic equation is:

$$ax^2 + bx + c = 0$$

The solution of the equation is:

$$x = \frac{-b \pm \sqrt{b^2 - 4ac}}{2a}$$

EXAMPLE 7.10

Solve the equation $3x^2 - 8x + 2 = 0$.

Comparing with $ax^2 + bx + c = 0$, we have $a = 3$, $b = -8$ and $c = 2$.

If your calculator has a built-in program for solving quadratic equations, go ahead and make use of it. If not, choose your own calculator sequence for the solution shown below. We would suggest that when you first find the value of the square root you put it into memory so that it can be recalled later when you are finding the other solution.

Substituting these values in the formula, we have

$$x = \frac{-(-8) \pm \sqrt{(-8)^2 - 4 \times 3 \times 2}}{2 \times 3}$$

$$= \frac{8 \pm \sqrt{64 - 24}}{6} = \frac{8 \pm \sqrt{40}}{6} = \frac{8 \pm 6.325}{6}$$

$\therefore$ either $x = \frac{8 + 6.325}{6}$ or $x = \frac{8 - 6.325}{6}$

The two solutions are therefore

$$x = 2.39 \quad \text{or} \quad x = 0.28 \quad \text{correct to 2 d.p.}$$

It is important that we check the solutions in case we have made an error. We may do this by substituting the values obtained in the left-hand side of the given equation and checking that the solution is zero, or approximately zero.

Thus when $x = 2.39$ we have LHS $= 3(2.39)^2 - 8(2.39) + 2 \approx 0$

and when $x = 0.28$ we have LHS $= 3(0.28)^2 - 8(0.28) + 2 \approx 0$

EXAMPLE 7.11

Solve the equation $2.13x^2 + 0.75x - 6.89 = 0$.

Comparing with $ax^2 + bx + c = 0$ we have $a = 2.13$, $b = 0.75$ and $c = -6.89$

$$x = \frac{-0.75 \pm \sqrt{(0.75)^2 - 4 \times 2.13 \times (-6.89)}}{2 \times 2.13}$$

$$= \frac{-0.75 \pm 7.698}{4.26}$$

$\therefore$ either $x = \frac{-0.75 + 7.698}{4.26}$ or $x = \frac{-0.75 - 7.698}{4.26}$

Hence $x = 1.631$ or $x = -1.983$ correct to 4 s.f.

Solution check

When $x = 1.631$

we have LHS $= 2.13(1.631)^2 + 0.75(1.631) - 6.89 \approx 0$

and when $x = -1.983$

we have LHS $= 2.13(-1.983)^2 + 0.75(-1.983) - 6.89 \approx 0$

EXAMPLE 7.12

Solve the equation $x^2 + 4x + 5 = 0$.

Here $a = 1$, $b = 4$ and $c = 5$

$$\therefore \quad x = \frac{-4 \pm \sqrt{4^2 - 4(1)(5)}}{2(1)} = \frac{-4 \pm \sqrt{16 - 20}}{2} = \frac{-4 \pm \sqrt{-4}}{2}$$

Now when a number is squared the answer must be a positive quantity because two quantities having the same sign are being multiplied together. Therefore, the square root of a negative quantity, such as -4 in the above equation, has no arithmetical meaning and is called an imaginary quantity. The equation $x^2 + 4x + 5 = 0$ is said to have imaginary or complex roots. Equations which have complex roots are beyond the scope of this book and are dealt with in more advanced mathematics.

Exercise 7.2

Solve the following equations by the factor method:

1) $x^2 - 36 = 0$

2) $4x^2 - 6.25 = 0$

3) $9x^2 - 16 = 0$

4) $x^2 + 9x + 20 = 0$

5) $x^2 + x - 72 = 0$

6) $3x^2 - 7x + 2 = 0$

7) $m^2 = 6m - 9$

8) $m^2 + 4m + 4 = 36$

9) $14q^2 = 29q - 12$

10) $9x + 28 = 9x^2$

Solve the following equations by using the quadratic formula:

11) $4x^2 - 3x - 2 = 0$

12) $x^2 - x + \frac{1}{4} = \frac{1}{9}$

13) $3x^2 + 7x - 5 = 0$

14) $7x^2 + 8x - 2 = 0$

15) $5x^2 - 4x - 1 = 0$

16) $2x^2 - 7x = 3$

17) $x^2 + 0.3x - 1.2 = 0$

18) $2x^2 - 5.3x + 1.25 = 0$

Solve the following equations:

19) $x(x + 4) + 2x(x + 3) = 5$

20) $x^2 - 2x(x - 3) = -20$

21) $\dfrac{2}{x + 2} + \dfrac{3}{x + 1} = 5$

22) $\dfrac{x + 2}{3} - \dfrac{5}{x + 2} = 4$

23) $\dfrac{6}{x} - 2x = 2$

24) $40 = \dfrac{x^2}{80} + 4$

25) $\dfrac{x + 2}{x - 2} = x - 3$

26) $\dfrac{1}{x + 1} - \dfrac{1}{x + 3} = 15$

PROBLEMS INVOLVING QUADRATIC EQUATIONS

Having learnt how to solve quadratic equations, we shall now see how they arise from engineering situations.

EXAMPLE 7.13

The distance s m moved by a vehicle in time t s with an initial velocity a m/s and a constant acceleration a m/s^2 is given by $s = ut + \frac{1}{2}at^2$.

Find the time taken to cover 84 m with a constant acceleration of 2 m/s^2 if the initial velocity is 5 m/s.

Using $s = 84$, $u = 5$ and $a = 2$

We have $84 = 5t + \frac{1}{2}2t^2$

from which $t^2 + 5t - 84 = 0$

Factorising gives $(t + 12)(t - 7) = 0$

$\therefore$ either $t + 12 = 0$ or $t - 7 = 0$

$\therefore$ either $t = -12$ or $t = 7$

Now the solution $t = -12$ is not acceptable since negative time has no meaning in this question. Thus, the required time is 7 seconds.

Solution check

When $t = 7$ we have LHS $= 7^2 + 5 \times 7 - 84 = 0$

EXAMPLE 7.14

A miniaturised circuit board is rectangular in shape. The diagonal of the rectangle is 15 mm long and one side is 2 mm longer than the other. Find the dimensions of the circuit board.

In Fig. 7.1 let length of BC be x mm. The length of CD is then $(x + 2)$ mm. $ABCD$ is right-angled and so by Pythagoras (Chapter 12):

$$x^2 + (x + 2)^2 = 15^2$$

$$x^2 + x^2 + 4x + 4 = 225$$

$$2x^2 + 4x - 221 = 0$$

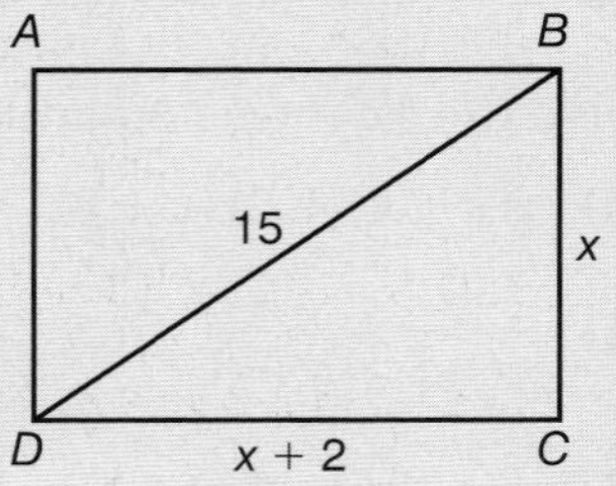

Fig. 7.1

Here, $a = 2$, $b = 4$ and $c = -221$

$$\therefore \quad x = \frac{-4 \pm \sqrt{4^2 - 4 \times 2 \times (-221)}}{2 \times 2}$$

$\therefore \quad x = 9.56$ or $x = -11.56$ correct to 2 d.p.

Since the answer cannot be negative, then $x = 9.56$ mm

and $$DC = 9.56 + 2 = 11.56\text{ mm}$$

Thus the circuit board has adjacent sides equal to 9.56 mm and 11.56 mm.

Solution check
When $x = 9.56$ we have LHS $= 2(9.56)^2 + 4(9.56) - 221 \approx 0$

EXAMPLE 7.15

A section of an air duct is shown by the full lines in Fig. 7.2.

a) Show that $w^2 - 2Rw + \dfrac{R^2}{4} = 0$

b) Find the value of w when $R = 2$ m.

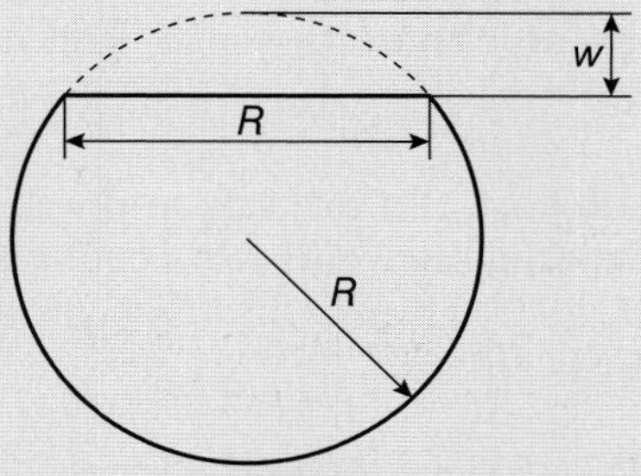

Fig. 7.2

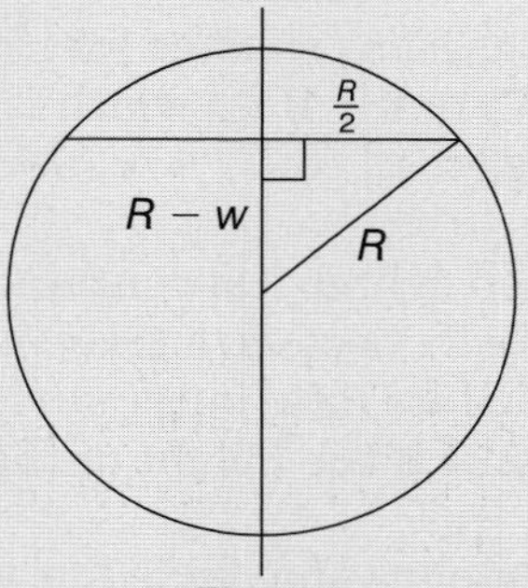

Fig. 7.3

a) Using the construction shown in Fig. 7.3 we have, by Pythagoras,

then $$(R - w)^2 + \left(\frac{R}{2}\right)^2 = R^2$$

∴ $$R^2 - 2Rw + w^2 + \frac{R^2}{4} = R^2$$

∴ $$w^2 - 2Rw + \frac{R^2}{4} = 0$$

b) When $R = 2$ $$w^2 - 4w + 1 = 0$$

Here $a = 1$, $b = -4$ and $c = 1$

∴ $$w = \frac{-(-4) \pm \sqrt{(-4)^2 - 4 \times 1 \times 1}}{2 \times 1}$$

Here $w = 3.732$ or 0.268 m correct to 3 d.p.

Now w must be less than 2 m, thus $w = 0.268$ mm.

Solution check

When $w = 0.268$ we have LHS $= (0.268)^2 - 4(0.268) + 1 \approx 0$

Exercise 7.3

1) The length L of a wire stretched tightly between two supports in the same horizontal line is given by

$$L = S + \frac{8D^2}{3S}$$

where S is the span and D is the (small) sag. If $L = 150$ and $D = 5$, find the value of S.

2) The profile of a pattern for a sheet metal infill plate is that of a right-angled triangle. The longest side is twice as long as one of the sides forming the right angle. If the remaining side is 80 mm long, find the length of the longest side.

3) A rectangular shutter for closing off a ventilator duct covers an area of $6175\ \text{mm}^2$. If its width is 30 mm greater than its depth, find its dimensions.

4) A closed cylindrical container is used as part of a test rig, and will eventually become a reservoir in an expansion circuit for a cooling liquid. If its total outer surface area is $29\,000\ \text{mm}^2$, find the value of its radius if the height of the container is 75 mm.

5) If a segment of a circle has a radius R, a height H and a length of chord W show that

$$R = \frac{W^2}{8H} + \frac{H}{2}$$

Rearrange this equation to give a quadratic equation for H and hence find H when $R = 12$ m and $W = 8$ m.

6) Fig. 7.4 shows a template whose area is $9690\ \text{mm}^2$. Find the value of r.

7) A pressure vessel is of the shape shown in Fig. 7.5, the radius of the vessel being r mm. If the surface area is $30\,000\ \text{mm}^2$ find r.

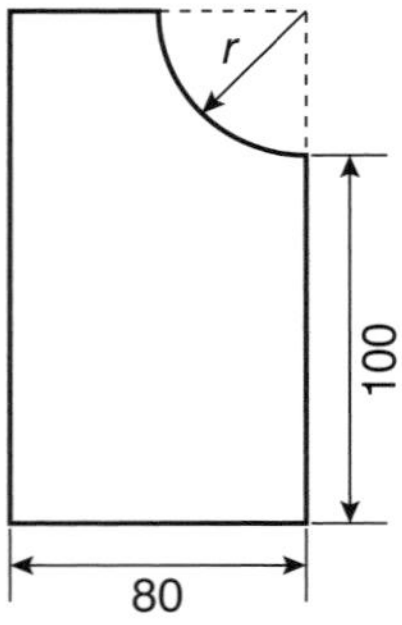

Fig. 7.4

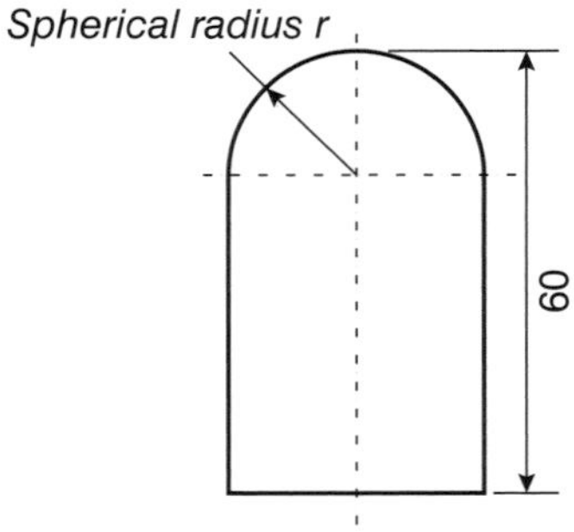

Fig. 7.5

8) The total iron loss in a transformer is given by the equation $P = 0.1f + 0.006f^2$. If $P = 20$ watts find the value of the frequency f.

9) The volume of a frustum of a cone is given by the formula $V = \frac{1}{3}\pi h(R^2 + rR + r^2)$ where h is the height of the frustum and R and r are the radii at the large and small ends respectively. If $h = 9$ m, $R = 4$ m and the volume is $337.2\ \text{m}^3$, what is the value of r?

10) A square steel plate is pierced by a square tool leaving a margin of 20 mm all round. The area of the hole is one third that of the original plate. What are the dimensions of the original plate?

11) The velocity v of a body in terms of time t is given by the expression $v = 3t^2 - 6t - 3$. Find the times at which the velocity is zero.

8 Indices

Index – base – power – laws of indices – positive, negative and fractional indices

Indices are an extremely useful tool in mathematics. One typical case is their use when large numbers, such as ten million – which is cumbersome to write – may be expressed concisely as 10^7. This is a neat form in which the 'base' ten is written with an index seven. Indices, which may be negative or fractional, are also used in mathematical relationships such as the law of expansion of gases, or the decay of an electric current.

You may already be familiar with the basic idea of indices. However, we start from scratch and show that it is just as easy to use indices for letters in algebra as it is for numbers in arithmetic.

INDEX, BASE AND POWER

Numbers may be written in many forms: you are probably familiar with 3^2. This is an example of a number with an index. The figure 2 gives the number of 3s to be multiplied together and is called the index (plural indices).

Thus $$3 \times 3 = 3^2$$

We also call 3 the base, and 3^2 is known as the second power of the base 3. Now we often use letters to represent numbers (algebra), and so the laws of arithmetic apply strictly to algebraic terms as well as numbers.

So, using letters, $$a \times a \times a = a^3$$

Here a^3 is the third power of the base a, and the index is 3.

Or $$y \times y \times y \times y = y^4$$

Here y^4 is the fourth power of the base y, and the index is 4.

Thus in the expression	x^n	is called the nth power of x
	x	is called the base
	n	is called the index

THE SIX LAWS OF INDICES

Law 1: Multiplication of Powers

Let us see what happens when we multiply powers of the same base together.

Now $5^2 \times 5^4 = (5 \times 5) \times (5 \times 5 \times 5 \times 5)$

$= 5 \times 5 \times 5 \times 5 \times 5 \times 5 = 5^6$

or $c^3 \times c^5 = (c \times c \times c) \times (c \times c \times c \times c \times c)$

$= c \times c \times c \times c \times c \times c \times c \times c = c^8$

In both the examples above we see that we could have obtained the result by adding the indices together.

Thus $5^2 \times 5^4 = 5^{2+4} = 5^6$

and $c^3 \times c^5 = c^{3+5} = c^8$

In general terms the law is

$$a^m \times a^n = a^{m+n}$$

We may apply this idea when multiplying more than two powers of the same base together.

Thus $7^2 \times 7^5 \times 7^9 = 7^{2+5} \times 7^9 = 7^{7+9} = 7^{16}$

We see that the same result would have been obtained by adding the indices, hence

$$7^2 \times 7^5 \times 7^9 = 7^{2+5+9} = 7^{16}$$

The law is:

When multiplying powers of the same base together add the indices

EXAMPLE 8.1

Simplify $m^5 \times m^4 \times m^6 \times m^2$

$$m^5 \times m^4 \times m^6 \times m^2 = m^{5+4+6+2} = m^{17}$$

Law 2: Division of Powers

Now let us see what happens when we divide powers of the same base

$$\frac{3^5}{3^2} = \frac{3 \times 3 \times 3 \times 3 \times 3}{3 \times 3} = 3 \times 3 \times 3 = 3^3$$

We see that the same result could have been obtained by subtracting the indices.

Thus $$\frac{3^5}{3^2} = 3^{5-2} = 3^3$$

In general terms the law is

$$\boxed{\frac{a^m}{a^n} = a^{m-n}}$$

When dividing powers of the same base subtract the index of the denominator from the index of the numerator

EXAMPLE 8.2

a) $\dfrac{4^8}{4^5} = 4^{8-5} = 4^3$

b) $\dfrac{z^3 \times z^4 \times z^8}{z^5 \times z^6} = \dfrac{z^{3+4+8}}{z^{5+6}} = \dfrac{z^{15}}{z^{11}} = z^{15-11} = z^4$

Law 3: Power of a Power

How do we simplify $(5^3)^2$?
One way is to proceed as follows:

$$(5^3)^2 = 5^3 \times 5^3 = 5^{3+3} = 5^6$$

We see that the same result would have been obtained if we multiplied the two indices together.

Thus $$(5^3)^2 = 5^{3\times 2} = 5^6$$

In general terms the law is

$$\boxed{(a^m)^n = a^{mn}}$$

When raising 'the power of a base' to a power, multiply the indices together

EXAMPLE 8.3

a) $(8^4)^3 = 8^{4\times 3} = 8^{12}$

b) $(p^2 \times q^4)^3 = (p^2)^3 \times (q^4)^3 = p^{2\times 3} \times q^{4\times 3} = p^6 q^{12}$

c) $\left(\dfrac{a^7}{b^5}\right)^6 = \dfrac{(a^7)^6}{(b^5)^6} = \dfrac{a^{7\times 6}}{b^{5\times 6}} = \dfrac{a^{42}}{b^{30}}$

Law 4: Zero Index

Now $$\frac{2^5}{2^5} = \frac{2\times2\times2\times2\times2}{2\times2\times2\times2\times2} = 1$$

but using the laws of indices

$$\frac{2^5}{2^5} = 2^{5-5} = 2^0$$

Thus $$2^0 = 1$$

Also $$\frac{c^4}{c^4} = \frac{c\times c\times c\times c}{c\times c\times c\times c} = 1$$

But using the laws of indices

Also $$\frac{c^4}{c^4} = c^{4-4} = c^0$$

Thus $$c^0 = 1$$

In general terms the law is

$$x^0 = 1$$

or

Any base raised to the index of zero is equal to 1

EXAMPLE 8.4

a) $25^0 = 1$ b) $(0.56)^0 = 1$ c) $(\frac{1}{4})^0 = 1$

Law 5: Negative Indices

Now $$\frac{2^3}{2^7} = \frac{2\times2\times2}{2\times2\times2\times2\times2\times2\times2} = \frac{1}{2\times2\times2\times2} = \frac{1}{2^4}$$

but using the laws of indices

$$\frac{2^3}{2^7} = 2^{3-7} = 2^{-4}$$

It follows that $2^{-4} = \dfrac{1}{2^4}$

Also $$\frac{d}{d^2} = \frac{d}{d \times d} = \frac{1}{d}$$

but using the laws of indices

$$\frac{d}{d^2} = \frac{d^1}{d^2} = d^{1-2} = d^{-1} = \frac{1}{d}$$

In general terms the law is

$$\boxed{x^{-n} = \frac{1}{x^n}}$$

EXAMPLE 8.5

a) $3^{-1} = \frac{1}{3^1} = \frac{1}{3}$

b) $5x^{-3} = 5 \times x^{-3} = 5 \times \frac{1}{x^3} = \frac{5}{x^3}$

c) $(2a)^{-4} = \frac{1}{(2a)^4} = \frac{1}{2^4 \times a^4} = \frac{1}{16a^4}$

d) $\frac{1}{z^{-5}} = \frac{1}{\frac{1}{z^5}} = 1 \div \frac{1}{z^5} = 1 \times \frac{z^5}{1} = z^5$

The Meaning of Positive, Zero and Negative Indices

$$\begin{aligned}
x^4 &= x \times x \times x \times x \\
x^3 &= x \times x \times x \\
x^2 &= x \times x \\
x^1 &= x \\
x^0 &= 1 \\
x^{-1} &= \frac{1}{x} \\
x^{-2} &= \frac{1}{x \times x} = \frac{1}{x^2} \\
x^{-3} &= \frac{1}{x \times x \times x} = \frac{1}{x^3}
\end{aligned}$$

Each line of the above sequence is obtained by dividing the previous line by x. The above sequence may help you to appreciate the meaning of positive and negative indices, and especially the zero index.

Remember: $(\text{elephants})^0 = 1$

Exercise 8.1

Simplify the following, giving each answer as a power:

1) $2^5 \times 2^6$	**2)** $a \times a^2 \times a^5$	**3)** $n^8 \div n^5$
4) $3^4 \times 3^7$	**5)** $b^2 \div b^5$	**6)** $10^5 \times 10^3 \div 10^4$
7) $z^4 \times z^2 \times z^{-3}$	**8)** $3^2 \times 3^{-3} \div 3^3$	**9)** $\dfrac{m^5 \times m^6}{m^4 \times m^3}$
10) $\dfrac{x^2 \times x}{x^6}$	**11)** $(9^3)^4$	**12)** $(y^2)^{-3}$
13) $(t \times t^3)^2$	**14)** $(c^{-7})^{-2}$	**15)** $\left(\dfrac{a^2}{a^5}\right)^3$
16) $\left(\dfrac{1}{7^3}\right)^4$	**17)** $\left(\dfrac{b^2}{b^7}\right)^{-2}$	**18)** $\dfrac{1}{(s^3)^3}$

Without using tables or calculating machines find the values of the following:

19) $\dfrac{8^3 \times 8^2}{8^4}$	**20)** $\dfrac{7^2 \times 7^5}{7^3 \times 7^4}$	**21)** $\dfrac{2^2}{2^2 \times 2}$
22) $2^4 \times 2^{-1}$	**23)** 2^{-2}	**24)** $\dfrac{1}{(10)^{-2}}$
25) $\dfrac{2^{-1}}{2}$	**26)** $\dfrac{24^0}{7}$	**27)** $(5^{-1})^2$
28) $3^{-3} \div 3^{-4}$	**29)** $\dfrac{7}{24^0}$	**30)** $\left(\dfrac{1}{5}\right)^{-2}$
31) 7×24^0	**32)** $\left(\dfrac{2}{3}\right)^{-3}$	**33)** $\left(\dfrac{2}{2^{-3}}\right)^{-2}$

Law 6: Fractional Indices

The cube root of 5 (written as $\sqrt[3]{5}$) is the number which, when multiplied by itself three times, gives 5.

Thus $\sqrt[3]{5} \times \sqrt[3]{5} \times \sqrt[3]{5} = 5$

But we also know that $5^{1/3} \times 5^{1/3} \times 5^{1/3} = 5$

Comparing these expressions $\sqrt[3]{5} = 5^{1/3}$

Similarly the fourth root of base d written as $(\sqrt[4]{d})$ is the number which, when multiplied by itself four times, gives d.

Thus $\sqrt[4]{d} \times \sqrt[4]{d} \times \sqrt[4]{d} \times \sqrt[4]{d} = d$

But we also know that $d^{1/4} \times d^{1/4} \times d^{1/4} \times d^{1/4} = d^{1/4+1/4+1/4+1/4} = d$

Comparing these expressions $\sqrt[4]{d} = d^{1/4}$

In general terms the law is

$$\sqrt[n]{x} = x^{\frac{1}{n}}$$

A fractional index represents a root – the denominator of the index denotes the root to be taken

SUMMARY OF THE SIX LAWS OF INDICES

Law 1	$a^m \times a^n = a^{m+n}$	Multiplication of powers
Law 2	$\dfrac{a^m}{a^n} = a^{m-n}$	Division of powers
Law 3	$(a^m)^n = a^{mn}$	Power of a power
Law 4	$a^0 = 1$	Zero index
Law 5	$a^{-n} = \dfrac{1}{a^n}$	Negative index
Law 6	$a^{\frac{1}{n}} = \sqrt[n]{a}$	Fractional index

As you work through the text examples make sure that you can identify, at each step, which law is being used. In this way, you will soon become familiar with each law and its use.

Number Examples Using Indices

Here are some examples in which law 6 is used. We do appreciate that the numerical answers may be found from your calculator, but if you work through the solutions as they are given here, it should help your understanding of indices.

EXAMPLE 8.6

Find the value of a) $25^{1/2}$ and b) $81^{1/4}$

a) $25^{1/2} = \sqrt{25} = 5$ (Note that for square roots the figure indicating the square root is usually omitted)

b) $81^{1/4} = \sqrt[4]{81} = 3$

EXAMPLE 8.7

Find the value of $8^{2/3}$.

Now we may write $\frac{2}{3}$ as either (i) $2 \times \frac{1}{3}$ or (ii) $\frac{1}{3} \times 2$

So using (i) $8^{2/3} = 8^{2\times\frac{1}{3}}$

$= (8^2)^{\frac{1}{3}}$ using law 3 for power of a power

$= \sqrt[3]{8^2}$ using law 6 for fractional indices

$= \sqrt[3]{64}$

$= 4$

Alternatively using (ii) $8^{2/3} = 8^{\frac{1}{3}\times 2}$

$= (8^{\frac{1}{3}})^2$ using law 3 for power of a power

$= (\sqrt[3]{8})^2$ using law 6 for fractional indices

$= (2)^2$

$= 4$

Both approaches give the same answer – but in this particular case which do you favour, and why?

EXAMPLE 8.8

Find the value of $16^{-3/4}$.

In the previous example, the second sequence is better as the arithmetic is simpler! Even more important here, so we will use the fact that $\frac{3}{4} = \frac{1}{4} \times 3$

So $16^{-3/4} = \dfrac{1}{16^{3/4}}$ using law 5 for negative indices

$= \dfrac{1}{16^{\frac{1}{4}\times 3}}$

$= \dfrac{1}{(16^{\frac{1}{4}})^3}$ using law 3 for power of a power

$= \dfrac{1}{(\sqrt[4]{16})^3}$ using law 6 for fractional indices

$= \dfrac{1}{(2)^3}$

$= \dfrac{1}{8}$

$= 0.125$

EXAMPLE 8.9

Find the value of $\dfrac{1}{(\sqrt{7})^{-2}}$.

$$\frac{1}{(\sqrt{7})^{-2}} = \frac{1}{\dfrac{1}{(\sqrt{7})^{-2}}} \quad \text{using law 5 for negative indices}$$

$$= 1 \div \frac{1}{(\sqrt{7})^{2}}$$

$$= 1 \times \frac{(\sqrt{7})^{2}}{1}$$

$$= (\sqrt{7})^{2}$$

$$= (7^{\frac{1}{2}})^{2} \quad \text{using law 6 for fractional indices}$$

$$= 7^{\frac{1}{2}\times 2} \quad \text{using law 3 for power of a power}$$

$$= 7^{1}$$

$$= 7$$

Exercise 8.2

Without using tables or calculating machines, find the values of the following:

1) $5^2 \times 5^{1/2} \times 5^{-3/2}$ **2)** $4 \div 4^{1/2}$ **3)** $8^{1/3}$

4) $64^{1/6}$ **5)** $8^{2/3}$ **6)** $25^{3/2}$

7) $(16^{1/4})^3$ **8)** $\dfrac{1}{9^{-3/2}}$ **9)** $\left(\dfrac{1}{4}\right)^{-1/2}$

10) $16^{0.5}$ **11)** $36^{-0.5}$ **12)** $(4^{-3})^{1/2}$

13) $\left(\dfrac{1}{4}\right)^{5/2}$ **14)** $\left(\dfrac{1}{16^{0.5}}\right)^{-3}$ **15)** $\dfrac{1}{(\sqrt{3})^{-2}}$

ALGEBRA EXAMPLES USING INDICES

EXAMPLE 8.10

Express each of the following as a single power:

a) $\sqrt{x^3}$ b) $\dfrac{1}{\sqrt[4]{a^5}}$ c) $\dfrac{(\sqrt{x})^4 x^{\frac{3}{4}}}{x^{\frac{1}{4}}}$

a) $\sqrt{x^3} = (x^3)^{\frac{1}{2}}$ using law 6 for fractional indices

$= x^{3\times\frac{1}{2}}$ using law 3 for power of a power

$= x^{3/2} = x^{1.5}$

b) $\dfrac{1}{\sqrt[4]{a^5}} = \dfrac{1}{(a^5)^{\frac{1}{4}}}$ using law 6 for fractional indices

$= \dfrac{1}{a^{5\times\frac{1}{4}}}$ using law 3 for power of a power

$= \dfrac{1}{a^{5/4}}$

$= a^{-5/4}$ using law 5 for negative index

$= a^{-1.25}$

c) $\dfrac{(\sqrt{x})^4 x^{\frac{3}{4}}}{x^{\frac{1}{4}}} = \dfrac{(x^{\frac{1}{2}})^4 x^{\frac{3}{4}}}{x^{\frac{1}{4}}}$ using law 6 for fractional indices

$= \dfrac{x^{\frac{1}{2}\times 4} x^{\frac{3}{4}}}{x^{\frac{1}{4}}}$ using law 3 for power of a power

$= \dfrac{x^2 x^{\frac{3}{4}}}{x^{\frac{1}{4}}} = \dfrac{x^{2+\frac{3}{4}}}{x^{\frac{1}{4}}}$ using law 1 for multiplication of powers

$= \dfrac{x^{\frac{11}{4}}}{x^{\frac{1}{4}}} = x^{\frac{11}{4}-\frac{1}{4}}$ using law 2 for division of powers

$= x^{\frac{10}{4}} = x^{2.5}$

Exercise 8.3

Simplify the following, expressing each answer as a single power:

1) $\sqrt{x}$ **2)** $\sqrt[5]{x^4}$ **3)** $\dfrac{1}{\sqrt{x}}$

4) $\dfrac{1}{\sqrt[3]{x}}$ 5) $\dfrac{1}{\sqrt[3]{x^4}}$ 6) $\sqrt{x^{-3}}$

7) $\dfrac{1}{\sqrt[3]{x^{-2}}}$ 8) $\dfrac{1}{\sqrt[4]{x^{-0.3}}}$ 9) $(\sqrt[3]{-x})^2$

10) $\sqrt{x^{2/3}}$ 11) $(\sqrt{x})^{2/3}$ 12) $\left(\dfrac{1}{\sqrt[3]{x^4}}\right)^{-3/4}$

13) $\dfrac{\sqrt[3]{a}}{a^2 \times \sqrt{a}}$ 14) $\dfrac{a^{-3}}{a^{2/3}}$ 15) $\left(\dfrac{x^3}{\sqrt{x^{-1.5}}}\right)$

16) $\dfrac{b^{5/2} \times b^{-3/2}}{b^{1/2}}$ 17) $\dfrac{m^{-3/4}}{m^{-5/2}}$ 18) $\dfrac{z^{2.3} \times z^{-1.5}}{z^{-3.5} \times z^2}$

19) $\dfrac{(x^{1/2})^3}{(x^3)^{1/2}}$ 20) $\dfrac{\sqrt{u}}{u^3}$ 21) $\dfrac{\sqrt[4]{y^3}}{\sqrt{y}}$

22) $\dfrac{(\sqrt[4]{n})^3}{\sqrt{n}}$ 23) $\dfrac{\sqrt[4]{x^2}}{\sqrt[7]{x^{-2}}}$ 24) $\dfrac{\sqrt[3]{t} \times \sqrt{t^3}}{t^{5/2}}$

Logarithms and Exponents 9

Base – index – logarithm power definition – bases 10 and e – the laws of logarithms – indicial equations – exponent calculations

LOGARITHMS

Logarithms – another tool in mathematics – are another way of expressing relationships which use indices. These are much easier to handle now that we have calculating machines; older people will tell nightmarish stories of their encounters with logarithmic tables, which are now virtually obsolete.

We will first see how the logarithmic definition is related to base numbers and indices, and then move on to the laws of logarithms and their use for numerical calculations and solving of indicial equations.

Logarithm Definition

We are familiar with an expression such as $9 = 3^2$

A similar algebraic equation is $N = b^x$

Now suppose we wish to find the value of x. It will be necessary to transpose the equation and make x the subject. Since we cannot do this using the usual methods, we have an alternative form using logarithms (logs).

> $\boldsymbol{N = b^x}$ has an alternative form $\boldsymbol{x = \log_b N}$
>
> $\boldsymbol{x}$ is the logarithm of $\boldsymbol{N}$ to the base $\boldsymbol{b}$

Some examples are:

We may write	$8 = 2^3$	in log form as	$\log_2 8 = 3$
or	$81 = 3^4$	in log form is	$\log_3 81 = 4$
$2 = \sqrt{4},\ 2 = 4^{\frac{1}{2}}$ or	$2 = 4^{0.5}$	in log form is	$\log_4 2 = 0.5$
$\dfrac{1}{4} = \dfrac{1}{2^2}$ or	$0.25 = 2^{-2}$	in log form is	$\log_2 0.25 = -2$

It is helpful to remember that **Number** = **Base**^{logarithm}

EXAMPLE 9.1

If $\log_7 49 = x$ find the value of x.

Writing the equation in index form we have $49 = 7^2$

or $7^2 = 7^x$

Since the bases are the same on both sides of the equation, the indices must be the same.

Thus $x = 2$

EXAMPLE 9.2

If $\log_b 8 = 3$ find the value of b.

Writing the equation in index form we have $8 = b^3$

or $2^3 = b^3$

Since the indices on both sides of the equation are the same, the bases must be the same.

Thus $b = 2$

SOME IMPORTANT VALUES OF LOGARITHMS

The Value of $\log_b 1$

Let $\log_b 1 = x$

then in index form $1 = b^x$

Now the only value of the index x which will satisfy this expression is zero.

Hence $\log_b 1 = 0$

Thus

To any base the value of $\log 1$ is zero

The Value of $\log_b b$

Let $\log_b b = x$

then in index form $b = b^x$

Now the only value of the index x which will satisfy the expression is unity.

Hence $\log_b b = 1$

Thus

The value of the log of a number to the same base is unity

The Value of $\log_b(-N)$

Let $\log_b(-N) = x$

then in index form $-N = b^x$

If we examine this expression we can see that whatever the value of the number N or whatever the value of the base b it is not possible to find a value for the index x which will satisfy the expression.

Hence $\log_b(-N)$ has no real value

Thus

Only positive numbers have real logarithms

Exercise 9.1

Express in logarithmic form:

1) $n = a^x$ **2)** $2^3 = 8$ **3)** $5^{-2} = 0.04$

4) $10^{-3} = 0.001$ **5)** $x^0 = 1$ **6)** $10^1 = 10$

7) $a^1 = a$ **8)** $e^2 = 7.39$ **9)** $10^0 = 1$

Find the value of x in each of the following:

10) $\log_x 9 = 2$ **11)** $\log_x 81 = 4$ **12)** $\log_2 16 = x$

13) $\log_5 25 = x$ **14)** $\log_3 x = 2$ **15)** $\log_4 x = 3$

16) $\log_{10} x = 2$ **17)** $\log_7 x = 0$ **18)** $\log_x 8 = 3$

19) $\log_x 27 = 3$ **20)** $\log_9 3 = x$ **21)** $\log_n n = 0$

BASES OF LOGARITHMS

Although logarithms can have any base, in practice only two are used – they are base 10 and base e.

Logarithms to the base 10

Logarithms to the base **10** are called **common logarithms** and are stated as $\mathbf{log_{10}}$, **log** or **lg**. When logarithmic tables were used to solve numerical problems, tables to this base are preferred as they are simpler to use than tables to any other base. Common logarithms are also used for scales on logarithmic graph paper and for calculations on the measurement of sound.

Logarithms to the base *e*

In higher mathematics, all logarithms are taken to the base e and are called **natural logarithms** and are stated as $\mathbf{log_e}$ or **ln**. They are also called Naperian or hyperbolic logarithms.

The mathematical constant e is called the natural base and has a value 2.718 28 correct to 5 decimal places

THE THREE LAWS OF LOGARITHMS

Law 1

Let	$\log_b M = x$	and	$\log_b N = y$
or in index form	$M = b^x$	and	$N = b^y$
Now	$MN = b^x \times b^y$		
∴	$MN = b^{x+y}$		
or in log form	$\log_b MN = x + y$		
and since	$x = \log_b M$	and	$y = \log_b N$
then			

$$\mathbf{\log_b MN = \log_b M + \log_b N}$$

The logarithm of two numbers multiplied together may be found by adding their individual logarithms

The example below shows how the law is used with numbers.

EXAMPLE 9.3

Find the value of $\log_{10}(5 \times 6)$ using Law 1 of logarithms.

Using Law 1 then $\log_{10}(5 \times 6) = \log_{10} 5 + \log_{10} 6$

For RHS: [AC] [lg] [5] [+] [lg] [6] [=] displays 1.477 121 3

This shows that $\log_{10} 5 + \log_{10} 6 = 1.477$ correct to 3 d.p.

For LHS: [AC] [lg] [(] [5] [×] [6] [)] [=] displays 1.477 121 3

This shows that $\log_{10}(5 \times 6)$ is the same and confirms the use of Law 1.

Law 2

Let	$\log_b M = x$	and	$\log_b N = y$
or in index form	$M = b^x$	and	$N = b^y$
Now	$\dfrac{M}{N} = \dfrac{b^x}{b^y}$		
$\therefore$	$\dfrac{M}{N} = b^{x-y}$		
or in log form	$\log_b \dfrac{M}{N} = x - y$		
and since	$x = \log_b M$	and	$y = \log_b N$

Then

$$\boldsymbol{\log_b \frac{M}{N} = \log_b M - \log_b N}$$

The logarithm of two numbers divided may be found by subtracting their individual logarithms

EXAMPLE 9.4

Find the value of $\log_e\left(\frac{6}{4}\right)$ using Law 2 of logarithms.

Using Law 2 then $\log_e\left(\frac{6}{4}\right) = \log_e 6 - \log_e 4$

For RHS: AC ln 6 − ln 4 = displays 0.405 465 1

This shows that $\log_e 6 - \log_e 4 = 0.405$ correct to 3 d.p.

Check this result yourself by calculating the value of $\log_e \dfrac{6}{4}$ or $\log_e 1.5$.

Law 3

Let	$\log_b M = x$
or in index form	$M = b^x$
Now	$M^n = (b^x)^n$
$\therefore$	$M^n = b^{nx}$
or in log form	$\log_b M^n = nx$
and since	$x = \log_b M$

then

$$\boldsymbol{\log_b M^n = n(\log_b M)}$$

The logarithm of a 'number raised to a power' may be found from multiplying the logarithm of the number by the index

EXAMPLE 9.5

Find the value of $\log_{10} 5^3$ using Law 3 of logarithms.

Using Law 3 then $\log_{10} 5^3 = 3\log_{10} 5$

For RHS: AC 3 × lg 5 = displays 2.096 91

This shows that $3\log_{10} 5 = 2.097$ correct to 3 d.p.

Check this result yourself by calculating the value of $\log_{10} 5^3$ or $\log_{10} 125$.

Combining the Laws

The algebraic example below uses all three laws.

EXAMPLE 9.6

Simplify $\log \dfrac{ab}{c^2}$ in terms of $\log a$, $\log b$ and $\log c$.

Base is of no importance here – our manipulation will suit any base.

Now $\log \dfrac{ab}{c^2} = \log ab - \log c^2$ using law 2 of logs for numbers divided

$= \log a + \log b - \log c^2$ using law 1 of logs for numbers multiplied together

$= \log a + \log b - 2\log c$ using law 3 of logs for number powers

CALCULATIONS USING LOGARITHMS

Most calculators have keys for both $\log_e$ (ln) and $\log_{10}$ (log or lg) so we may calculate using logarithms of either base.

To Find the Logarithm of a Number

EXAMPLE 9.7

Find the value of a) $\log_e 3.4$ and b) $\log_{10} 0.876$

a) Using the sequence [AC] [ln] [3.4] [=] displays 1.223 775 4

This shows that $\log_e 3.4 = 1.224$ correct to 3 d.p.

b) and the sequence [AC] [lg] [0.876] [=] displays −0.057 495 8

This shows that $\log_{10} 0.876 = -0.0575$ correct to 4 d.p.

To Find a Number when Given its Logarithm

EXAMPLE 9.8

Find the number whose a) natural logarithm is 0.5461
b) logarithm to the base 10 is 1.723

a) If N is our number then $\log_e N = 0.5461$

or in index form $N = e^{0.5461}$

This process is called finding the antilogarithm, to the base e, of 0.5461 and the calculator sequence, using [SHIFT] [ln] to obtain [e^x] is:

[AC] [SHIFT] [ln] [0.5461] [=] giving 1.7265 correct to 4 d.p.

or, in other words, $\text{antilog}_e\, 0.5641 = 1.7265$

b) Here our antilog will be to find $10^{1.723}$. Using [SHIFT] [lg] for [10^x]:

[AC] [SHIFT] [lg] [1.723] [=] gives 52.84 correct to 2 d.p.

thus $\text{antilog}_{10}\, 1.723 = 52.84$

SUMMARY OF THE LAWS OF LOGARITHMS

Law 1	$\log_b MN$	$=$	$\log_b M + \log_b N$
Law 2	$\log_b \dfrac{M}{N}$	$=$	$\log_b M - \log_b N$
Law 3	$\log_b M^n$	$=$	$n(\log_b M)$

Exercise 9.2

1) Using the laws of logarithms express the following in terms of $\log a$, $\log b$, $\log c$ or $\log d$ as appropriate:

a) $\log a^2 b$ **b)** $\log \dfrac{ac^3}{b^4}$ **c)** $\log \dfrac{ab}{cd}$

2) Find the values, correct to 3 d.p., of:

a) $\log_e 3.76$ **b)** $\log_e 0.34$ **c)** $\log_{10} 35$ **d)** $\log_{10} 0.078$

3) Find the numbers, correct to 4 s.f., whose natural logarithms are:

a) 2.76 **b)** 0.09 **c)** −3.46 **d)** −0.543

4) Find the numbers, correct to 3 s.f., whose logarithms to the base 10 are:

a) 1.93 **b)** 0.297 **c)** −0.0056 **d)** −0.576

5) Evaluate $\log_{10} 12$. Check the value obtained by finding the value of $\log_e (3 \times 4)$, resulting from the use of logarithmic Law 1.

6) Evaluate $\log_{10} 1.25$ and check your result by using Law 2 of logarithms on $\log_{10}\left(\frac{5}{4}\right)$ and finding the answer.

7) Evaluate $\ln 32$ and verify your result by finding the value of $\ln 2^5$ and using the third law of logarithms.

INDICIAL EQUATIONS

These are equations in which the number to be found is an index, or part of an index.

The method of solution is to reduce the given equation to an equation involving logarithms, as the following examples will illustrate.

EXAMPLE 9.9

If $8.79^x = 67.75$ find the value of x.

Now taking logarithms of both sides of the given equation we have

$$\log 8.79^x = \log 67.65$$

$$\therefore \quad x(\log 8.79) = \log 67.65$$

$$\therefore \quad x = \frac{\log 67.65}{\log 8.79}$$

The base of the logarithms has not yet been chosen, since the above procedure is true for any base value. So one way is:

AC | lg | 67.65 | ÷ | lg | 8.79 | = giving 1.94 for x, correct to 3 s.f.

It is a good idea to check your answer by substituting 1.94 in the LHS of the original equation and verifying that it gives the RHS value – try this for yourself.

EXAMPLE 9.10

Find the value of x if $1.793^{(x+3)} = 20^{0.982}$.

Now taking logarithms of both sides of the given equation we have

$$\log 1.793^{(x+3)} = \log 20^{0.982}$$

$$(x+3)(\log 1.793) = (0.982)(\log 20)$$

$$x+3 = \frac{(0.982)(\log 20)}{\log 1.793}$$

$$x = \frac{(0.982)(\log 20)}{\log 1.793} - 3$$

This time we will use natural logs in the following sequence:

AC | 0.982 | × | ln | 20 | ÷ | ln | 1.793 | − | 3 | =

giving 2.04 correct to 3 s.f.

Exercise 9.3

Evaluate the following:

1) $11.57^{0.3}$ **2)** $15.26^{2.15}$ **3)** $0.6327^{0.5}$

4) $0.065\,21^{3.16}$ **5)** $27.15^{-0.4}$

Find the value of x in the following:

6) $3.6^x = 9.7$ **7)** $0.9^x = 2.176$

8) $\left(\frac{1}{7.2}\right)^x = 1.89$ **9)** $1.4^{(x+2)} = 9.3$

10) $21.9^{(3-x)} = 7.334$ **11)** $2.79^{(x-1)} = 4.377^x$

12) $\left(\frac{1}{0.64}\right)^{(2+x)} = 1.543^{(x+1)}$ **13)** $\frac{1}{0.9^{(x-2)}} = 8.45$

EXPONENTS

The exponent functions e^x and e^{-x} are of interest to engineers mainly because they are expressions which represent growth and decay – for instance, in electrical circuits. Later you will see their graphs, but it is important at this stage that you should be able to handle expressions in which these functions occur.

Calculations Involving Exponent Functions e^x and e^{-x}

EXAMPLE 9.11

Evaluate $50\,e^{2.16}$.

A sequence of operations, using [SHIFT] [ln] to obtain [e^x], is:

[AC] [50] [×] [SHIFT] [ln] [2.16] [=] giving 434 correct to 3 s.f.

EXAMPLE 9.12

Evaluate $200\,e^{-3.14}$.

The sequence of operations would then be:

[AC] [200] [×] [SHIFT] [ln] [−] [1.34] [=] giving 52.4 correct to 3 s.f.

EXAMPLE 9.13

Formula $R = \dfrac{(0.42)S}{l} \times \log_e \dfrac{d_2}{d_1}$ refers to the insulation resistance of a wire.

Find the value of R when $S = 2000$, $l = 120$, $d_1 = 0.2$ and $d_2 = 0.3$.

Substituting the given values gives:

$$R = \frac{0.42 \times 2000}{120} \times \log_e \frac{0.3}{0.2}$$

and so:

[AC] [0.42] [×] [2000] [÷] [120] [×] [ln] [(] [0.3] [÷] [0.2] [)] [=]

gives 2.84 to 2 d.p.

EXAMPLE 9.14

In a capacitive circuit the instantaneous voltage across the capacitor is given by $v = V(1 - e^{-t/CR})$ where V is the initial supply voltage, R ohms the resistance, C farads the capacitance and t seconds the time from the instant of connecting the supply voltage.

If $V = 200$, $R = 10\,000$ and $C = 20 \times 10^{-6}$ find the time when the voltage v is 100 volts.

Substituting given values $\quad 100 = 200(1 - e^{-t/20\times10^{-6}\times10\,000})$

thus $\quad \dfrac{100}{200} = 1 - e^{-t/0.2}$

or $\quad 0.5 = 1 - e^{-5t}$

$\therefore \quad e^{-5t} = 1 - 0.5$

so $\quad e^{-5t} = 0.5$

rearranging in log form $\quad \log_e 0.5 = -5t$

$$t = -\frac{\log_e 0.5}{5}$$

Thus [AC] [–] [ln] [0.5] [÷] [5] [=] gives 0.139 seconds to 3 s.f.

Exercise 9.4

1) Find the values of:

a) $70\,e^{2.5}$ **b)** $150\,e^{-1.34}$ **c)** $3.4\,e^{-0.445}$

2) The formula $L = 0.000\,644\left[\left(\log_e \dfrac{d}{r}\right) + \dfrac{1}{4}\right]$ is used for self-inductance of parallel conductors. Find L when $d = 50$ and $r = 0.25$.

3) The inductance L microhenrys of a straight aerial is given by the formula: $L = \dfrac{1}{500}\left[\left(\log_e \dfrac{4l}{d}\right) - 1\right]$ where l mm is the length of the aerial and d mm its diameter. Calculate the inductance of an aerial 5 m long and 2 mm diameter.

4) Find the value of $\log_e \left(\dfrac{c_1}{c_2}\right)^2$ when $c_1 = 4.7$ and $c_2 = 3.5$.

5) If $T = R\log_e\left(\dfrac{a}{a-b}\right)$ find T when, $R = 28$, $a = 5$ and $b = 3$.

6) When a chain of length $2l$ is suspended from two points $2d$ apart on the same horizontal level, $d = c\log_e\left(\dfrac{l+\sqrt{l^2+c^2}}{c}\right)$.

If $c = 80$ and $l = 200$ find d.

7) The instantaneous value of the current when an inductive circuit is discharging is given by the formula $i = Ie^{-Rt/L}$. Find the value of this current, i, when $I = 6$, $R = 30$, $L = 0.5$ and $t = 0.005$.

8) In a circuit in which a resistor is connected in series with a capacitor the instantaneous voltage across the capacitor is given by the formula

$$v = V(1 - e^{-t/CR})$$

Find v when $V = 200$, $C = 40 \times 10^{-6}$, $R = 100\,000$ and $t = 1$.

9) In the formula $v = Ve^{-Rt/L}$ the value of $v = 50$, $V = 150$, $R = 60$ and $L = 0.3$. Find the corresponding value of t.

10) The instantaneous charge in a capacitive circuit is given by $q = Q(1 - e^{-t/CR})$. Find the value of t when $q = 0.01$, $Q = 0.015$, $C = 0.0001$ and $R = 7000$.

Functions and Graphs 10

Graphs of linear equations – axes and scales – interpolation and extrapolation – the law of a straight line – graphs of experimental data – the logarithmic curve – the exponent curve

GRAPHS

In newspapers, television, business reports, technical papers and government publications, use is made of pictorial illustrations to compare quantities. These diagrams help the reader to understand what deductions may be drawn from the quantities represented. The most common sort of diagram is the graph. An everyday example would be industrial output against time in months. But for us, as engineers, a more likely example would be acceleration of a vehicle against time in seconds.

Location of a Point

Engineers are often concerned about positioning, or locating, a point on a plane. An example of such a plane is the paper on which you are writing, or the flat surface table of a CNC drilling machine.

You are probably aware of Ordnance Survey maps which have horizontal and vertical grid lines. These are suitably numbered and enable exact positioning by giving a grid reference. Our positioning system is similar, the grid reference being called Cartesian co-ordinates (named after a mathematician called Descartes).

Axes of Reference and Coordinates

The graphs which follow will all be based on Cartesian (or rectangular) axes. We take two lines at right angles to each other, Fig. 10.1, which are called axes of reference. Generally the horizontal axis is known as the x-axis, the vertical line as the y-axis. The values of x and y which locate a point are known as the *co-ordinates* of the point.

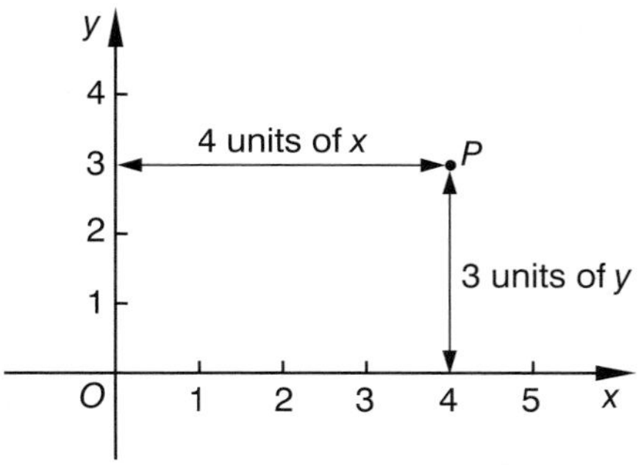

Fig. 10.1

Point P has an x co-ordinate 4 and a y co-ordinate 3, shown there as (4, 3).

If the point (0, 0) lies at the intersection of the axes it is known as the origin and is denoted by $\boldsymbol{O}$.

Axes and Scales

By good positioning of the axes on the graph paper and careful choice of scales (which need not be the same on each axis) the easier it will be to plot points and draw an accurate graph. To start with you may find this rather tedious, but with practice everything falls into place.

You may appreciate some advice on the choice of a scale on an axis. The scale should be as large as possible so that the points may be plotted with the greatest possible accuracy – this means that you should make the plot cover the whole sheet of graph paper, not just a small area in the bottom left-hand corner!

The difference between a good scale and a bad scale is how easy it is to read intermediate decimal values: try plotting 1.7 or 2.3 on the 'terrible' scales shown below and you will see why they are so named.

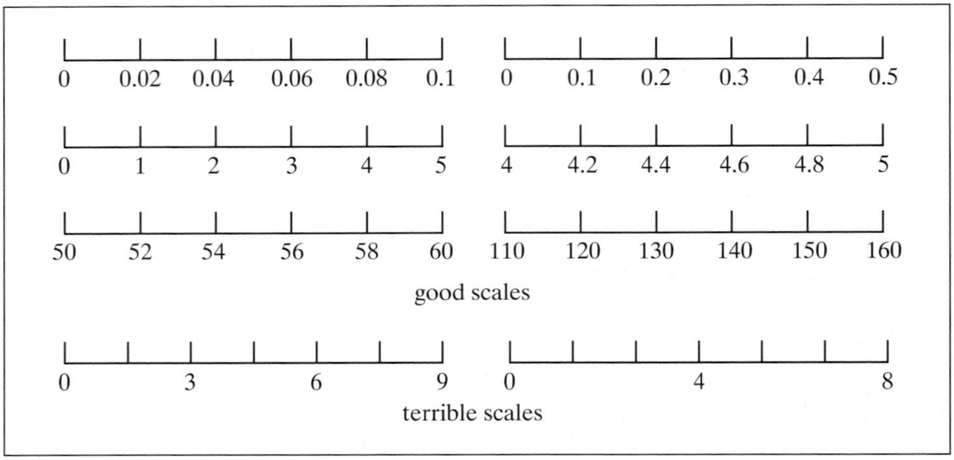

INTERPOLATION AND EXTRAPOLATION

The following example illustrates these terms.

EXAMPLE 10.1

The table below gives the corresponding values of x and y. Plot this information and from the graph find:

a) the value of y when $x = -3$

b) the value of x when $y = 2$

x	-4	-2	0	2	4	6
y	-2.0	-1.6	0	1.4	2.5	3.0

The graph is shown plotted in Fig. 10.2 and it is a smooth curve. This means that we may use the graph to find corresponding values of x and y between those given in the original table of values.

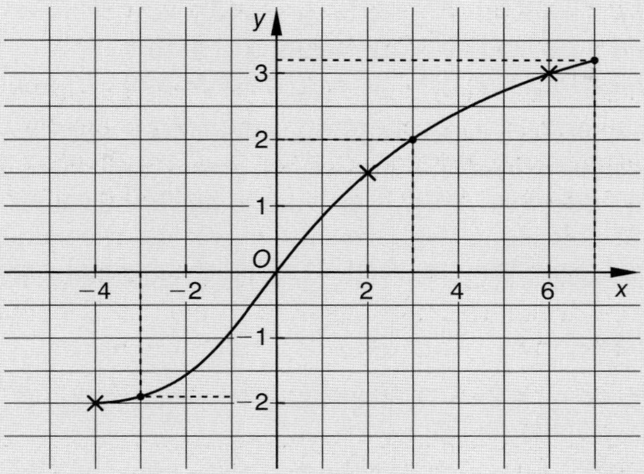

Fig. 10.2

By using the constructions shown

a) the value of y is -1.9 when $x = -3$

b) the value of x is 3 when $y = 2$

Using a graph in this way to find values of x and y not given in the original table of values is called *interpolation*.

If we extend the curve so that it follows the general trend we can estimate corresponding values of x and y which lie just beyond the range of the given value. Thus by extending the curve we can find the probable value of y when $x = 7$. This is found to be 3.2. Finding a probable value in this way is called *extrapolation*. An extrapolated value can usually be relied upon but in some cases it may contain a substantial amount of error. Extrapolated values must therefore be used with care.

It must be clearly understood that interpolation and extrapolation should only be used if the graph is a straight line or a smooth curve.

GRAPHS OF LINEAR EQUATIONS

Linear equations produce straight line graphs – these are very useful as they are straightforward to draw and their equations are simple when compared with others. Here you will learn how to choose axes and appropriate scales, draw a line which fits the plotted points and then calculate the relevant results.

Graphs of Simple Equations

Consider the equation: $y = 2x + 5$

We can give x any value we please and calculate a corresponding value for y.

Thus when $x = 0$ $y = 2 \times 0 + 5 = 5$
and $x = 1$ $y = 2 \times 1 + 5 = 7$
and $x = 2$ $y = 2 \times 2 + 5 = 9$ and so on.

The value of y therefore depends on the value allocated to x. We therefore call y the *dependent variable*. Since we can give x any value we please, we call x the *independent variable*. It is usual to mark the values of the independent variable along the horizontal x-axis and the values of the dependent variable are then marked off along the vertical y-axis.

EXAMPLE 10.2

Draw the graph of $y = 2x - 5$ for values of x between -3 and 4.

We must first decide on which x values to use – here the choice is reasonably easy, say, -3, -2, -1, 0, 1, 2, 3 and 4 so when, for example, $x = -2$ then $y = 2(-2) - 5 = -9$.

Similar calculations for the other values enable the graph shown in Fig. 10.3 to be plotted. This graph is a straight line.

Equations of the type $y = 2x - 5$, where the highest power of the variables x and y is the first, are called equations of the first degree. They are also called linear equations. In general

> Linear equations produce straight line graphs

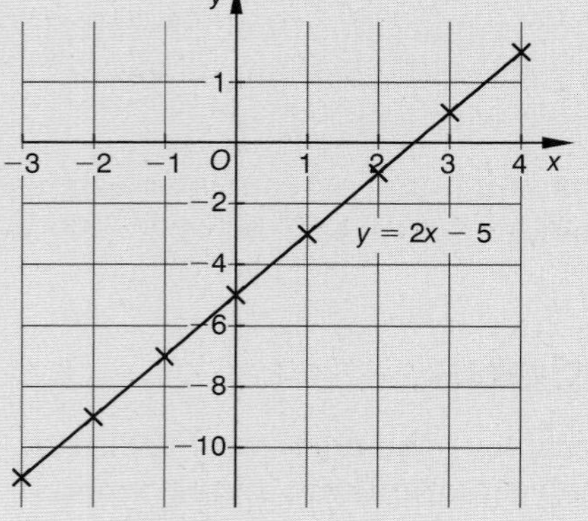

Fig. 10.3

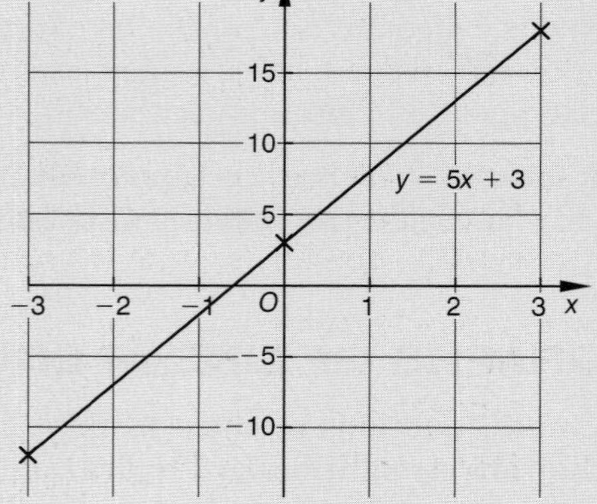

Fig. 10.4

EXAMPLE 10.3

By means of a graph show the relationship between x and y in the equation $y = 5x + 3$. Plot the graph between $x = -3$ and $x = 3$.

The given equation is linear so the graph will be a straight line. Although we can draw a straight line graph using only two points, it is usual to take three points, the third acting as a check on the other two.

x	-3	0	$+3$	The graph is shown in Fig. 10.4
$y = 5x + 3$	-12	3	$+18$	

The Law of a Straight Line

As we have seen already a straight line results from plotting a linear equation, which is an equation of the first degree.

A straight line graph is probably the commonest form of graph and this is why we study it first. It is even more important because we can often reduce more complicated equations to a straight line form.

In Fig 10.5 the point B is any point on the line shown and has coordinates x and y. Point A is where the lines cuts the y-axis and has coordinates $x = 0$ and $y = c$.

In $\triangle ABC$ $\quad \dfrac{BC}{AC} = \tan\theta$

$\therefore \quad BC = (\tan\theta) \times AC$

but $\quad y = BC + CD$

thus $\quad y = (\tan\theta)AC + CD$

or $\quad y = mx + c$

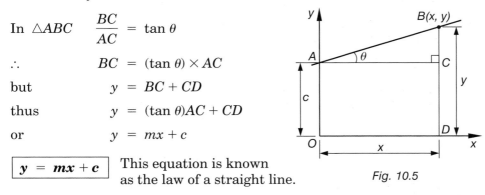

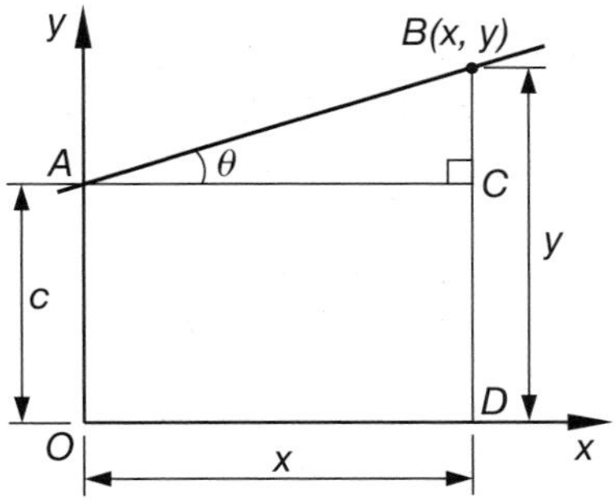

Fig. 10.5

$\boxed{y = mx + c}$ This equation is known as the law of a straight line.

***c* is the intercept on the *y*-axis**

Care must be taken as this only applies if the zero of the scale along the x-axis is at the intersection of the x and y axes.

***m* is the gradient**

In mathematics, the gradient* of a line is defined as the tangent of angle θ.

Hence in Fig. 10.5 the gradient $m = \tan\theta = \dfrac{BC}{AC}$.

*Care should be taken not to confuse this with the gradient given on maps, railways, etc. which is the sine of the angle (not the tangent) e.g. a railway slope of 1 in 100 is one unit vertically for every 100 units measured along the slope.

Positive and negative gradients are shown in Figs 10.6 and 10.7.

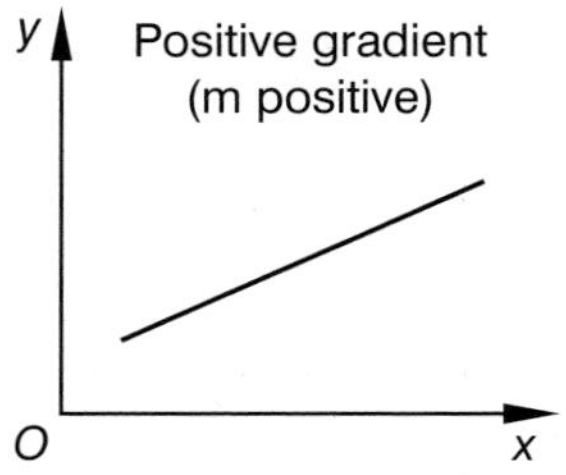

Fig. 10.6

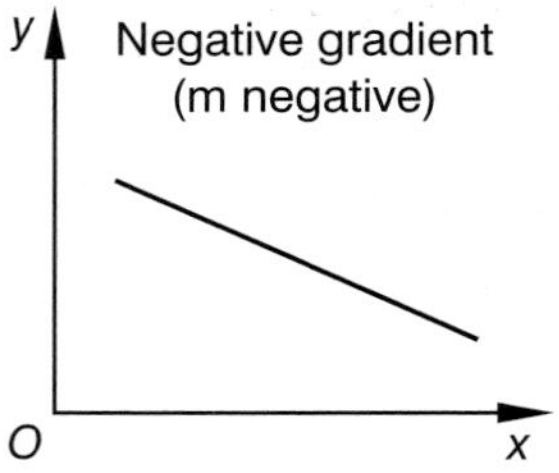

Fig. 10.7

Two special cases – zero gradient and infinite gradient – are shown in Figs 10.8 and 10.9.

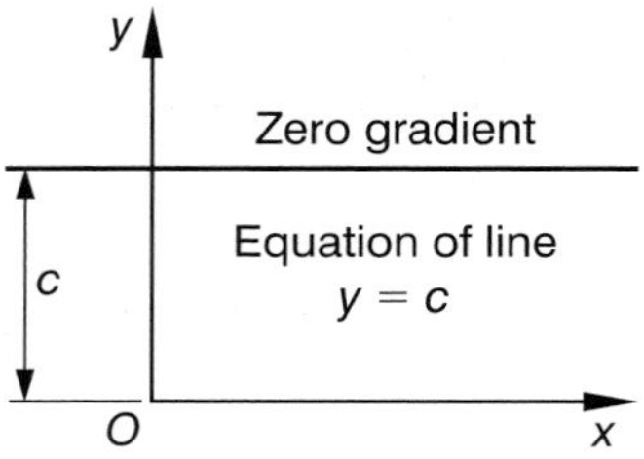

Fig. 10.8

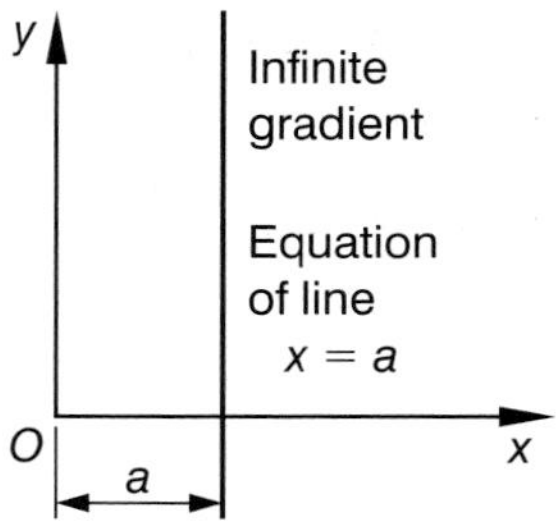

Fig. 10.9

LINEAR EQUATIONS AND THEIR GRAPHS

Linear equations which are not stated in standard straight line form must be rearranged if they are to be compared the with standard equation $y = mx + c$.

EXAMPLE 10.4

a) The equation $y = x + 1$

may be written as $y = 1x + 1$

Now comparing with $y = mx + c$

then the gradient $m = 1$

and the intercept $c = 1$

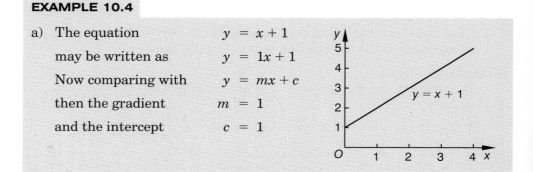

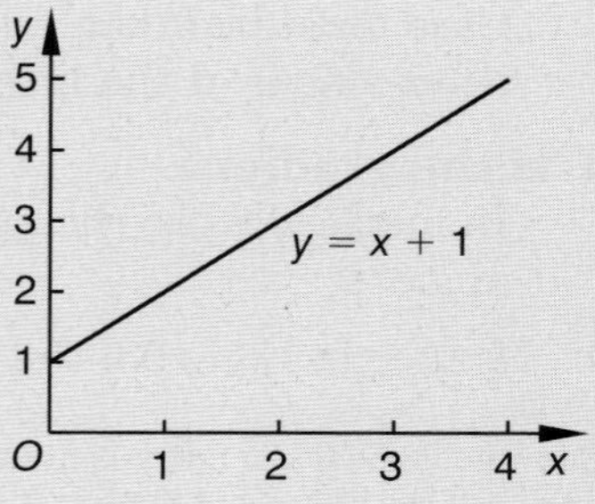

b) The equation $y = 2x - 1.5$
may be compared with $y = mx + c$
then the gradient $m = 2$
and the intercept $c = -1.5$

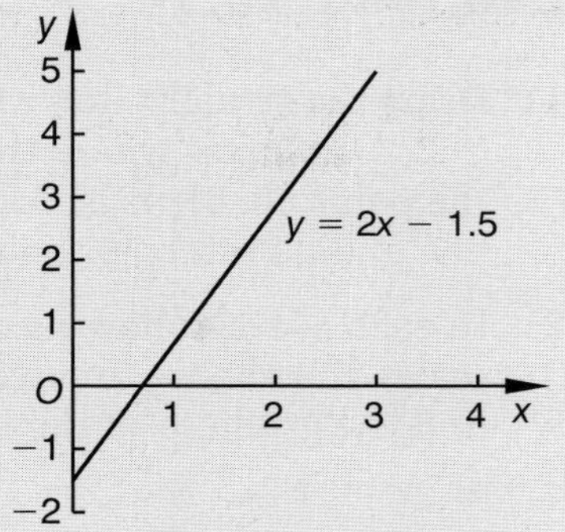

c) The equation $2y + x = 4$
must be rearranged $y = -\frac{1}{2}x + 2$
Now comparing with $y = mx + c$
then the gradient $m = -\frac{1}{2}$
and the intercept $c = 2$

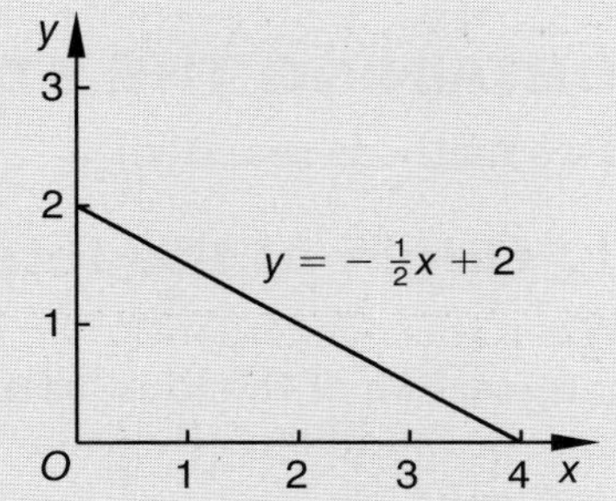

d) The equation $3y = x$
must be rearranged $y = \frac{1}{3}x + 0$
Now comparing with $y = mx + c$
then the gradient $m = \frac{1}{3}$
and the intercept $c = 0$

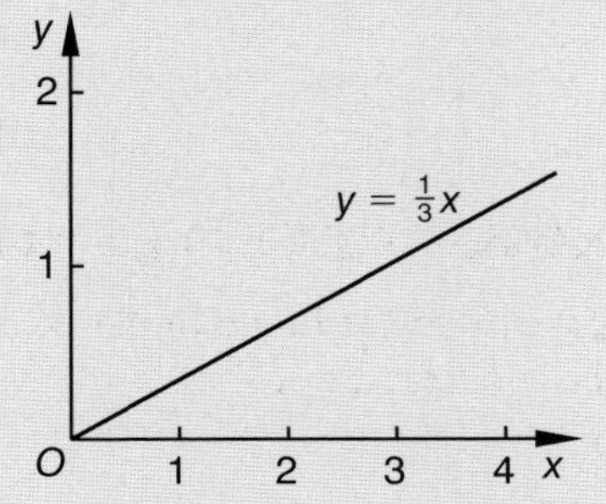

e) The equation $y = -2$
may be written as $y = 0x - 2$
Now comparing with $y = mx + c$
then the gradient $m = 0$
and the intercept $c = -2$

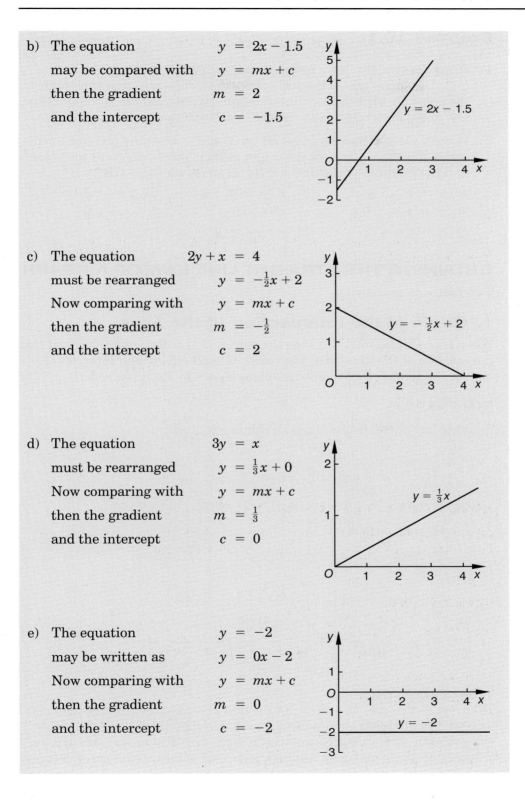

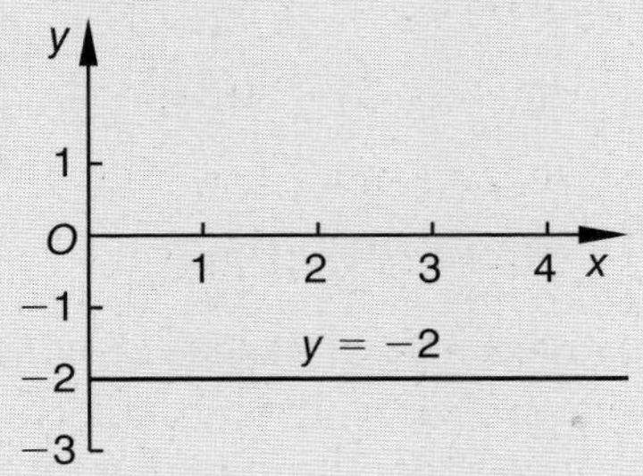

Exercise 10.1

1) Draw the straight line which passes through the points (4, 7) and (−2, 1) on axes where the scales have been chosen so that the origin, the point (0, 0), is at their intersection. Hence, find the gradient of the line and its intercept on the y-axis, and state the equation of the line.

2) In each of the following cases set up x and y axes and arrange for the scales you choose to have the origin at their intersection. In each case find the gradient of the line and its intercept on the y-axis:

a) $y = x + 3$	b) $y = -3x + 4$	c) $y = -3.1x - 1.7$
d) $y = 4.3x - 2.5$	e) $x = -1$	f) $y = 2.9$
g) $x = y + 4$	h) $x + 2y = 3$	j) $2x/y = 3.6$

OBTAINING THE STRAIGHT LINE LAW OF A GRAPH

Two methods are used:

1. Origin at the Intersection of the Axes

When it is convenient to arrange the origin O, i.e. the point (0, 0), at the intersection of the axes, then the values of gradient m and intercept c may be found directly from the graph as shown in Example 10.5.

EXAMPLE 10.5

Find the law of the straight line shown in Fig. 10.10.

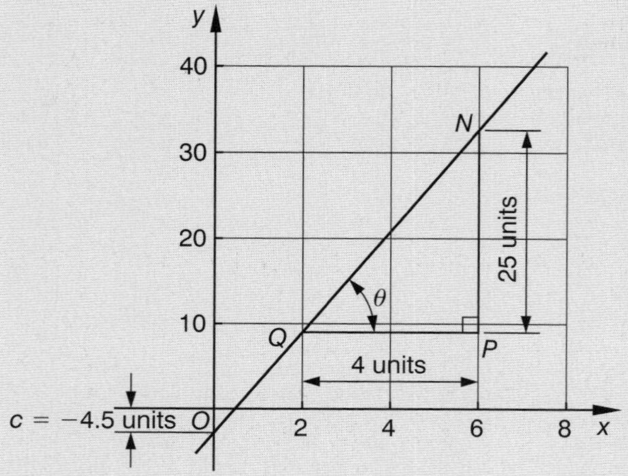

Fig. 10.10

To find gradient m

Take any two points Q and N on the line and construct the right-angled $\triangle QPN$. This triangle should be of reasonable size, since a small triangle will probably give an inaccurate result. Note that if we can measure to an accuracy of 1 mm using an ordinary rule, this error in a length of 20 mm is much more significant than the same error in a length of 50 mm. The lengths of NP and QP are then found using the scales of the y- and x-axes. Direct lengths of these lines, as would be obtained using an ordinary rule, e.g. both in centimetres, must not be used – the scales of the axes must be taken into account.

$$\therefore \qquad \text{Gradient} \quad m = \tan\theta = \frac{NP}{QP} = \frac{25}{4} = 6.25$$

To find intercept c

This is measured using the scale of the y-axis.

$$\therefore \qquad \text{Intercept} \quad c = -4.5$$

The standard equation of a straight line is $y = mx + c$

$\therefore$ the required equation is $y = 6.25x + (-4.5)$

i.e. $y = 6.25x - 4.5$

2. Origin *not* at the Intersection of the Axes

This method is applicable for all problems – hence it may also be used when the origin O is at the intersection of the axes.

If a point lies on a line then the coordinates of that point satisfy the equation of that line, e.g. the point $(2, 7)$ lies on the line $y = 2x + 3$ because if $x = 2$ is substituted in the equation then $y = 2 \times 2 + 3 = 7$ which is the correct value as given for y.

So we choose two points which lie on the given straight line, and substitute their coordinates into the standard equation $y = mx + c$.

The two equations which result are then solved simultaneously to find the values of m and c.

EXAMPLE 10.6

Determine the law of the straight line shown in Fig. 10.11.

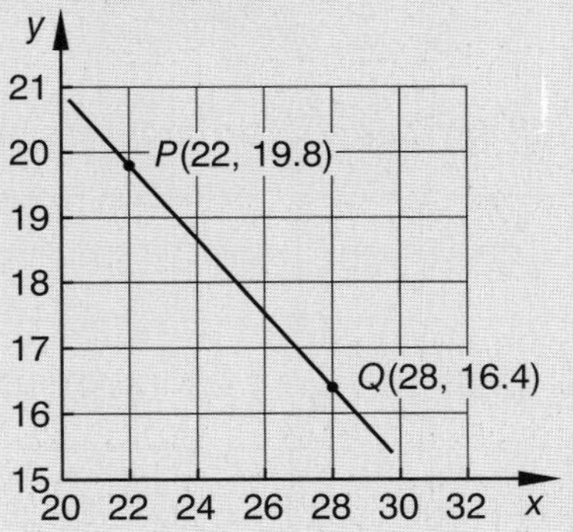

Fig. 10.11

Choose two convenient points P and Q and find their coordinates. Again these points should not be close together, but as reasonably far apart as is convenient. Their coordinates are as shown in Fig. 10.11. Remember when you substitute these values it is the second co-ordinate which is put in for y. It is a common error to use the first co-ordinate – so beware and avoid this pitfall!

Let the equation of the line be $\quad y = mx + c$

Now $P(22, 19.8)$ lies on the line $\quad \therefore\ 19.8 = m(22) + c$

and $Q(28, 16.4)$ lies on the line $\quad \therefore\ 16.4 = m(28) + c$

To solve these two equations simultaneously we must first eliminate one of the unknowns. In this case c will disappear if the second equation is subtracted from the first, giving

$$19.8 - 16.4 = m(22) - m(28) + c - c$$

or $$3.4 = (22 - 28)m$$

$\therefore$ $$m = \frac{3.4}{-6} = -0.567$$

To find c the value $m = -0.567$ may be substituted into either of the original equations. Choosing the first equation we get

$$19.8 = -0.567(22) + c$$

giving $$c = 19.8 + 0.567(22) = 32.3$$

Hence the required law is $$y = -0.567x + 32.3$$

Exercise 10.2

1) A straight line passes through the points $(-2, -3)$ and $(3, 7)$. Without drawing the line find the values of m and c in the equation $y = mx + c$.

2) The width of keyways for various shaft diameters are given below:

Diameter of shaft D (mm)	10	20	30	40	50	60	70	80
Width of key-way W (mm)	3.75	6.25	8.75	11.25	13.75	16.25	18.75	21.25

Show that D and W are connected by a law of the type $W = aD + b$ and find the values of a and b.

3) During an experiment to find the coefficient of friction between two metallic surfaces the following results were obtained:

Load W (N)	10	20	30	40	50	60	70
Friction force F (N)	1.5	4.3	7.6	10.4	13.5	15.6	18.8

Show that F and W are connected by a law of the type $F = aW + b$ and find the values of a and b.

4) In a test on a certain lifting machine it is found that an effort of 50 N will lift a load of 324 N and that an effort of 70 N will lift a load of 415 N. Assuming that the graph of effort plotted against load is a straight line, find the probable load that may be lifted by an effort of 95 N.

GRAPHS OF EXPERIMENTAL DATA

Best Fit Straight Line

One of the most important applications of the straight line is the determination of a law connecting two quantities obtained from an experiment. These readings will usually contain errors due to inaccurate measurement and other experimental flaws. If the points, when plotted, show a trend towards a straight line, this is usually accepted and the best fit straight line is drawn. *This line may not pass through any of the points* but we must make an attempt to ensure an even spread above and below the line, ignoring any odd points which are obviously wrong.

A word of warning! Often students work through examples of straight line graphs and get the idea that all experimental results give straight line graphs. This is far from the truth. We usually test the possibility first, and if unsuccessful we try other relationships.

EXAMPLE 10.7

Hooke's law states that for an elastic material, up to the limit of proportionality, the stress σ is directly proportional to the strain ϵ it produces. In equation form this is $\sigma = E\epsilon$ where the constant E is called the modulus of elasticity of the material.

Find the value of E using the following results obtained in an experiment.

σ MN/m^2	125	110	95	80	63	54	38
$\epsilon \times 10^{-4}$	6.00	5.22	4.66	3.82	3.67	2.69	1.68

In engineering materials, stress is always denoted by the Greek letter σ (sigma), whilst strain is denoted by ϵ (epsilon). In this experiment σ and ϵ are the variables, since their values change. The modulus of elasticity is denoted by E and is a constant, since its value is fixed for a particular material.

We are told that the experiment will result in a straight line, or thereabouts. For us to compare the equation $\sigma = E\epsilon$ with the standard straight line equation $y = mx + c$ we must plot σ on the vertical axis, and ϵ on the horizontal axis. We can see immediately that the intercept on the y-axis c will be zero. This means our graph will pass through the origin $\boldsymbol{O}$. Also the gradient m will be E on our graph.

Inspection of the values shows that it is convenient to arrange for the origin i.e. the point $\boldsymbol{O}$, (0, 0), to be at the intersection of the axes. We have chosen the scales as shown in Fig. 10.12 and plotted the points.

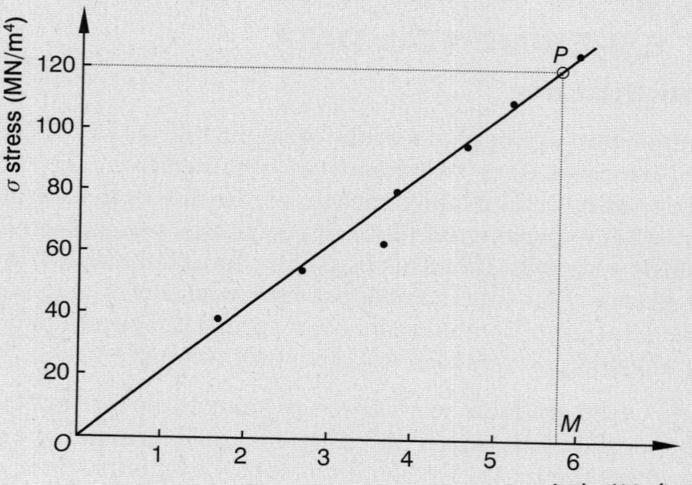

Fig. 10.12

Since the values are the result of an experiment we will not expect the points to lie exactly on a straight line. We know that the graph passes through the origin and this helps us in drawing the 'best' straight line through the points. Judgement is needed here – for instance the point $(3.67 \times 10^{-4}, 63)$ is obviously an incorrect result as it lies well away from the line of the other points, and so we should ignore this point.

It is likely that we shall all draw different straight lines and so our results may vary a little, but we expect that, since the results come from an experiment.

To find gradient E we select a suitable right-angled $\triangle POM$. This triangle should be as large as conveniently possible, not a pathetic little specimen as is often seen!!!

The gradient is given by $\dfrac{PM}{OM} = \dfrac{120}{5.8 \times 10^{-4}} = 207\,000$

The units of the ratio $\dfrac{PM}{OM}$ will be those of PM, i.e. MN/m^2, since OM represents strain which has no units (this is because strain is the ratio of two lengths).

Hence the modulus of elasticity of the material, $E = 207\,000$ MN/m^2.

EXAMPLE 10.8

The resistance R ohms of a field winding is measured at various temperatures $t°$C and the results are recorded in the table below:

$t°$C	22	26	33	38	47	54	60	66	75
R ohms	108	111	116	117	119	123	126	127	132

It is thought that the law connecting R and t is of the form $R = a + bt$. Verify that this is true and then find the law of the line. Find also the value of the temperature when the resistance is 128 ohms.

To test if the given law is true we must plot values of R on the vertical axis and those of t on the horizontal axis, and hope we get a plot of points which can justify drawing the best straight line through them.

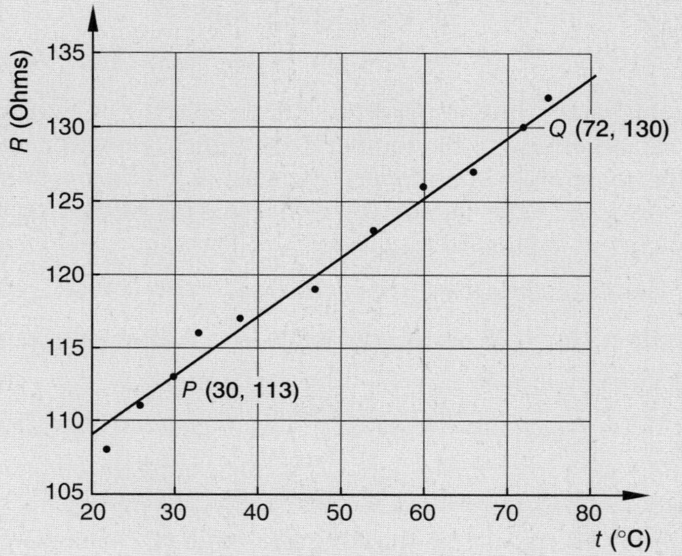

Fig. 10.13

On plotting the points (Fig. 10.13) it will be noticed that they deviate from a straight line. Since the data are experimental we must expect errors in observation and measurement but the general trend would seem to be about a straight line – so we draw what we think is the 'best' straight line through the points.

Since the points follow approximately a straight line we can say that the equation connecting R and t is of the form $R = bt + a$.

If we compare our equation with the straight line law $y = mx + c$ we can see that the gradient is b instead of m, and the intercept on the y-axis is a instead of c.

Because the origin is not at the intersection of the axes, to find the values of constants a and b we choose **two points which lie on the line**. These two points may, or may not, be given values. They must be as far apart as conveniently possible in order to obtain maximum accuracy.

We have chosen the points $P(30, 113)$ and $Q(72, 130)$

The point $P(30, 113)$ lies on the line $\therefore \quad 113 = a(30) + b$

The point $Q(72, 130)$ lies on the line $\therefore \quad 130 = a(72) + b$

Now subtracting the first equation from the second we get

$$130 - 113 = a(72 - 30)$$

$$\therefore \quad a = \frac{17}{42} = 0.405$$

Now substituting the value $a = 0.405$ into the first equation we get

$$130 = 0.405(72) + b$$

$$\therefore \quad b = 130 - 0.405(72) = 101$$

It is debatable as to what accuracy we should give the answer – strictly only to 2 s.f. according to the temperature values. However, as long as we mention this, then we will assume 3 s.f. accuracy. The most dangerous error is for us to give the calculated results to a far greater accuracy than the original given data justifies *without qualifying our statement*.

Hence the required law of the line is $R = 0.405t + 101$

To find t when, $R = 128$ ohms, the value $R = 128$ is substituted into the equation giving

$$128 = 0.405t + 101$$

$$\therefore \quad t = \frac{128 - 101}{0.405} = 66.7\,^\circ\text{C}$$

This value may be verified by checking the value of t corresponding to $R = 128$ on the straight line in Fig. 10.13.

Exercise 10.3

1) The rate of a spring, λ, is defined as force per unit extension, hence for a load, F N producing an extension x mm the law is $F = \lambda x$. Find the value of λ in units of N/m using the following values obtained from an experiment:

F (N)	20	40	60	80	100	120	140
x (mm)	37	79	111	156	197	229	270

2) A circuit contains a resistor having a fixed resistance of R ohms. The current I amperes, and the potential difference V volts are related by the expression $V = IR$. Find the value of R given the following results obtained from an experiment:

V (volts)	3	7	11	13	17	20	24	29
I (amperes)	0.066	0.125	0.209	0.270	0.324	0.418	0.495	0.571

3) During a test to find how the power of a lathe varied with the depth of cut, results were obtained as shown in the table. The speed and feed of the lathe were kept constant during the test.

Depth of cut d (mm)	0.51	1.02	1.52	2.03	2.54	3.0
Power P (W)	0.89	1.04	1.14	1.32	1.43	1.55

Show that the law connecting d and P is of the form $P = ad + b$ and find the law. Hence find the value of d when P is 1.2 watts.

4) During a test with a thermocouple pyrometer the e.m.f. (E millivolts) was measured against the temperature at the hot junction (t °C) and the following results were obtained:

t	200	300	400	500	600	700	800	900	1000
E	6	9.1	12.0	14.8	18.2	21.0	24.1	26.8	30.2

The law connecting t and E is supposed to be $E = at + b$. Test if this is so and find suitable values for a and b.

5) The following results were obtained from an experiment on a set of pulleys. W is the load raised and E is the effort applied. Plot these results and obtain the law connecting E and W.

W(N)	15	20	25	30	35	40	45
E(N)	2.3	2.7	3.2	3.8	4.3	4.7	5.3

GRAPHS OF NON-LINEAR RELATIONSHIPS

The recognition of shapes, and the layout of curves, as related to their equations is important to us as technologists. We will take a look at the parabola which is often used for the shape of headlamp reflectors, since a bulb placed at its focus will produce reflected rays which are parallel. We will also consider exponent curves, where x is replaced by t for time, which illustrate growth and decay. These are of particular interest to electrical engineers in the behaviour of electrical charges, currents and voltages – also scientists in population growth and radioactive decay.

There are many other familiar curves such as the circle, the ellipse, the cubic curve, and the logarithmic graph.

How to Tackle Plotting an Unknown Curve from an Equation

When faced with 'plotting' an equation, how do we decide what values of x to use? If we have seen something like it previously this experience will help – if not then it is a case of trial and error. Most curves have an 'interesting' portion and this is generally what is needed – for the parabola this portion is as shown in Fig. 10.14.

With no guidance at all, start by substituting $-4,\ -3,\ -2,\ -1,\ 0,\ 1,\ 2,\ 3,\ 4,$ for x and find the corresponding value(s) of y. It may also help to consider the value(s) of x when $y = 0$.

Make a rough sketch on scrap paper and this will help you to decide on any further values needed, and also where to put the graph on your sheet of paper – it is not always necessary to have squared graph paper to get the information you need about a curve.

The Parabola

The simplest form of a parabola is given by the equation $y = x^2$ with the axis of symmetry vertical as shown in Fig. 10.14. This is the interesting part of the graph, since it easy to see where the rest of the curve will be.

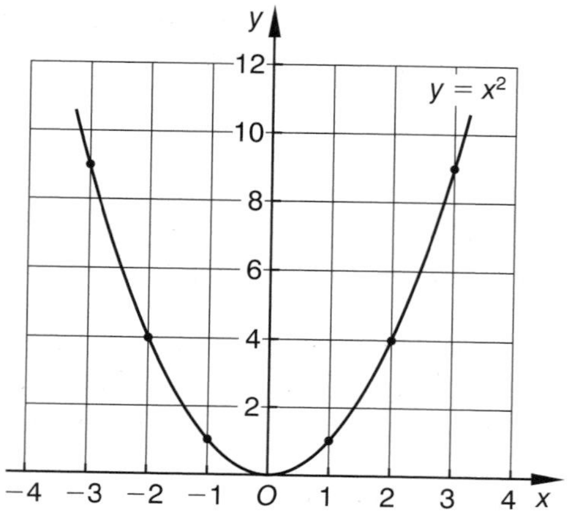

Fig. 10.14

The Exponent Curve

The curve of e^t, using a time base

In technology, reference to the exponent curve is usually based on time. Thus the curves are plotted on a time t base and not an x base.

Curves of exponent functions which have equations of the type $y = e^t$ or $y = e^{-t}$ are called exponent graphs. We may plot the curves using values obtained from a calculator.

For convenience both the curves are shown plotted on the same axes in Fig. 10.15. Although the range of values chosen for t is limited, the overall shape of the curves is clearly shown.

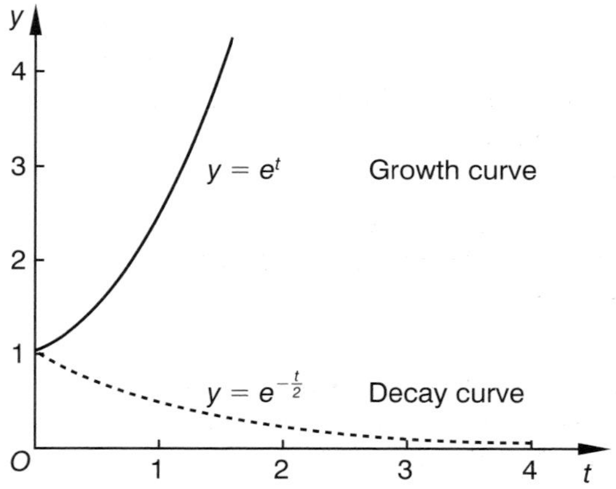

Fig. 10.15

Practical applications based on growth and decay start from a given instant. This means we are dealing with actual (or real) times which, in numerical terms, are positive values of t. Thus only portions of the curves to the right of the vertical axis are generally used.

Exercise 10.4

Sketch (or plot if you have time) the graphs of the examples given – see if you know the name of each curve – these are given in the answers.

1) $x^2 + y^2 = 9$ Try values of x from -4 *to* $+4$. Remember that square roots have plus and minus values, and that as far as we are concerned the square roots of negative numbers do not exist!

2) $xy = 1$ Try the usual values of x.

3) $y = \log_e x$ Use your calculator and you may find that you will need more values of x between 0 to 1, say 0.25, 0.5, 0.75 to enable you to see the shape of the curve here.

4) $y = x^3 - x^2 - 6x$ Start with the usual values of x and, as in question 3), you may need some intermediate values to sort out the shape of the graph.

5) $\dfrac{x^2}{4} + \dfrac{y^2}{9} = 1$ Try and sort this one out without any help, the only clue being that you will almost certainly know two names for the curve.

Areas and Volumes 11

Plane areas – prism – cylinder – cone – frustum of cone – sphere – pyramid

AREAS AND PERIMETERS

Most complicated forms may be divided into simple shapes such as rectangles, triangles and circles. This means, of course, that we must be familiar with the areas and perimeters of these basic figures. Engineers constantly use areas: for instance, stress is calculated from force and area, as is pressure. Another example is electrical conductivity, which depends on the cross-sectional area of the conductor through which the current flows.

Rectangle

$$\text{Area} = l \times b$$
$$\text{Perimeter} = 2l + 2b$$

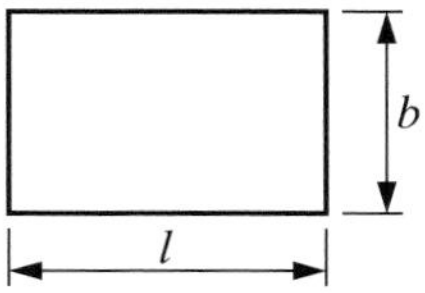

EXAMPLE 11.1

Find the area of the section shown in Fig. 11.1.
The section can be split up into three rectangles as shown. The total area can be found by calculating the areas of the three rectangles separately and then adding these together.

Thus,

$$\text{Area of rectangle 1} = 15 \times 40 = 600\ \text{mm}^2$$
$$\text{Area of rectangle 2} = 120 \times 10 = 1200\ \text{mm}^2$$
$$\text{Area of rectangle 3} = 20 \times 70 = 1400\ \text{mm}^2$$
$$\text{Total area of section} = 600 + 1200 + 1400 = 3200\ \text{mm}^2$$

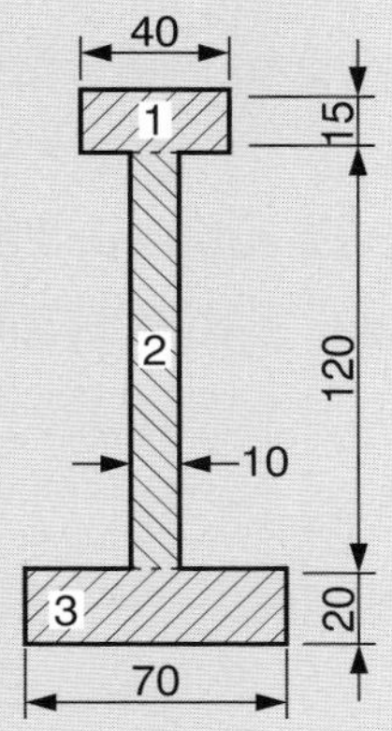

Fig. 11.1

Parallelogram

$$\text{Area} = b \times h$$

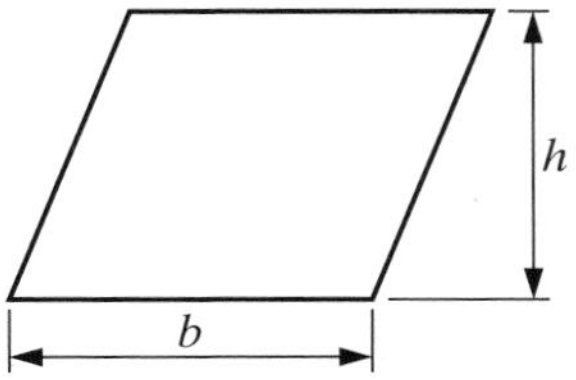

EXAMPLE 11.2

Find the area of the parallelogram shown in Fig. 11.2.

First find the vertical height h. In $\triangle BCE$:
$h = BC \times \sin 60° = 3 \times 0.866 = 2.598$

$$\text{Area of parallelogram} = \text{base} \times \text{height}$$
$$= 5 \times 2.598$$
$$= 13.0\ \text{m}^2$$

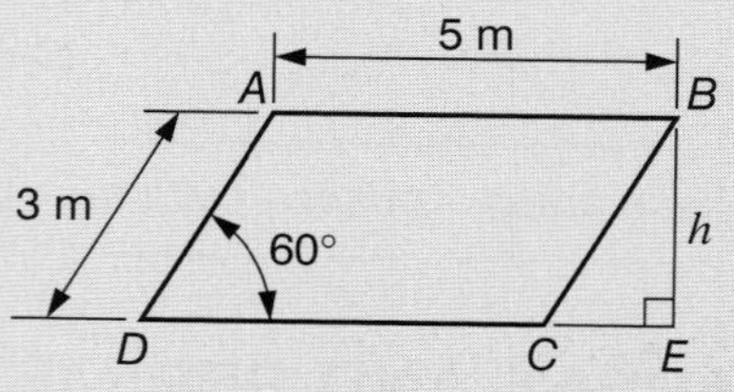

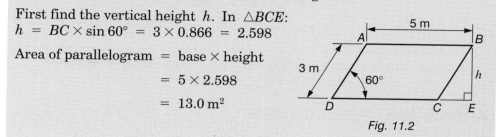

Fig. 11.2

Triangle

$$\text{Area} = \tfrac{1}{2} \times b \times h$$

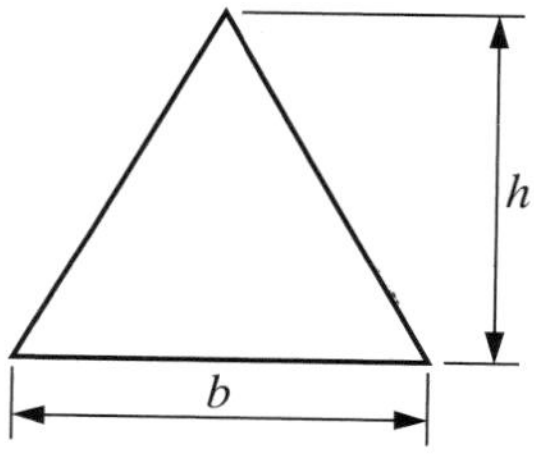

EXAMPLE 11.3

The inner shape of a pattern in a large hall is a regular octagon (8-sided polygon) which is 5 m across flats (Fig. 11.3). Find its area.

Angle subtended at centre by a side of the octagon $= \dfrac{360°}{8} = 45°$

Now $\triangle AOB$ is isosceles, since $OA = OB$.

$\therefore \quad \angle AOC = \dfrac{45°}{2} = 22.5°$

But $\quad OC = \dfrac{5}{2} = 2.5$ m

Also $\quad \dfrac{AC}{OC} = \tan 22.5°$

$\therefore \quad AC = OC \times \tan 22.5°$

$= 2.5 \times 0.4142 = 1.036$ m

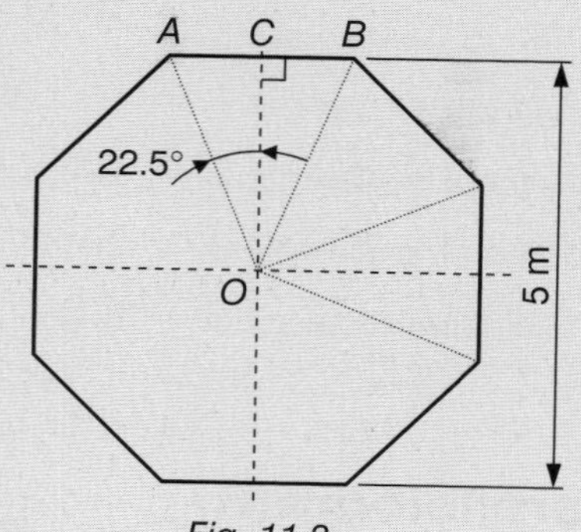

Fig. 11.3

Thus $\quad$ Area of $\triangle AOB = AC \times OC = 1.036 \times 2.5 = 2.59\ \text{m}^2$

$\therefore \quad$ Area of octagon $= 2.59 \times 8 = 20.7\ \text{m}^2$

Trapezium (or Trapezoid)

$$\text{Area} = \tfrac{1}{2} \times h \times (a + b)$$

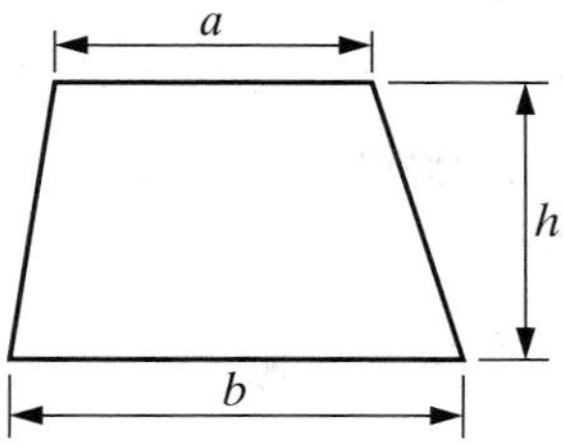

EXAMPLE 11.4

Fig. 11.4 shows the cross-section of a retaining wall. Calculate its cross-sectional area.

Since the section is a trapezium:

$$\begin{aligned} \text{Area} &= \tfrac{1}{2} \times h \times (a + b) \\ &= \tfrac{1}{2} \times 6 \times (2 + 3) \\ &= 15\,\text{m}^2 \end{aligned}$$

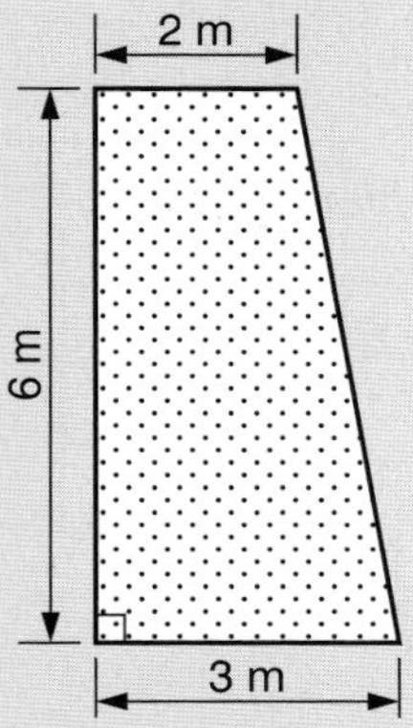

Fig. 11.4

Circle

$$\begin{aligned} \text{Area} &= \pi r^2 = \frac{\pi d^2}{4} \\ \text{Circumference} &= 2\pi r = \pi d \end{aligned}$$

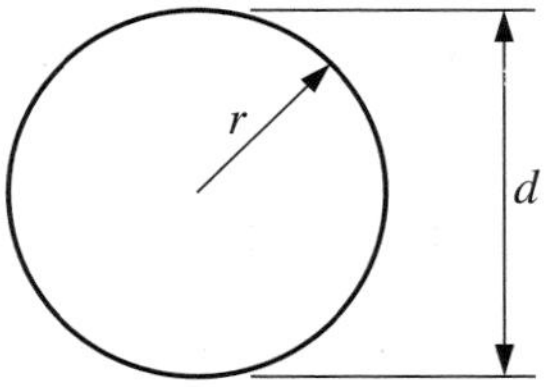

EXAMPLE 11.5

A pipe has an outside diameter of 32.5 mm and an inside diameter of 25 mm. Calculate the cross-sectional area of the shaft (Fig. 11.5).

Cross-sectional area

= (outer circle area) − (inner circle area)

$$= \frac{\pi(32.5)^2}{4} - \frac{\pi(25)^2}{4} = 339\,\text{mm}^2$$

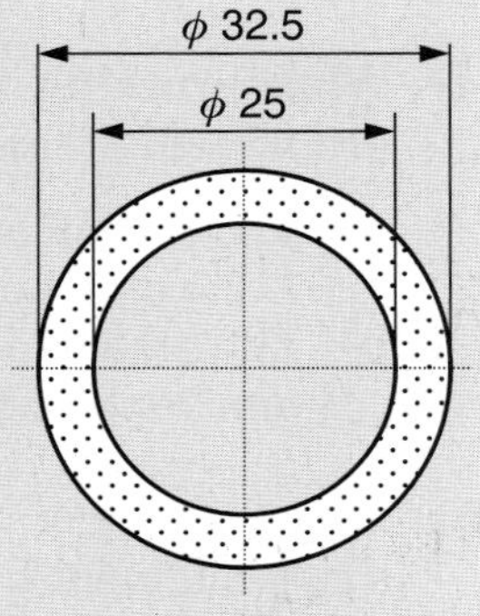

Fig. 11.5

Exercise 11.1

1) The area of a rectangular metal plate is $220\ mm^2$. If its width is 25 mm, find its length.

2) A rectangular sheet metal plate has a length of 147.5 mm and a width of 86.5 mm.
Find its area in m^2.

3) Find the areas of the cross-sections of the aluminium extrusions shown in Fig. 11.6.

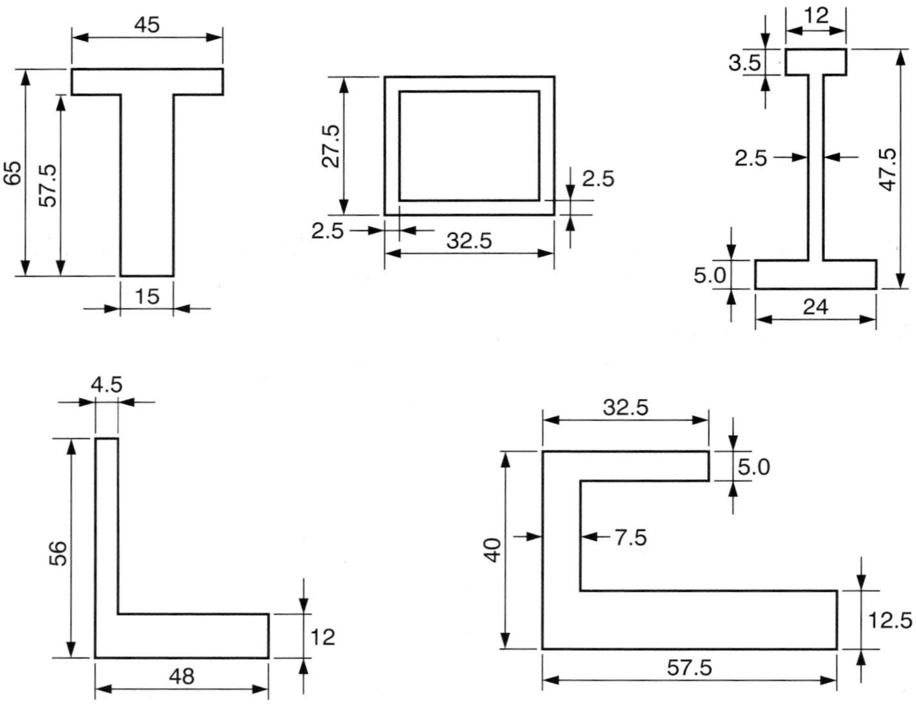

Fig. 11.6

4) Whilst working on the specification for a new kitchen appliance, a draughtsman has the problem of finding the values of two areas:

a) The area of a parallelogram if two adjacent sides measure 112.5 mm and 10.5 mm, and the angle between them is 49°.
b) The area of a trapezium whose parallel sides are 75 mm and 82 mm long respectively, and whose vertical height is 39 mm.

5) In the course of working out the cost of some bright drawn steel bars, a cost engineer has to find their masses. This means finding their volumes which, in turn, means finding the values of the cross-sectional areas which have the following shapes:

A regular hexagon	a)	which is 40 mm wide across flats,
	b)	which has sides 50 mm long
A regular octagon	c)	which is 20 mm wide across flats
	d)	which has sides 20 mm long.

6) If the area of cross-section of a circular shaft is 700 mm^2, find its diameter.

7) A company which manufactures reciprocating engines requires the value of the shaded area in Fig. 11.7 as this is the cross-sectional area of flow of a liquid coolant channel.

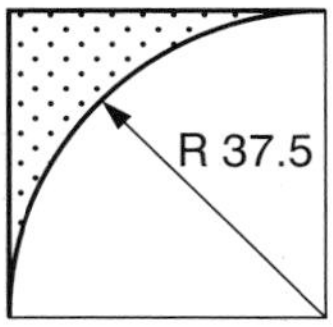

Fig. 11.7

8) A hollow shaft has a cross-sectional area of 868 mm^2. If its inside diameter is 7.5 mm, calculate its outside diameter.

9) Find the area of the blank shown in Fig. 11.8.

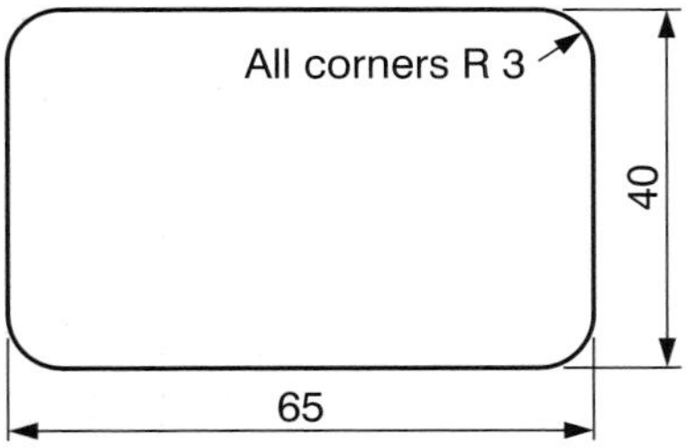

Fig. 11.8

10) How many revolutions will a wheel make in travelling 2 km if its diameter is 700 mm?

11) A rectangular piece of insulating material is required to wrap round a pipe which is 560 mm diameter. Allowing 150 mm for overlap, calculate the width of material required.

VOLUMES AND SURFACE AREAS

As with perimeters and areas, so volumes and surface areas can be just as important in engineering. The same technique of subdividing awkward solids is used, so once again we must be familiar with the surface areas and volumes of the component shapes, e.g. cylinders, spheres, etc. Areas are used in heat radiation and conduction problems for example, and volumes in finding the masses of components.

EXAMPLE 11.6

A piece of timber has the cross-section shown in Fig. 11.9. If its length is 300 mm, find its volume and total surface area.

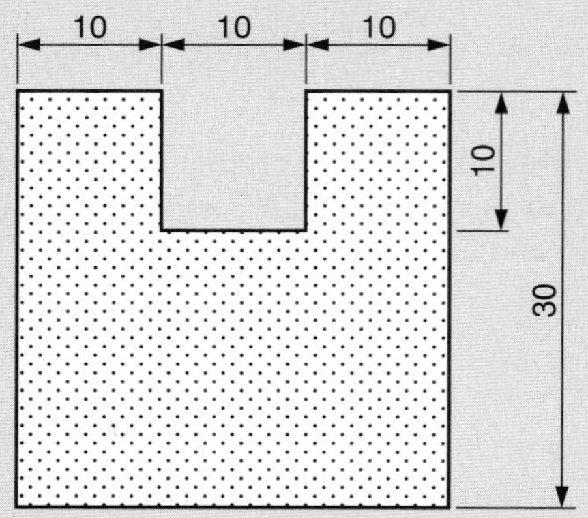

Fig. 11.9

$$\text{Area of cross-section} = (30 \times 30) - (10 \times 10) = 800\ \text{mm}^2$$

$$\text{Volume} = (\text{Area of cross-section}) \times (\text{Length})$$

$$= 800 \times 300 = 240\,000\ \text{mm}^3$$

$$\text{Perimeter of cross-section} = (3 \times 30) + (5 \times 10) = 140\ \text{mm}$$

$$\text{Total surface area} = (\text{Perimeter of cross-section} \times \text{Length}) + (\text{Area of ends})$$

$$= (140 \times 300) + (2 \times 800) = 43\,600\ \text{mm}^2$$

EXAMPLE 11.7

A steel bar has the cross-section shown in Fig. 11.10. If it is 3 m long, calculate its volume, total surface area and mass.

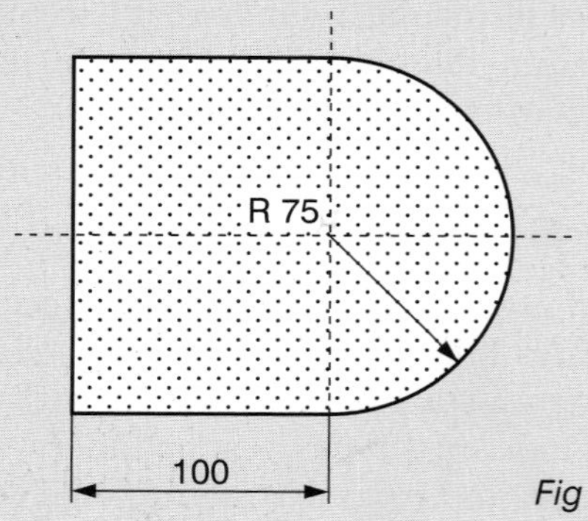

Fig 11.10

$$\text{Area of cross-section} = \tfrac{1}{2}\times\pi\times 75^2 + 100\times 150 = 23\,840\text{ mm}^2$$

$$= \frac{23\,840}{(1000)^2} = 0.023\,84\text{ m}^2$$

$$\therefore \quad \text{Volume of solid} = 0.023\,84 \times 3 = 0.0715\text{ m}^3$$

$$\text{Perimeter of cross-section} = \pi\times 75 + 2\times 100 + 150 = 585.6\text{ mm}$$

$$= \frac{585.6}{1000} = 0.5856\text{ m}$$

$$\text{Lateral surface area} = 0.5856\times 3 = 1.757\text{ m}^2$$

$$\text{Surface area of ends} = 2\times 0.023\,84 = 0.048\text{ m}^2$$

$$\therefore \quad \text{Total surface area} = 1.757 + 0.048 = 1.81\text{ m}^2$$

If we use the density of steel of 7900 kg/m^3 and

knowing that $\quad$ mass = volume × density

then $\quad$ $\text{mass of bar} = 0.0715 \times 7900\ \cancel{m^3} \times \dfrac{kg}{\cancel{m^3}}$

$= 565$ kg $\quad$ correct to 3 s.f.

Cylinder

$$\text{Volume} = \pi r^2 h$$

$$\text{Curved surface area} = 2\pi r h$$

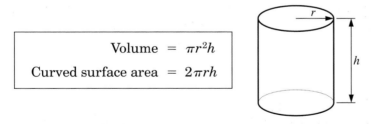

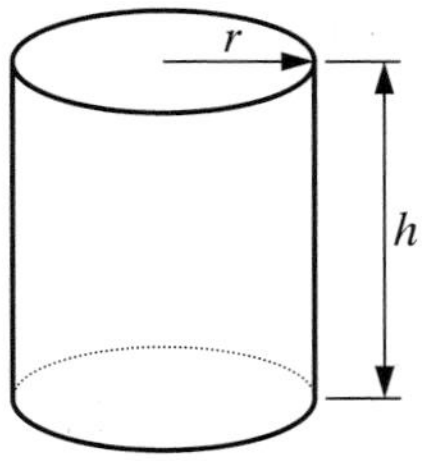

EXAMPLE 11.8

A cylindrical can holds 18 litres of petrol. Find the depth of the petrol if the can has a diameter of 600 mm.

Now 18 litres = 18×10^6 mm^3

and if the depth of the petrol is h mm

Then $\quad$ $\text{Volume of petrol} = \pi(\text{radius})^2 \times h$

$$\therefore \quad 18\times 10^6 = \pi\times 300^2 \times h$$

$$\therefore \quad h = \frac{18\,000\,000}{\pi\times 90\,000} = 63.7\text{ mm}$$

EXAMPLE 11.9

A metal bar of length 200 mm and diameter 75 mm is melted down and cast into washers 2.5 mm thick with an internal diameter of 12.5 mm and external diameter 25 mm. Calculate the number of washers obtained assuming no loss of metal.

$$\text{Volume of original bar of metal} = \pi \times 37.5^2 \times 200 = 883\,600\ \text{mm}^3$$

$$\text{Volume of one washer} = \pi \times (12.5^2 - 6.25^2) \times 2.5 = 920.4\ \text{mm}^3$$

$$\text{Number of washers obtained} = \frac{883\,600}{920.4} = 960$$

Cone

$$\text{Volume} = \tfrac{1}{3}\pi r^2 h$$

$$\text{Curved surface area} = \pi r l$$

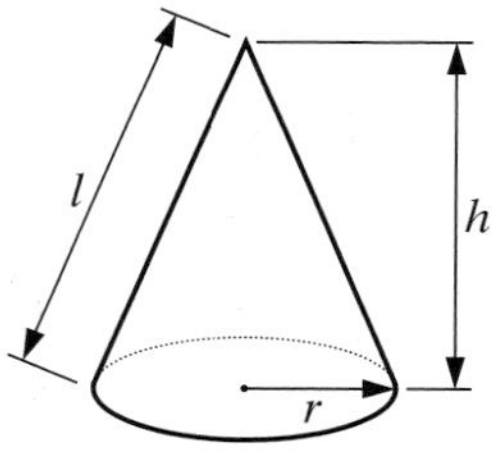

EXAMPLE 11.10

A hopper is in the form of an inverted cone. It has a maximum internal diameter of 2.4 m and an internal height of 2.1 m.

a) If the hopper is lined with lead, calculate the area of lead used.

b) Determine the capacity of the hopper.

a) The slant height may be found by using Pythagoras' theorem on the triangle shown in Fig. 11.11.

$$l^2 = r^2 + h^2 = 1.2^2 + 2.1^2 = 5.85$$

$$l = \sqrt{5.85} = 2.42\ \text{m}$$

$$\text{Surface area} = \pi r l = \pi \times 1.2 \times 2.42 = 9.12\ \text{m}^2$$

Hence the area of lead required is $9.12\ \text{m}^2$

b) $\text{Volume} = \tfrac{1}{3}\pi r^2 h = \tfrac{1}{3} \times \pi \times 1.2^2 \times 2.1 = 3.17\ \text{m}^3$

Hence the capacity of the hopper is $3.17\ \text{m}^3$

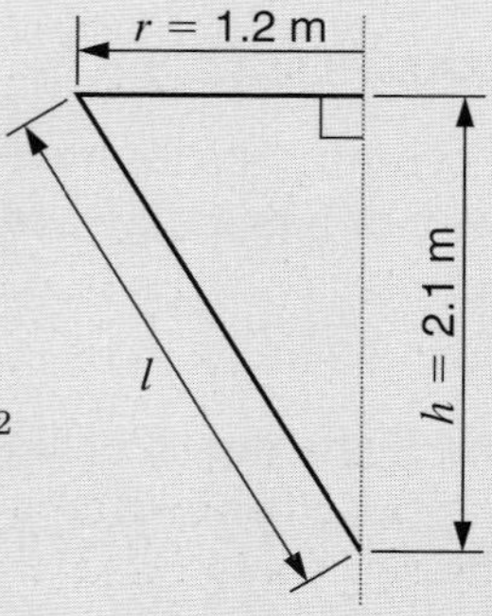

Fig. 11.11

Frustum of a Cone

A *frustum* (or *frustrum*) is the portion of a cone or pyramid between the base and a horizontal slice which removes the pointed portion.

$$\text{Volume} = \tfrac{1}{3}\pi h(R^2 + Rr + r^2)$$

$$\text{Curved surface area} = \pi l(R + r)$$

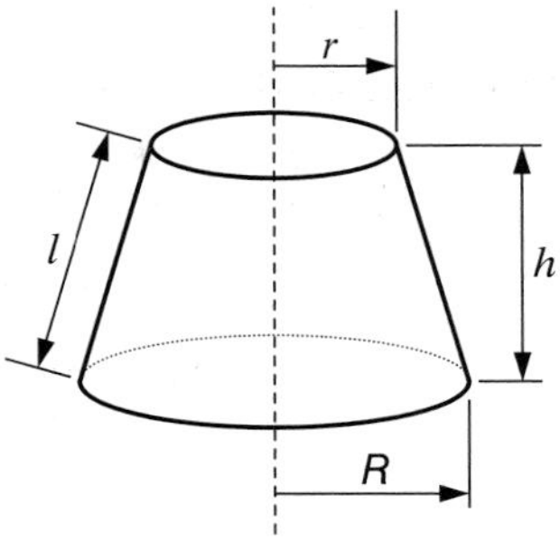

EXAMPLE 11.11

A concrete column is shaped like a frustum of a cone. The radius at the top is 0.6 m and the base radius is 0.9 m. Calculate the height of the column if the volume of concrete is 5 m³.

Now $\quad \text{Volume} = \tfrac{1}{3}\pi h(R^2 + Rr + r^2)$

$\therefore \quad 5 = \tfrac{1}{3} \times \pi \times h \times (0.9^2 + 0.9 \times 0.6 + 0.6^2) = 1.791\,h$

giving $\quad h = 2.79\text{ m}$

EXAMPLE 11.12

The bowl shown in Fig. 11.12 is made from sheet steel and has an open top. Calculate the total cost of painting the vessel (inside and outside) at a cost of 1p per 10 000 mm².

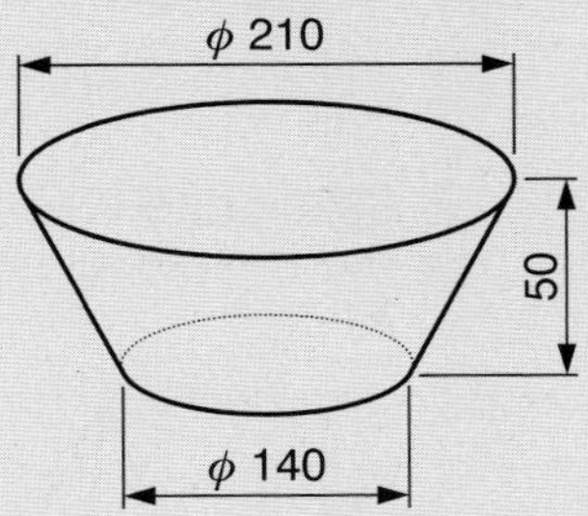

Fig. 11.12

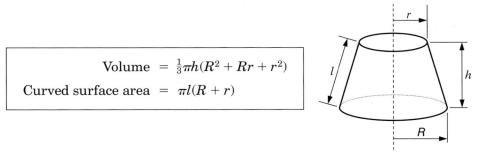

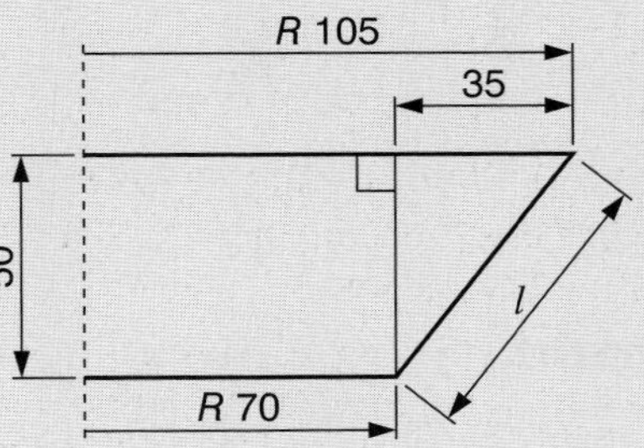

Fig. 11.13

Fig. 11.13 shows a half section of the bowl. Using Pythagoras' theorem on the right-angled triangle

$$l^2 = 50^2 + 35^2$$

$$\therefore \quad l = 61.0\text{ mm}$$

Now the required total surface area, i.e. inside and outside

$$= 2\{\text{Curved surface area}\} + 2\{\text{Base area}\}$$
$$= 2\{\pi l(R+r)\} + 2\{\pi r^2\}$$
$$= 2\{\pi(61)(105+70)\} + 2\{\pi 70^2\} = 97\,900\ \text{mm}^2$$

At 1p per $10\,000\ \text{mm}^2$, total cost $= \dfrac{97\,900}{10\,000} = 9.79\ \text{p}$

Sphere

$$\text{Volume} = \tfrac{4}{3}\pi r^3$$
$$\text{Surface area} = 4\pi r^2$$

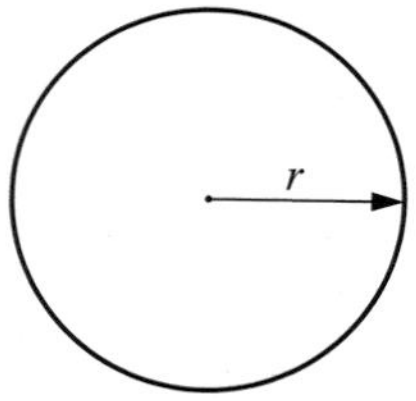

EXAMPLE 11.13

A metal end cap is in the shape of a hemisphere. Its internal and external diameters are 48 mm and 50 mm respectively.

a) Calculate the volume of metal used in its construction.

b) If the inside is to be painted, calculate the area to be covered.

a) If R is the outside radius and r the inside radius, then the

$$\text{hemispherical volume} = \tfrac{1}{2}\left(\tfrac{4}{3}\pi R^3 - \tfrac{4}{3}\pi r^3\right)$$
$$= \tfrac{1}{2}\times\tfrac{4}{3}\times\pi\times(R^3 - r^3)$$
$$= \tfrac{2}{3}\times\pi\times(25^3 - 24^3) = 3770\ \text{mm}^3$$

b)
$$\text{inside area of dome} = \tfrac{1}{2}\times 4\pi r^2$$
$$= \tfrac{1}{2}\times 4\times\pi\times 24^2 = 3620\ \text{mm}^2$$

Pyramid

$$\text{Volume} = \tfrac{1}{3}A\,h$$

Surface area = (Sum of the areas of the triangles forming the sides) + (the area of the base)

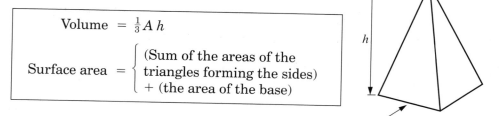

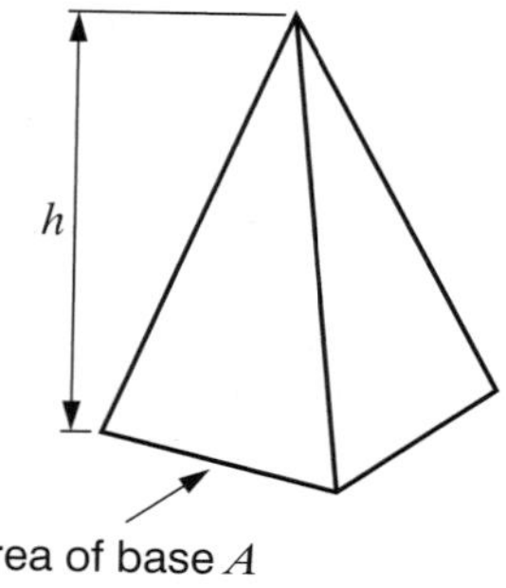

EXAMPLE 11.14

Find the volume and total surface area of a symmetrical pyramid whose base is a rectangle 7 m × 4 m and whose height is 10 m.

$$\text{Volume} = \tfrac{1}{3}Ah$$
$$= \tfrac{1}{3} \times (7 \times 4) \times 10 = 93.3\,\text{mm}^3$$

To find the surface area

From Fig. 11.14 the surface area consists of two sets of equal triangles (that is $\triangle ABC$ and $\triangle ADE$, and also $\triangle ABE$ and $\triangle ACD$) together with the base $BCDE$. To find the area of $\triangle ABC$ we must find the slant height AH. From the apex, A, drop a perpendicular AG on to the base and draw GH perpendicular to BC. H is then the mid-point of BC.

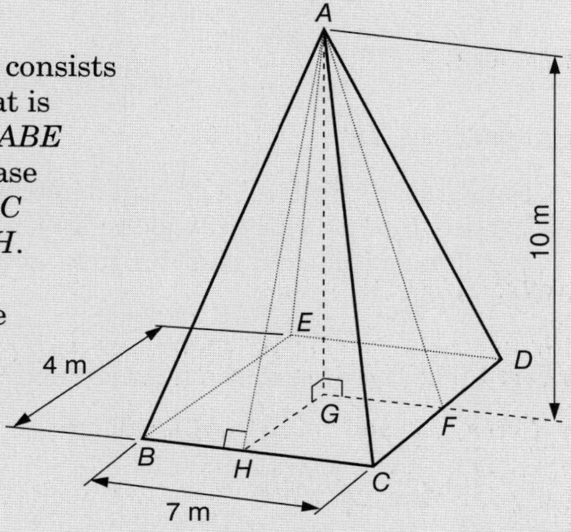

Fig. 11.14

In $\triangle AHG$, $\angle AGH = 90°$ and using Pythagoras' theorem

$$AH^2 = AG^2 + HG^2 = 10^2 + 2^2 = 104$$
$$AH = \sqrt{104} = 10.2\,\text{m}$$
$$\text{Area of } \triangle ABC = \tfrac{1}{2} \times \text{base} \times \text{height} = \tfrac{1}{2} \times 7 \times 10.2 = 35.7\,\text{m}^2$$

Similarly

$$AF^2 = AG^2 + GF^2 = 10^2 + 3.5^2 = 112.3$$
$$\therefore \quad AF = \sqrt{112.3} = 10.6\,\text{m}$$
$$\therefore \quad \text{Area of } \triangle ACD = \tfrac{1}{2} \times \text{base} \times \text{height} = \tfrac{1}{2} \times 4 \times 10.6 = 21.2\,\text{m}^2$$
$$\text{Total surface area} = (2 \times 35.7) + (2 \times 21.2) + (7 \times 4)$$
$$= 142\,\text{m}^2$$

Frustrum of a Pyramid

$$\text{Volume} = \tfrac{1}{3}h(A + \sqrt{Aa} + a)$$

$$\text{Surface area} = \begin{cases} \text{(Sum of the areas of the} \\ \text{trapeziums forming the sides)} \\ + \text{(areas of top and base)} \end{cases}$$

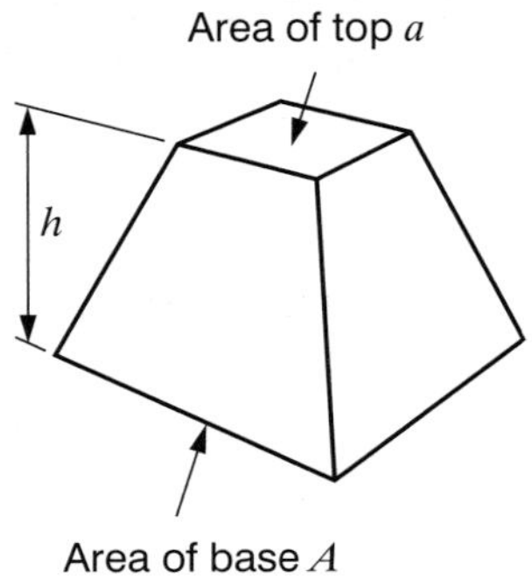

EXAMPLE 11.15

A casting has a length of 2 m and its cross-section is a regular hexagon. The casting tapers uniformly along its length. The hexagon has an edge 200 mm long at one end and 100 mm at the other. Calculate the volume of the casting.

In Fig. 11.15 the area of the hexagon of 200 mm side = 6 × Area $\triangle ABO$.

In $\triangle AOC$, $\angle AOC = 30°$, $AC = 100$ mm

and $\tan \angle AOC = \dfrac{AC}{OC}$

giving
$$OC = \frac{AC}{\tan \angle AOC} = \frac{100}{\tan 30°} = 173 \text{ mm}$$

$$\text{Area of } \triangle ABO = \tfrac{1}{2} \times 200 \times 173$$

$$\text{Area of hexagon} = 6 \times \tfrac{1}{2} \times 200 \times 173 = 103\,800 \text{ mm}^2$$

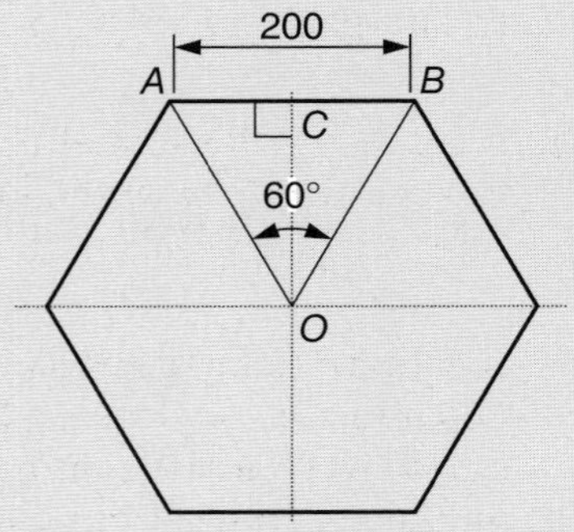

Fig. 11.15

The area of the hexagon of 100 mm side can be found in the same way. Work this out for yourself and you will arrive at 25 950 mm^2.

The casting is a frustum of a pyramid with $A = 103\,800$, $a = 25\,950$ and $h = 2000$.

$$\text{Volume} = \tfrac{1}{3}h\{A + \sqrt{Aa} + a\}$$
$$= \tfrac{1}{3} \times 2000 \times \{103\,800 + \sqrt{103\,800 \times 25\,950} + 25\,950\}$$
$$= 1.21 \times 10^8 \text{ mm}^3$$

Exercise 11.2

1) A block of lead 0.15 m by 0.1 m by 0.075 m is hammered out to make a square sheet 10 mm thick. What is the length of the side of the square?

2) Calculate the volume of metal in a pipe which has a bore of 50 mm, a thickness of 8 mm and a length of 6 m.

3) A hot water cylinder whose length is 1.12 m is to hold 200 litres. Find the diameter of the cylinder in millimetres.

4) Calculate the heating surface (in square metres) of a steam pipe whose external diameter is 60 mm and whose length is 8 m.

5) A metal bucket is 400 mm deep. It is 300 mm diameter at the top and 200 mm diameter at the bottom. Calculate the number of litres of water that the bucket will hold assuming that it is a frustum of a cone.

6) It is required to replace two pipes with bores of 28 mm and 70 mm respectively with a single pipe which has the same area of flow. Find the bore of this single pipe.

7) A totally enclosed metal container shaped like a pyramid has a square base of side 2 m and a height of 4 m. Calculate its volume and its total surface area.

8) A column is a regular octagon (8-sided polygon) in cross section. It is 460 mm across flats at the base and it tapers uniformly to 300 mm across flats at the top. If it is 3.6 m high, calculate the volume of material required to make it.

9) A bucket used on a crane is in the form of a frustum of a pyramid. Its base is a square of 600 mm side and its top is a square of 750 mm side. It has a depth of 800 mm.

a) Calculate, in cubic metres, the volume of cement that it will hold.

b) Twenty of these buckets of cement are emptied into a cylindrical cavity 4 m diameter. Calculate the depth to which the cavity will be filled.

10) The ball of a float valve is a sphere of 200 mm diameter. It is immersed in water to a depth of 100 mm. How many litres of water does it displace?

11) A hopper is in the form of a frustum of a rectangular pyramid. The top is 4 m long and 3 m wide, whilst the bottom is 2 m long and 1.5 m wide. If it is 2 m deep, calculate the volume of the hopper and the total inner surface area of the inclined faces.

12) A tub holding 58 litres of water when full is shaped like the frustum of a cone. If the radii at the ends of the tub are 400 mm and 300 mm respectively, calculate the height of the tub.

Trigonometry and the Circle 12

Theorem of Pythagoras – basic trigonometrical ratios – reciprocal ratios – identities – radians – degrees – circle components – length of arc – area of sector

THE THEOREM OF PYTHAGORAS

The first part of this section will remind you of the theorem of Pythagoras. Builders, for example, find the '3, 4, 5' triangle extremely useful for setting out right angles when marking out the bases for buildings.

We must first remind ourselves that in a right-angled triangle the hypotenuse is the longest side and always lies opposite to the right-angle.

Pythagoras' theorem states:

> In a right-angled triangle, the square on the hypotenuse is equal to the sum of the squares on the other two sides

A right-angled triangle is shown in Fig. 12.1 with **the squares** drawn on the sides. According to Pythagoras:

$$\text{Area 1} = \text{Area 2} + \text{Area 3}$$

$$a^2 = b^2 + c^2$$

so if $b = 3$ and $c = 4$

$$a^2 = 3^2 + 4^2$$

$$= 9 + 16 = 25$$

giving $a = 5$

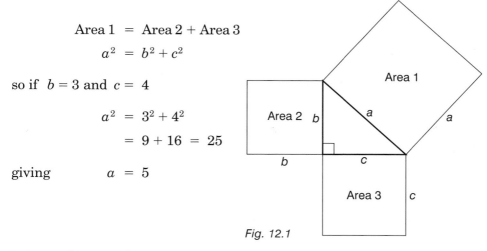

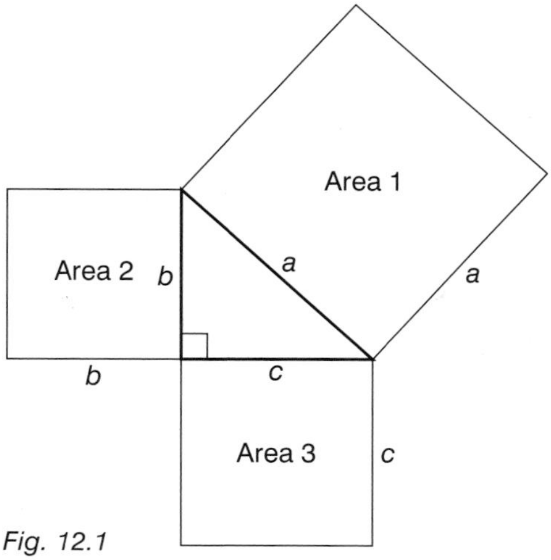

Fig. 12.1

It is worth remembering that a triangle with sides 3, 4 and 5 is right angled. You may have to mark out a large right-angle on the ground, perhaps for the base of a garage – a protractor or set-square will not be accurate enough, but you can make the '3, 4, 5' triangle to as large a scale as you wish.

Triangles with sides '5, 12, 13' and '7, 24, 25' are also right-angled.

EXAMPLE 12.1

Four holes are bored in a plate as shown in Fig. 12.2. If D is midway between B and C, find the distance between A and D.

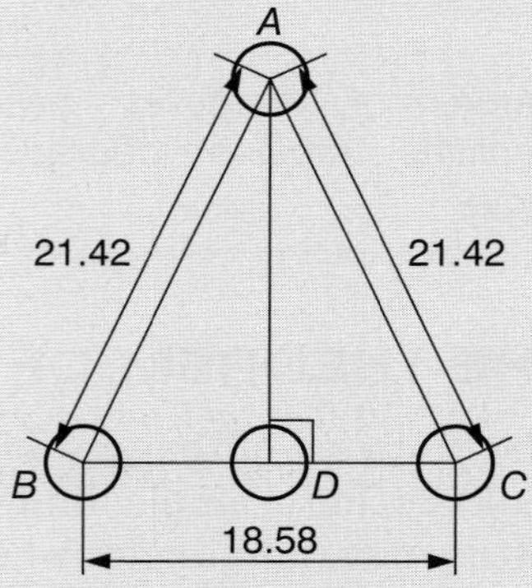

Fig. 12.2

Now $\triangle ABC$ is isosceles since it has two equal sides. The line AD bisects the base and is therefore perpendicular to BC.

Therefore $\triangle ACD$ is right-angled and so:

$$AC^2 = CD^2 + AD^2$$

or $$AD^2 = AC^2 - CD^2$$

$$= 21.42^2 - 9.289^2 = 372.5$$

$$\therefore \quad AD = \sqrt{372.5} = 19.30\text{ mm}$$

Exercise 12.1

1) Two holes are bored in a plate to the dimensions shown in Fig. 12.3. To check the holes dimension m is required. What is this dimension?

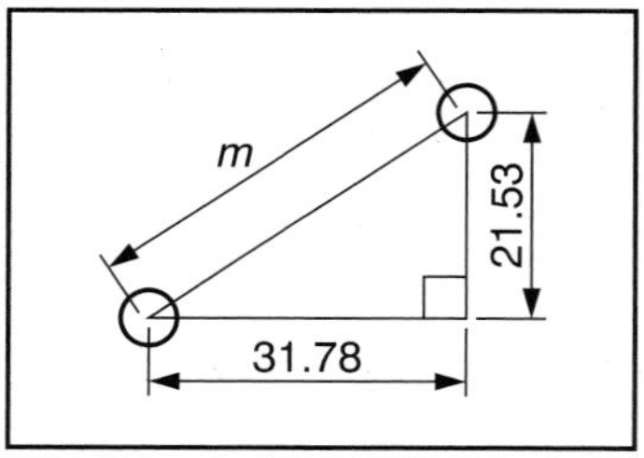

Fig. 12.3

2) Fig. 12.4 shows part of a drawing. If the holes are drilled correctly, what should be dimension x?

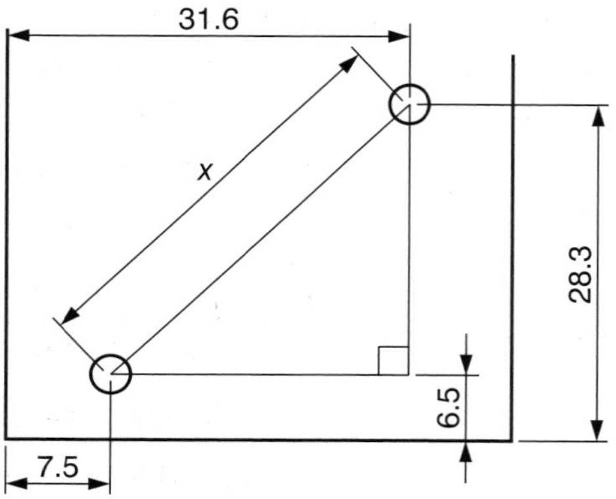

Fig. 12.4

3) Fig. 12.5 shows a round bar of 30 mm diameter which has a flat machined on it. Find the width of the flat.

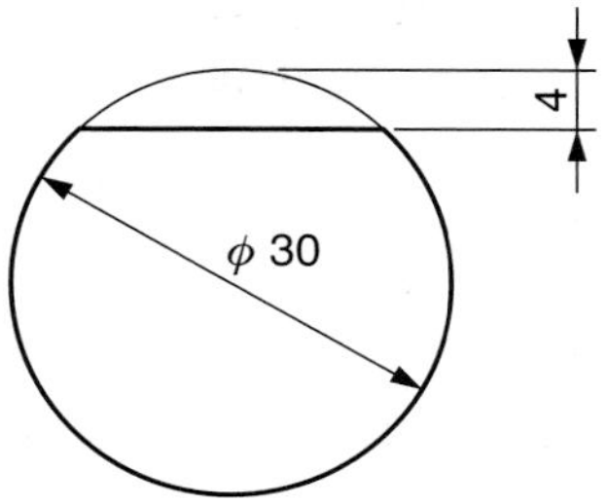

Fig. 12.5

4) Fig. 12.6 shows a bar which has two opposite flats milled on it. Find the distance d between the flats.

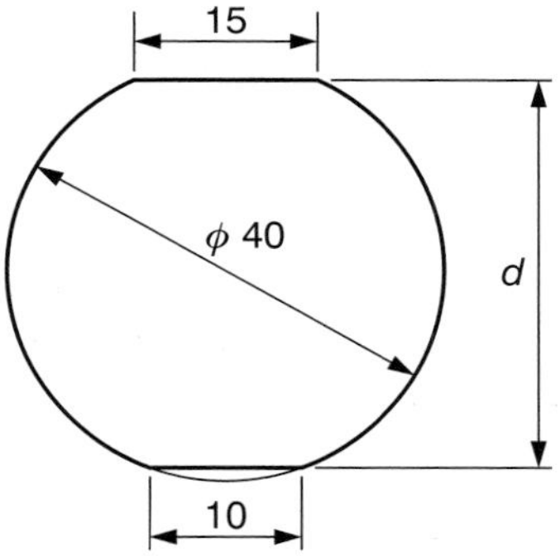

Fig. 12.6

BASIC TRIGONOMETRIC RATIOS

As engineers we are used to having certain basic tools for any particular job. In this case they are called the 'sine', the 'cosine' and the 'tangent' which are basic trigonometric ratios in a right-angled triangle.

This right-angled triangle is labelled with standard notation, as shown in Fig. 12.7. Here the angles are labelled A, B and C (in any order), and the sides are labelled a, b and c with each side opposite to its corresponding angle. The three basic trig. ratios are:

$$\text{the sine of an angle} = \frac{\text{the side opposite the angle}}{\text{hypotenuse}}$$

$$\text{the cosine of an angle} = \frac{\text{the side adjacent to the angle}}{\text{hypotenuse}}$$

$$\text{the tangent of an angle} = \frac{\text{the side opposite the angle}}{\text{the side adjacent to the angle}}$$

Abbreviations for sine, cosine and tangent are sin, cos and tan.

$$\sin B = \frac{AC}{BC} \quad \text{or} \quad \sin B = \frac{b}{a}$$

$$\cos B = \frac{AB}{BC} \quad \text{or} \quad \cos B = \frac{c}{a}$$

$$\tan B = \frac{AC}{AB} \quad \text{or} \quad \tan B = \frac{b}{c}$$

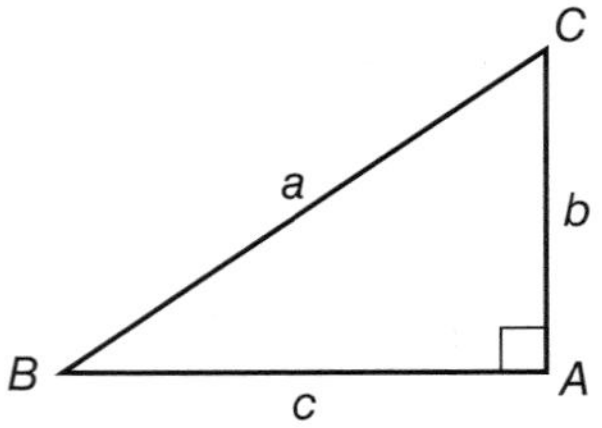

Fig. 12.7

EXAMPLE 12.2

Find the sides marked x, correct to 3 s.f, in Figs 12.8, 12.9, and 12.10.

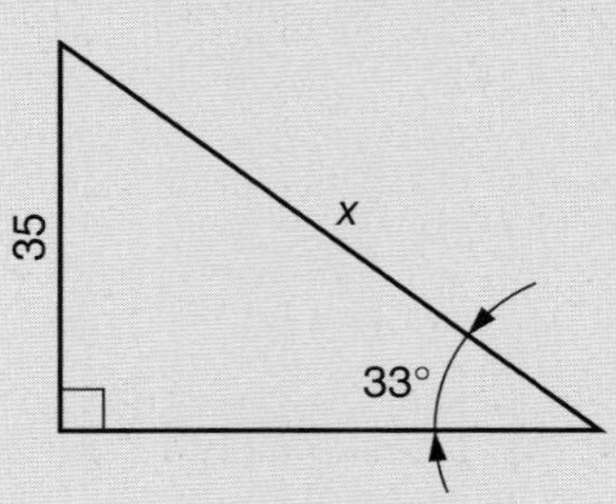

Fig. 12.8

$$\sin 33° = \frac{35}{x}$$

$$x = \frac{35}{\sin 33°} = \frac{35}{0.545} = 64.3\text{ mm}$$

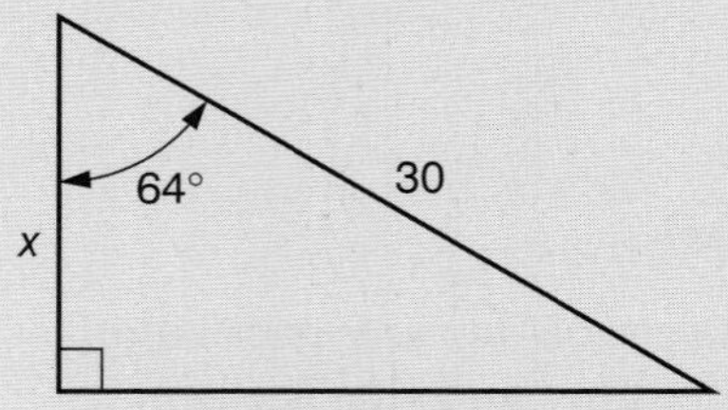

Fig. 12.9

$$\frac{x}{30} = \cos 64°$$

$$x = 30 \times \cos 64°$$

$$= 30 \times 0.4384 = 13.2\text{ mm}$$

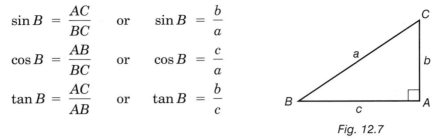

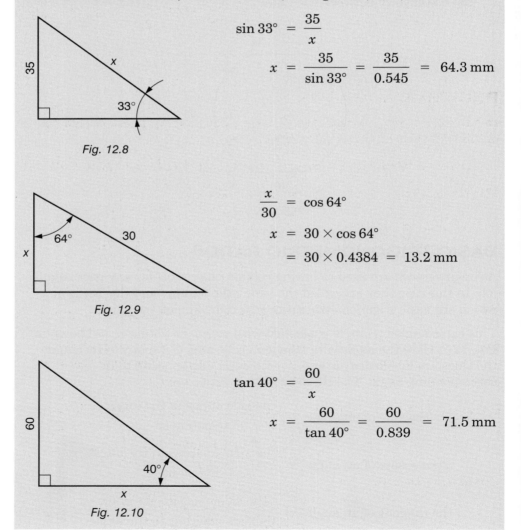

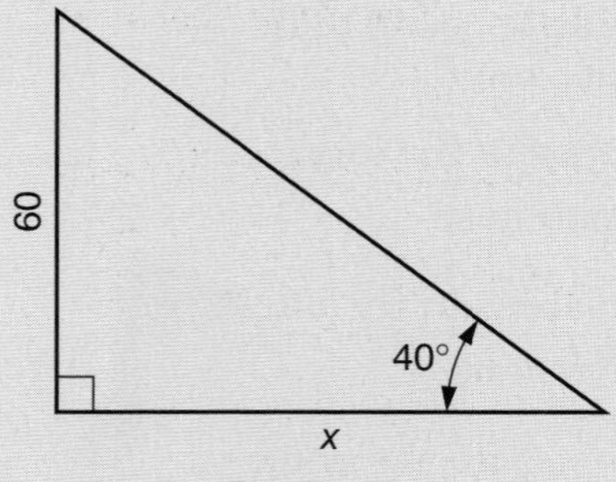

Fig. 12.10

$$\tan 40° = \frac{60}{x}$$

$$x = \frac{60}{\tan 40°} = \frac{60}{0.839} = 71.5\text{ mm}$$

EXAMPLE 12.3

Find the angles marked θ in Figs 12.11 and. 12.12 correct to 3 s.f.

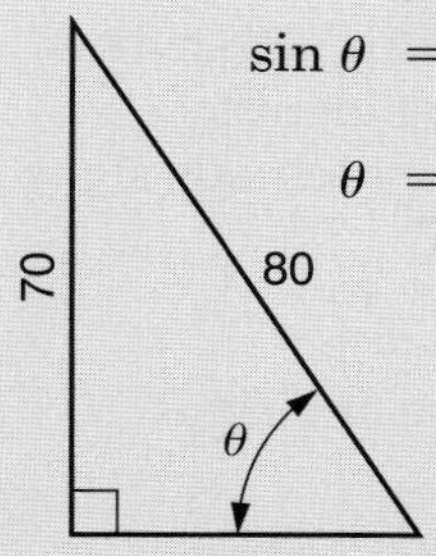

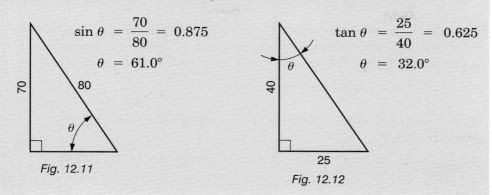

$$\sin\theta = \frac{70}{80} = 0.875$$

$$\theta = 61.0°$$

Fig. 12.11

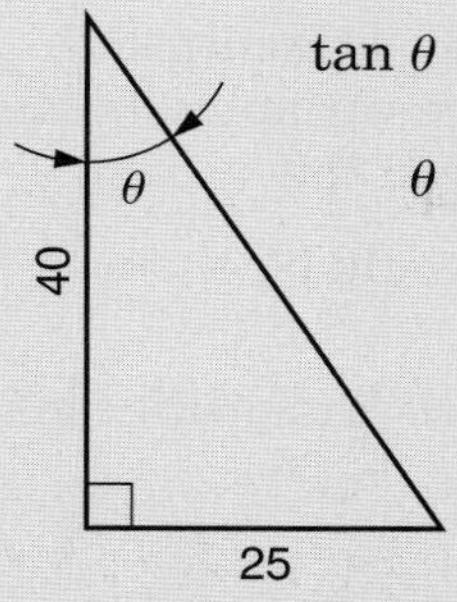

$$\tan\theta = \frac{25}{40} = 0.625$$

$$\theta = 32.0°$$

Fig. 12.12

RECIPROCAL RATIOS

In addition to sin, cos and tan there are three other ratios that may be obtained from a right-angled triangle. These are:

cosecant (abbreviation cosec), secant (sec) and cotangent (cot)

The three reciprocal ratios are defined as follows:

$$\operatorname{cosec} A = \frac{1}{\sin A} \qquad \sec A = \frac{1}{\cos A} \qquad \cot A = \frac{1}{\tan A}$$

The reciprocal of x is $\frac{1}{x}$. Hence the similar names for these trig. ratios.

Formulae in technical reference books often include reciprocal ratios. Before use you should rewrite the formula in terms of the more familiar ratios, namely sin, cos, and tan.

For example, the formula used for checking the form of a metric thread:

$$M = D - \frac{5p}{6}\cot\theta + d(\operatorname{cosec}\theta + 1)$$

can be rewritten as:

$$M = D - \frac{5p}{6}\left(\frac{1}{\tan\theta}\right) + d\left(\frac{1}{\sin\theta} + 1\right)$$

TRIGONOMETRIC IDENTITIES

A statement of the type $\operatorname{cosec} A \equiv \dfrac{1}{\sin A}$ is called an *identity*.

The sign $\equiv$ means 'is identical to'. Any statement using this sign is true for all values of the variables, i.e. the angle A in the above identity.
In practice, however, the $\equiv$ sign is often replaced by the $=$ (equals sign) and the identity would be given as $\operatorname{cosec} A = \dfrac{1}{\sin A}$.

Many trigonometrical identities may be verified by the use of a right-angled triangle.

EXAMPLE 12.4

To show that $\tan A = \dfrac{\sin A}{\cos A}$

The sides and angles of the triangle may be labelled in any way providing that A is *not* the 90° angle (Fig. 12.13).

Now $\quad \sin A = \dfrac{a}{b}$

and $\quad \cos A = \dfrac{c}{b}$

and $\quad \tan A = \dfrac{a}{c}$

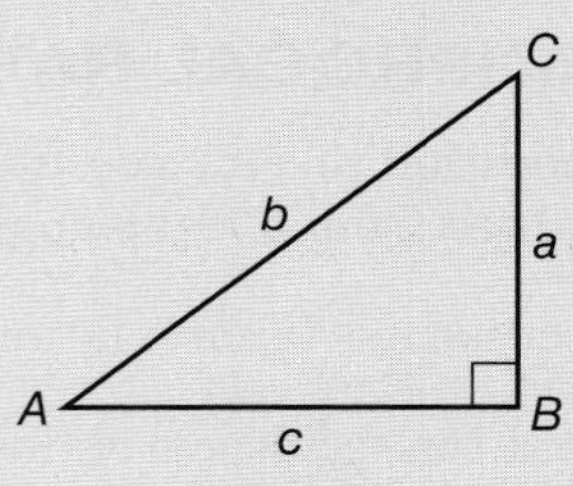

Fig. 12.13

Hence from the given identity,

$$\text{RHS} = \frac{\sin A}{\cos A} = \frac{a/b}{c/b} = \frac{ab}{bc} = \frac{a}{c} = \tan A = \text{LHS}$$

EXAMPLE 12.5

To show that $\sin^2 A + \cos^2 A = 1$

In Fig. 12.13 $\quad \sin A = \dfrac{a}{b} \quad \therefore \quad \sin^2 A = \left(\dfrac{a}{b}\right)^2 = \dfrac{a^2}{b^2}$

$\quad \cos A = \dfrac{c}{b} \quad \therefore \quad \cos^2 A = \left(\dfrac{c}{b}\right)^2 = \dfrac{c^2}{b^2}$

$\therefore \quad \text{LHS} = \sin^2 A + \cos^2 A = \dfrac{a^2}{b^2} + \dfrac{c^2}{b^2} = \dfrac{a^2 + c^2}{b^2}$

But by Pythagoras' theorem, $a^2 + c^2 = b^2$

$\therefore \quad \text{LHS} = \dfrac{b^2}{b^2} = 1 = \text{RHS}$

Thus $\quad \sin^2 A + \cos^2 A = 1$

Exercise 12.2

Find the lengths of the sides marked x in triangles 1) to 6):

1)

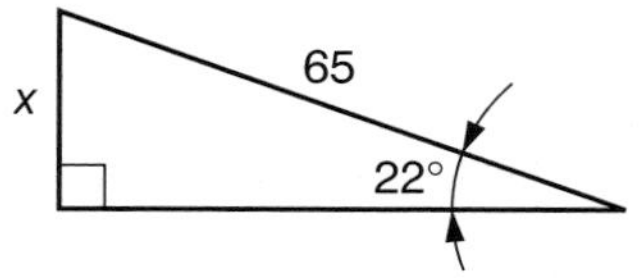

2)

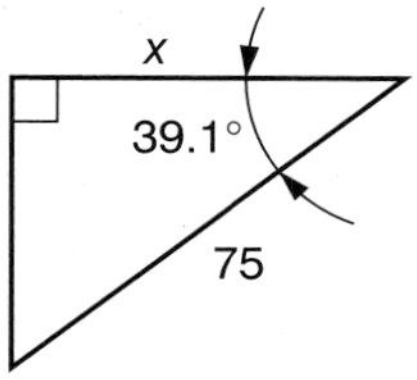

3)

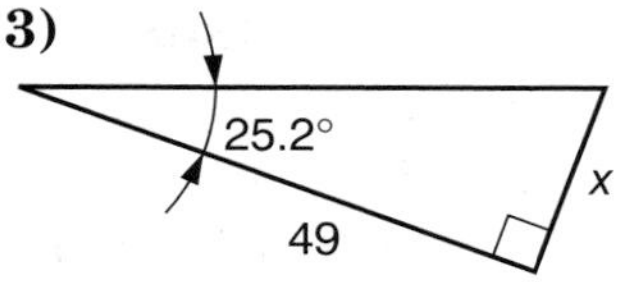

4)

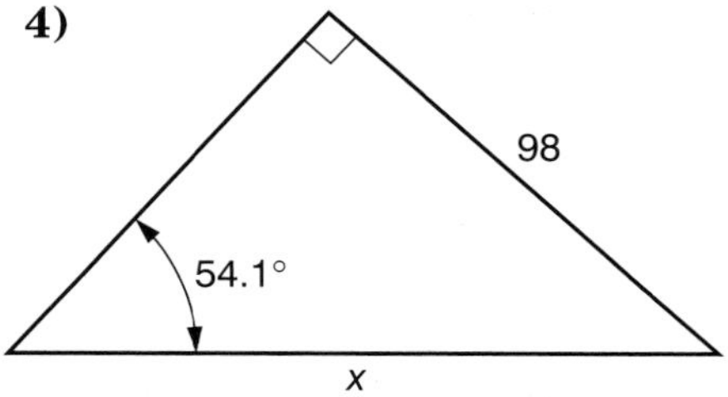

5)

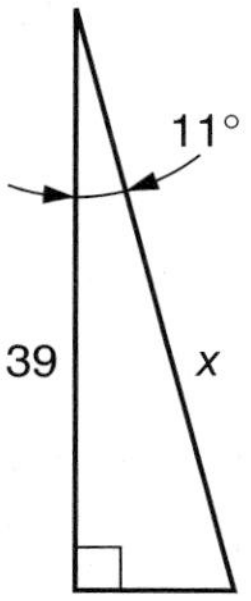

6)

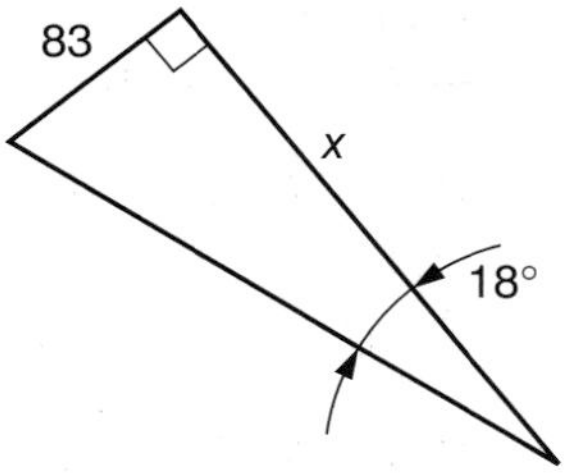

Find the angles marked θ in triangles 7) to 9):

7)

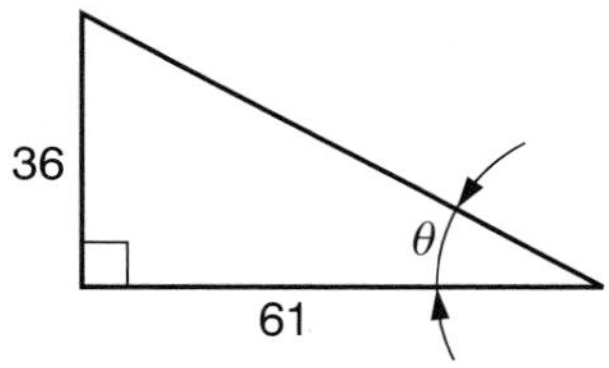

8)

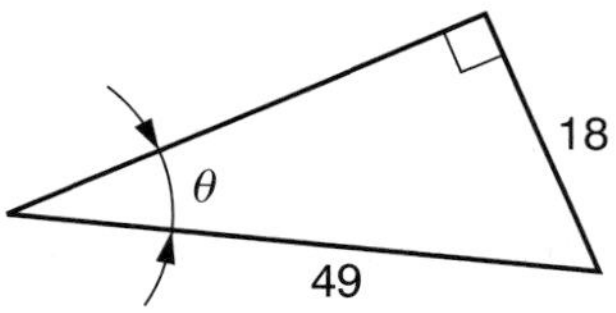

9)

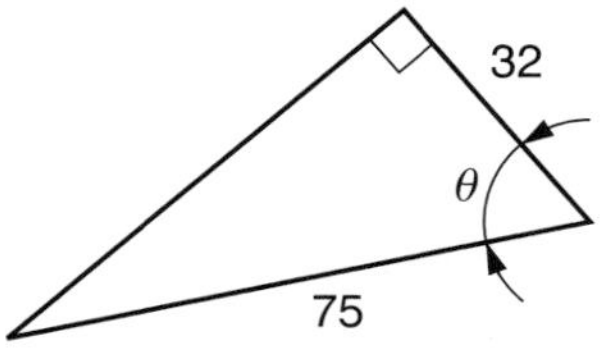

10) The altitude of an isosceles triangle is 86 mm and each of the equal angles is 29°. Calculate the lengths of the equal sides.

TRIGONOMETRY AND THE CIRCLE

The circle is a figure that keeps cropping up in life generally, but especially in technology. An alternative measure of an angle is associated with the circle, namely the radian. This measure is important especially when we study waveforms – sine and cosine graphs.

Radian Measure

We have seen that an angle is usually measured in degrees but there is another way of measuring an angle. In this, the unit is known as the radian (abbreviation rad).

Referring to Fig. 12.14 gives:

$$\text{Angle in radians} = \frac{\text{length of arc}}{\text{radius of circle}}$$

$$\theta \text{ radians} = \frac{l}{r}$$

$$l = r\theta$$

Hence $\quad \text{Length of arc} = r\theta$

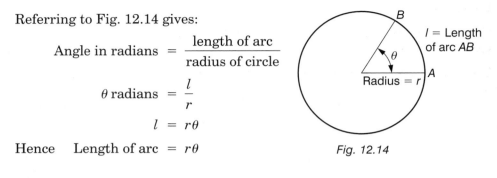

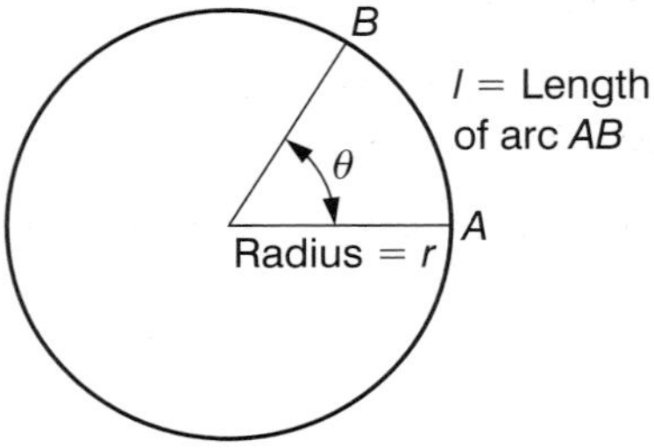

Fig. 12.14

Relation between Radians and Degrees

For a full 360° circle the arc will be the circumference $2\pi r$

thus $\quad \text{Full circle angle} = \frac{\text{circumference}}{\text{radius}} = \frac{2\pi r}{r} = 2\pi \text{ radians}$

giving $\quad 360° = 2\pi \text{ radians}$

so $\quad 1 \text{ radian} = \frac{360°}{2\pi} = 57.3 \text{ degrees}$

To convert from degrees to radians	To convert from radians to degrees
$\text{angle} = \frac{\pi(\theta°)}{180} \text{ radians}$	$\text{angle} = \left(\frac{180}{\pi} \times \theta\right) \text{ degrees}$

More often than not we use ratios of π for angles measured in radians, rather than using a numerical value. Here are the most used angles:

$30° = \frac{\pi(30)}{180} = \frac{\pi}{6} \text{ rad}$		$45° = \frac{\pi}{4} \text{ rad}$	$60° = \frac{\pi}{3} \text{ rad}$
$90° = \frac{\pi}{2} \text{ rad}$	$180° = \pi \text{ rad}$	$270° = \frac{3\pi}{2} \text{ rad}$	$360° = 2\pi \text{ rad}$

Degrees, Minutes and Seconds

Modern calculating methods make the use of decimal degrees (e.g. 36.783°) more likely than the use of minutes and seconds.

EXAMPLE 12.6

Convert 29° 37′ 29″ to radians stating the answer correct to 5 significant figures.

The first step is to convert the given angle into degrees and decimals of a degree.

$$29^\circ\ 37'\ 29'' = 29 + \frac{37}{60} + \frac{29}{3600} = 29.625^\circ$$

$$= \frac{\pi \times 29.625}{180} = 0.517\,05 \text{ radians}$$

Many scientific calculators will convert degrees, minutes and seconds into decimal degrees, and vice versa, using special keys – instructions for use of these keys will be given in the accompanying booklet.

EXAMPLE 12.7

Convert 0.089 35 radians into degrees.

$$0.089\,35 \text{ radians} = \frac{0.089\,35 \times 180}{\pi} = 5.119^\circ$$

Components of a Circle

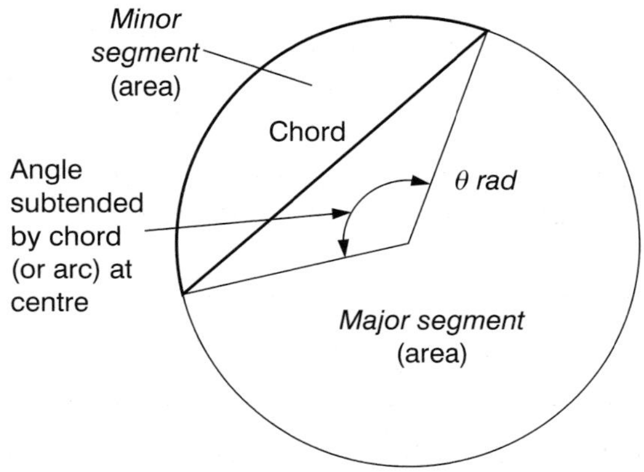

Fig. 12.15

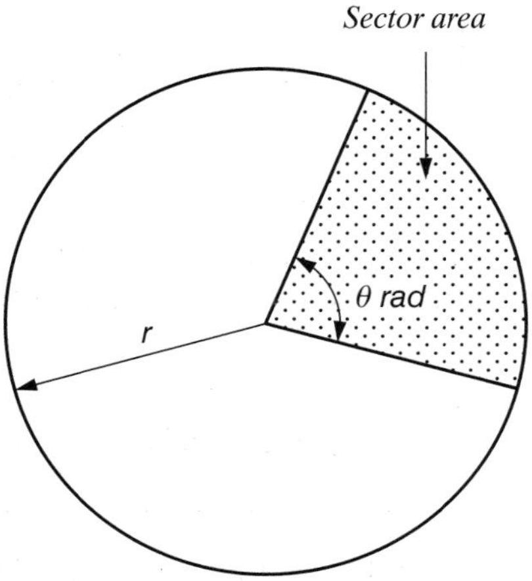

Fig. 12.16

Useful Properties of Radii, Chords and Tangents

You will, no doubt, be familiar with most of the information given here, but it is included as most of these properties are used regularly in fine measurement calculations.

1) If two circles are tangential to each other then the straight line which passes through the centres of the circles also passes through the point of tangency.

   Thus the line AB joining the centres of the circles also passes through the point of tangency C (Fig. 12.17) and AB is perpendicular to DE.

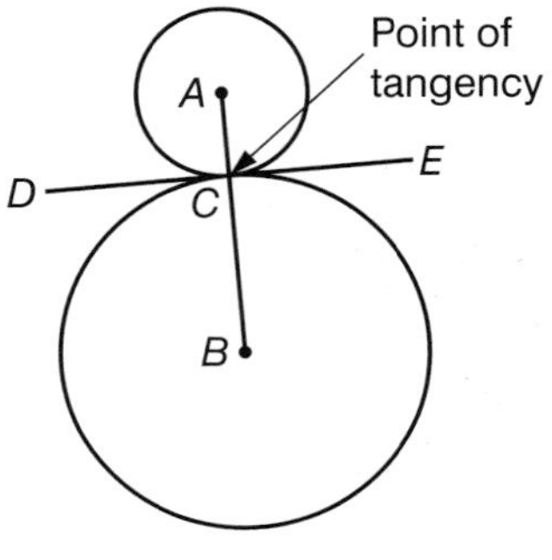

Fig. 12.17

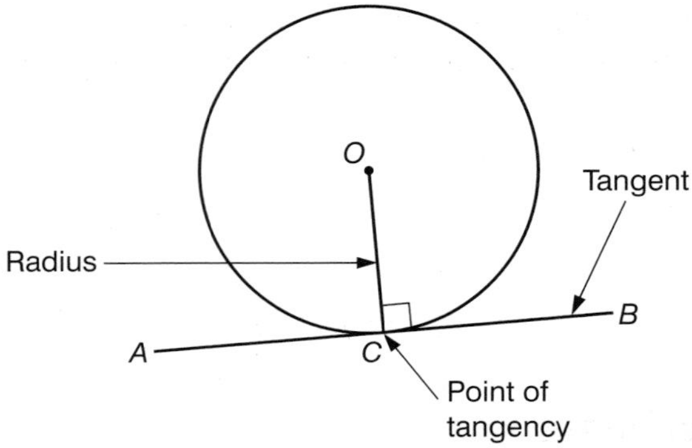

Fig. 12.18

2) If a line is tangential to a circle then it is at right angles to a radius drawn to the point of tangency.

   Thus if AB is a tangent with C the point of tangency then the radius OC is at right angles to AB (Fig. 12.18).

3) If, from a point outside a circle, tangents are drawn to the circle then their lengths are equal.

   Thus in Fig. 12.19 the lengths AC and BC are equal. It can also be proved that $\angle ACB$ is bisected by CO, O being the centre of the circle.

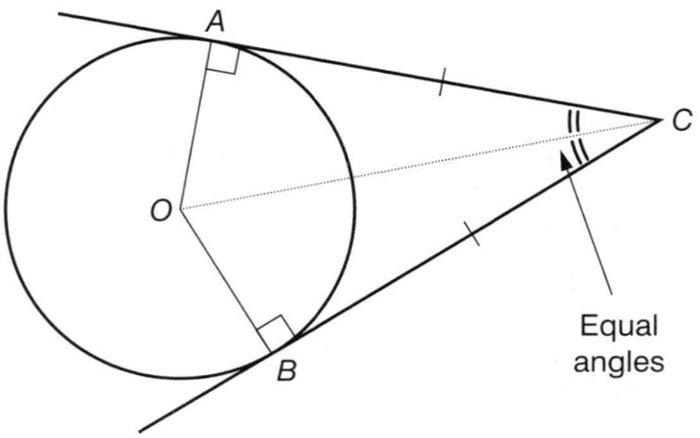

Fig. 12.19

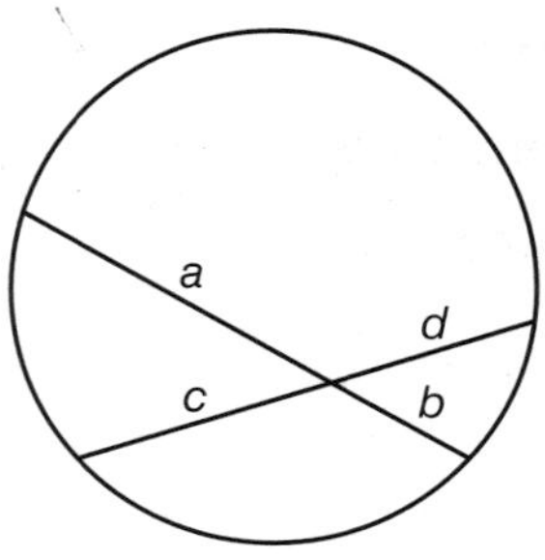

Fig. 12.20

4) If two chords intersect each other in a circle then the product of the segments of the one equals the product of the segments of the other. In Fig. 12.20:

$$a \times b = c \times d$$

Length of Arc, and Area of Sector

The area of a circle $= \pi r^2$ and so by proportion (Fig. 12.16),

$$\text{Area of sector} = \pi r^2 \times \frac{\theta}{2\pi} = \frac{1}{2} r^2 \theta$$

Remember that it is assumed that θ is measured in radians unless any other measurement is denoted, e.g. degrees.

Summary

Length of arc	$=$	$r\theta$	$=$	$2\pi r\left(\frac{\theta^\circ}{360}\right)$
Area of sector	$=$	$\frac{1}{2}r^2\theta$	$=$	$\pi r^2\left(\frac{\theta^\circ}{360}\right)$

EXAMPLE 12.8

Calculate a) the length of arc of a circle whose radius is 8 m and which subtends an angle of 56° at the centre, and b) the area of the sector so formed.

a) $\text{Length of arc} = 2\pi r \times \frac{\theta^\circ}{360} = 2 \times \pi \times 8 \times \frac{56}{360} = 7.82 \text{ m}$

b) $\text{Area of sector} = \pi r^2 \times \frac{\theta^\circ}{360} = \pi \times 8^2 \times \frac{56}{360} = 31.28 \text{ m}^2$

EXAMPLE 12.9

Find the angle of a sector of radius 35 mm and area 1020 mm^2.

Now $\quad \text{Area of sector} = \frac{1}{2}r^2\theta$

and using the given values of area $= 1020 \text{ m}^2$ and $r = 35$ mm

we have $\quad 1020 = \frac{1}{2}(35)^2\theta$

from which $\quad \theta = \frac{1020 \times 2}{35^2} = 1.67 \text{ rad}$

$$= \frac{180 \times 1.67}{\pi} = 95.7^\circ$$

EXAMPLE 12.10

Water flows in a 400 mm diameter pipe to a depth of 300 mm.

Calculate (a) the wetted perimeter of the pipe and

(b) the area of cross-section of the water.

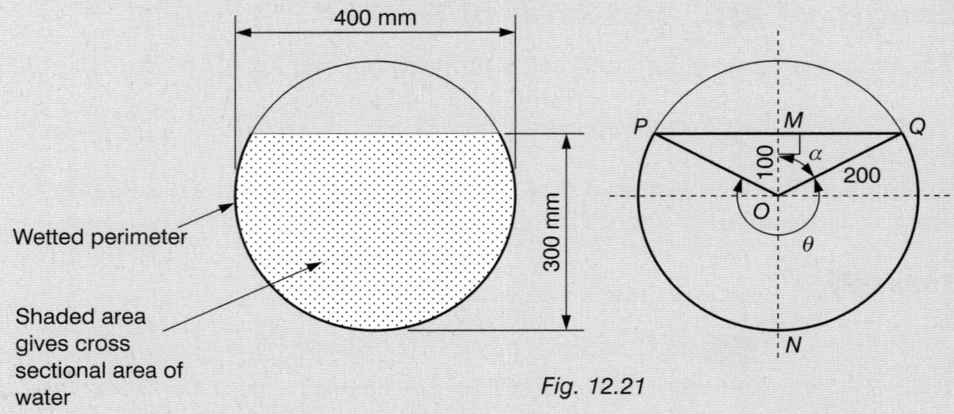

Fig. 12.21

a) From Fig. 12.21 the right-angled triangle MQO

$$\cos\alpha = \frac{OM}{OQ} = \frac{100}{200} = 0.5$$

$$\therefore \quad \alpha = 60^\circ$$

now $$\theta + 2\alpha = 360^\circ$$

$$\therefore \quad \theta = 360^\circ - 2(60^\circ) = 240^\circ$$

but $$\text{Wetted perimeter} = \text{arc } PNQ$$

$$= 2\pi r\left(\frac{\theta^\circ}{360}\right) = 2\pi(200)\left(\frac{240}{360}\right)$$

$$= 838\text{ mm}$$

b) Also from $\triangle MQO$

$$\sin\alpha = \frac{MQ}{OQ}$$

$$\therefore \quad MQ = OQ\sin\alpha = 200\sin 60^\circ = 173.2\text{ mm}$$

Now $$\begin{pmatrix}\text{Cross-sectional}\\ \text{area of water}\end{pmatrix} = \begin{pmatrix}\text{Area of}\\ \text{sector } PNQ\end{pmatrix} + \begin{pmatrix}\text{Area of}\\ \text{triangle } POQ\end{pmatrix}$$

$$= \pi r^2\left(\frac{\theta^\circ}{360}\right) + \tfrac{1}{2}(PQ)(MO)$$

$$= \pi(200)^2\left(\frac{240}{360}\right) + \tfrac{1}{2}(2 \times 173.2)(100)$$

$$= 101\,000\text{ mm}^2$$

Exercise 12.3

1) Convert the following angles to radians stating the answers correct to 4 significant figures:

a) $35°$ **b)** $83° 28'$ **c)** $19° 17' 32''$ **d)** $43.66°$

2) Convert the following angles to degrees, minutes and seconds correct to the nearest second:

a) 0.1732 radians **b)** 1.5632 radians **c)** 0.0783 radians

3) If r is the radius and θ is the angle subtended by an arc, find the length of arc when:

a) $r = 2$ m, $\theta = \pi/6$ rad. **b)** $r = 34$ m, $\theta = 38° 40'$

4) If l is the length of an arc, r is the radius and θ the angle subtended by the arc, find θ when:

a) $l = 9.4$ m, $r = 4.5$ m **b)** $l = 14$ mm, $r = 79$ mm

5) An animal feed hopper incorporates a hinged shutter door which is in the shape of the sector of a circle. The length round the arc is 70 mm and the angle subtended at the centre is 45°. We need to know the length of one of the straight sides, which will be hinged, and in addition, the area covered by the shutter.

6) The cross-section of a mechanical component is shown in Fig. 12.22. It is necessary to know the value of the shaded area.

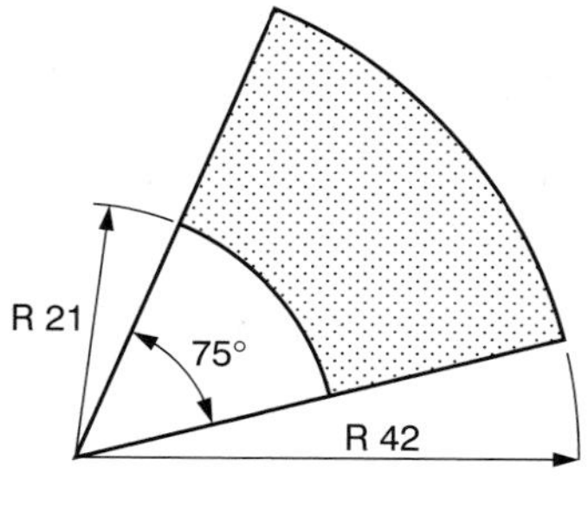

Fig. 12.22

7) We are trying to adapt an optical instrument to fit one of the items which our company manufactures. A chord 26 mm long has been ground on to the flat surface of a circular glass lens which has an effective diameter of 35 mm. You have been asked to calculate:

a) The lengths of the arcs into which the effective circumference is divided.

a) The area of the lens in the minor segment.

8) A flat is machined on a circular bar of 15 mm diameter, the maximum depth of cut being 2 mm. Find the area of the cross-section of the finished bar.

9) Water flows in a 300 mm diameter drain to a depth of 100 mm. Calculate the wetted perimeter of the drain and the area of cross-section of the water.

13 Trigonometry and Solving Angles

The sine rule – the ambiguous case – the circumscribing circle – the cosine rule – area of a triangle

SOLUTION OF TRIANGLES

Solving a triangle means finding all the unknown sides and angles. One way is to draw the triangle to scale and measure using a rule and protractor but this is rather tedious and the accuracy of the answers is limited. Trigonometry, however, can readily be used and, using a calculator, any desired degree of accuracy is possible.

'Any old triangle' is called, in mathematics, a scalene triangle – a triangle having no special features: no right angle, all angles different and no sides of the same length. This chapter covers the use of the sine and cosine rules. These are the two rules necessary for solving scalene triangles, unless you wish to break them down into right-angled triangle components. Direct practical applications include an example of a simple crane framework and an electrical phasor diagram.

When we have found the three missing elements in the solution of a triangle problem we are said to have 'solved the triangle'.

THE SINE RULE

The sine rule may be used when either of the following is known:

1) one side and any two angles; or
2) two sides and an angle opposite to one of these sides.
   (In this case two solutions may be found giving rise to what is called the 'ambiguous case', see Example 13.2)

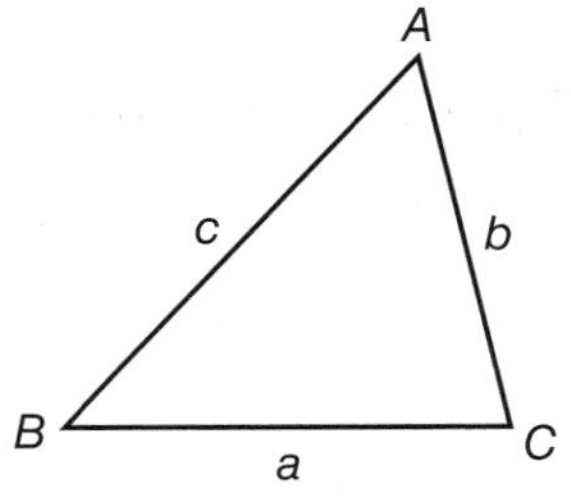

Fig. 13.1

Using the notation of Fig. 13.1 the sine rule states:

$$\frac{a}{\sin A} = \frac{b}{\sin B} = \frac{c}{\sin C}$$

EXAMPLE 13.1

Solve the triangle ABC given that $A = 42°$, $C = 72°$ and $b = 61.8$ mm.

The triangle should be drawn for reference as shown in Fig. 13.2 but there is no need to draw it to scale.

Since $\angle A + \angle B + \angle C = 180°$ then $\angle B = 180° - 42° - 72° = 66°$

The sine rule states

$$\frac{a}{\sin A} = \frac{b}{\sin B}$$

$$\therefore \quad a = \frac{b \sin A}{\sin B} = \frac{61.8 \times \sin 42°}{\sin 66°} = 45.3\text{ mm}$$

$$\frac{c}{\sin C} = \frac{b}{\sin B}$$

$$\therefore \quad c = \frac{b \sin C}{\sin B} = \frac{61.8 \times \sin 72°}{\sin 66°} = 64.3\text{ mm}$$

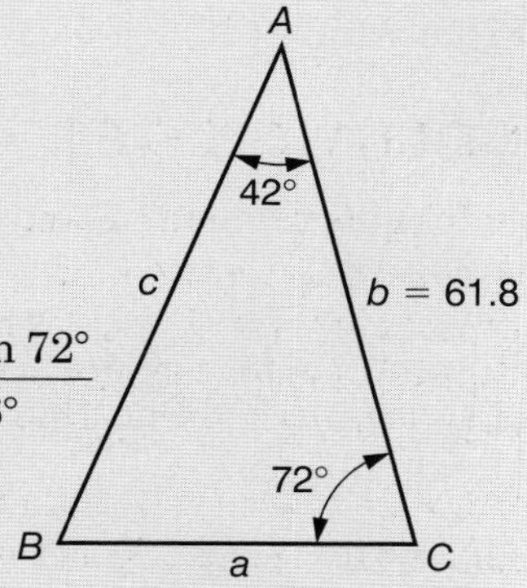

Fig. 13.2

The complete solution is:

$$\angle B = 66°, \quad a = 45.3\text{ mm} \quad \text{and} \quad c = 64.3\text{ mm}$$

A rough check on sine rule calculations may be made by remembering that in any triangle, the longest side lies opposite the largest angle and the shortest side lies opposite the smallest angle.

Thus in the previous example:

Smallest angle $= 42° = A$ and Shortest side $= a = 45.3$ mm

Largest angle $= 72° = C$ and Longest side $= c = 64.3$ mm

The Ambiguous Case

Look at these two triangles:

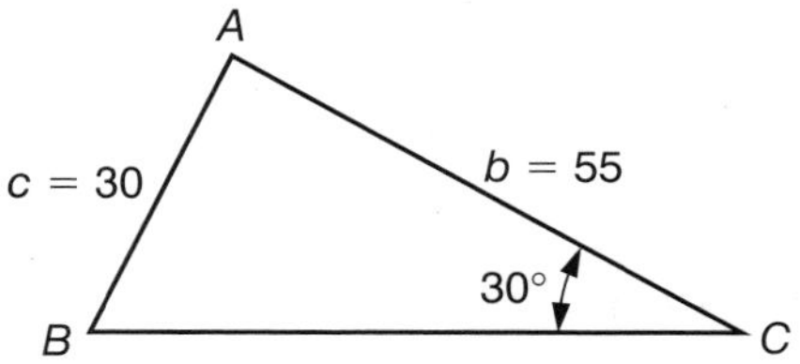

Fig. 13.3

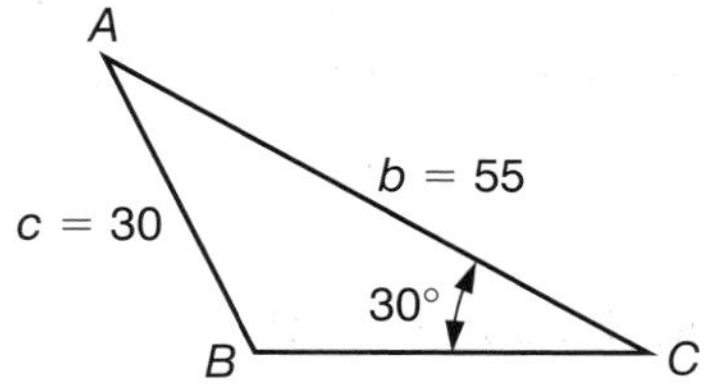

Fig. 13.4

and now consider the next example:

EXAMPLE 13.2

Solve $\triangle ABC$ if $b = 55\text{ mm}$, $c = 30\text{ mm}$ and $\angle C = 30°$.

Since we are given two sides and an angle, we look to the sine rule.

So using $$\frac{b}{\sin B} = \frac{c}{\sin C}$$

From which $$\sin B = \frac{b \sin C}{c} = \frac{55 \times \sin 30°}{30} = 0.9167$$

Giving $$\angle B = 66.4°$$

Now, no doubt, you will have noticed that the given data would fit either of the triangles, Fig. 13.3 or Fig. 13.4. This is why it is called the ambiguous case.

But how is it that we have worked through using trigonometry and found only one value for $\angle B = 66.4°$ which is clearly only suitable for Fig. 13.3?

Where does the other value of $\angle B$ come from? In fact, there are two angles between $0°$ and $180°$ which have the same sine value. These are supplementary angles and therefore add up to $180°$.

Hence the other value of $$\angle B = 180° - 66.4° = 113.6° \text{ which fits Fig. 13.4}$$

Although your calculator will only produce one value of angle for a specified sine value, it is possible to verify that $\sin 113.6° = 0.9167$ (see Chapter 14 for inverse trigonometric ratios).

We will now find the full solutions for both triangles.

When $\angle B = 66.4°$

$$\angle A = 180° - 66.4° - 30° = 83.6°$$

Now $$\frac{a}{\sin A} = \frac{c}{\sin C}$$

$$\therefore \quad a = \frac{c \sin A}{\sin C} = \frac{30 \times \sin 83.6°}{\sin 30°} = 59.6\text{ mm}$$

When $\angle B = 113.6°$

$$\angle A = 180° - 113.6° - 30° = 36.4°$$

$$\frac{a}{\sin A} = \frac{c}{\sin C}$$

$$a = \frac{c \sin A}{\sin C} = \frac{30 \times \sin 36.4°}{\sin 30°} = 35.6\text{ mm}$$

The ambiguous case may be seen clearly by constructing the given triangle geometrically as follows (Fig. 13.5).

Using a full size scale draw $AC = 55$ mm and draw CX such that $ACX = 30°$. Now with centre A and radius 30 mm describe a circular arc to cut CX at B and B'.

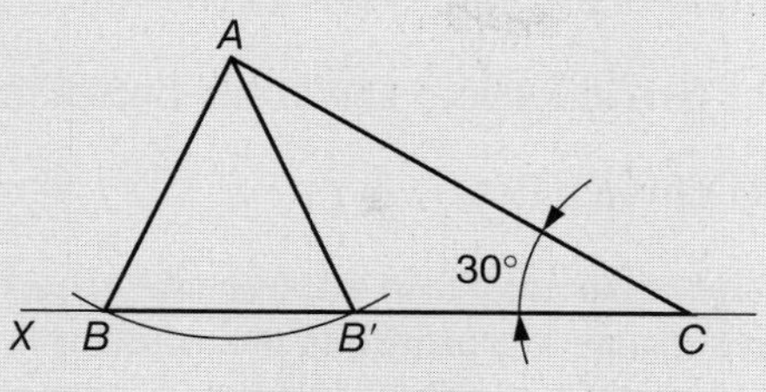

Fig. 13.5

Then ABC represents the triangle shown in Fig. 13.3 and $AB'C$ represents the triangle shown in Fig. 13.4.

As long as you are aware of the two possible solutions, where this occurs in an engineering situation, there is almost always an indication as to which shape of triangle is required.

Use of the Sine Rule to Find the Diameter (*D*) of the Circumscribing Circle of a Triangle

Using the notation of Fig. 13.6

$$\frac{a}{\sin A} = \frac{b}{\sin B} = \frac{c}{\sin C} = D$$

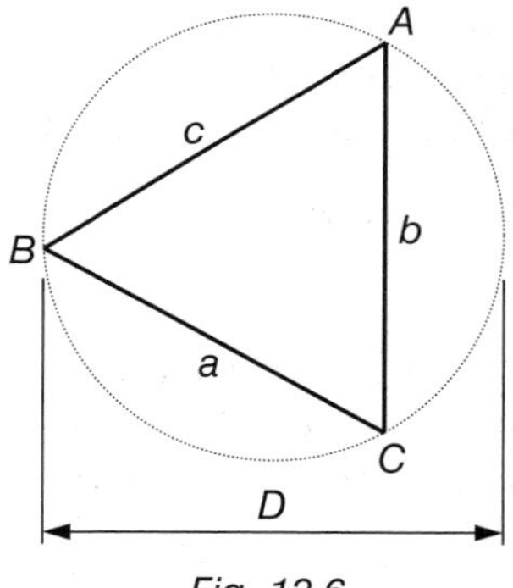

Fig. 13.6

The rule is useful when we wish to find the pitch circle diameter of a ring of holes.

EXAMPLE 13.3

In Fig. 13.7 three holes are positioned by the angle and dimensions shown. Find the pitch circle diameter.

We are given $\angle B = 41°$ and $b = 112.5$ mm

$$\therefore \quad D = \frac{b}{\sin B} = \frac{112.5}{\sin 41°}$$

$$= 171.5 \text{ mm}$$

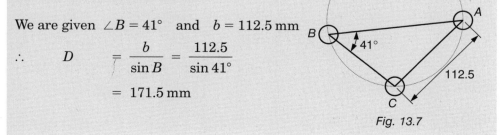

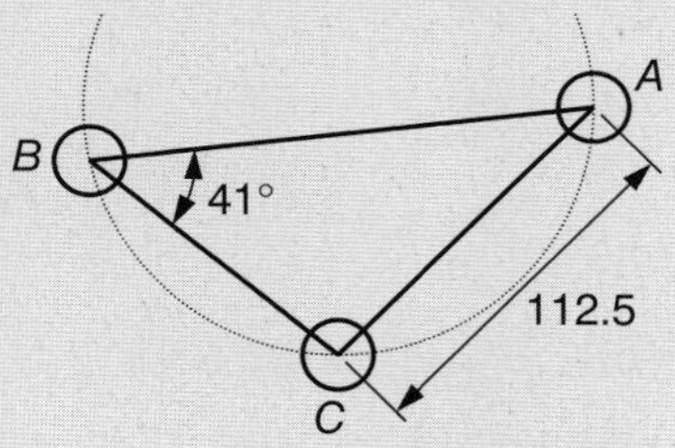

Fig. 13.7

THE COSINE RULE

The cosine rule is used in all cases where the sine rule cannot be used. These are when either of the following is known:

(1) two sides and the angle between them, or

(2) three sides.

Whenever possible we use the sine rule because the calculations are easier. In solving a triangle it is sometimes necessary to start with the cosine rule and then, having found one of the unknown elements, to finish off using the sine rule.

The cosine rule states:

$$\begin{aligned} a^2 &= b^2 + c^2 - 2bc\cos A \\ \text{or} \quad b^2 &= a^2 + c^2 - 2ac\cos B \\ \text{or} \quad c^2 &= a^2 + b^2 - 2ab\cos C \end{aligned}$$

EXAMPLE 13.4

Solve the triangle ABC if $a = 70$ mm, $b = 40$ mm and $\angle C = 64°$.

Referring to Fig. 13.8, to find the side c we use

$$c^2 = a^2 + b^2 - 2ab\cos C$$

$$= 70^2 + 40^2 - 2 \times 70 \times 40 \times \cos 64°$$

$$\therefore \quad c = \sqrt{4044} = 63.6 \text{ mm}$$

We now use the sine rule to find $\angle A$:

$$\frac{a}{\sin A} = \frac{c}{\sin C}$$

$$\sin A = \frac{a \sin C}{c} = \frac{70 \times \sin 64°}{63.6}$$

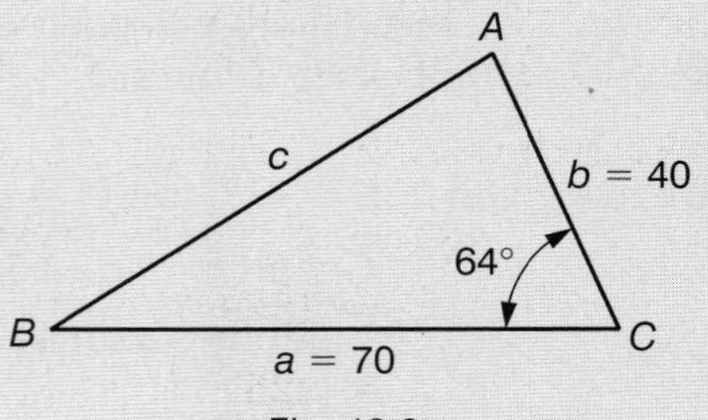

Fig. 13.8

Thus $A = 81.6°$

and $B = 180° - 81.6° - 64° = 34.4°$

EXAMPLE 13.5

The mast AB of a jib crane (Fig. 13.9) is 3 m long and the tie BC is 2.4 m long. If the jib AC is 4.8 m long, find the angle B between the mast and the tie.

Here we shall use $b^2 = a^2 + c^2 - 2ac\cos B$

Since we require B, we shall make B the subject of the equation.

Adding $2ac\cos B$ to both sides:

$$2ac\cos B + b^2 = a^2 + c^2 - \cancel{2ac\cos B} + \cancel{2ac\cos B}$$

and subtracting b^2 from both sides:

$$2ac\cos B + \cancel{b^2} - \cancel{b^2} = a^2 + c^2 - b^2$$

and finally dividing both sides by $2ac$:

$$\frac{\cancel{2ac}\cos B}{\cancel{2ac}} = \frac{a^2 + c^2 - b^2}{2ac}$$

Giving $\cos B = \dfrac{a^2 + c^2 - b^2}{2ac}$

hence $\cos B = \dfrac{2.4^2 + 3^2 - 4.8^2}{2 \times 2.4 \times 3}$

$= -0.5750$

or $B = \text{inv}\cos(-0.5750)$

giving $B = 125°$

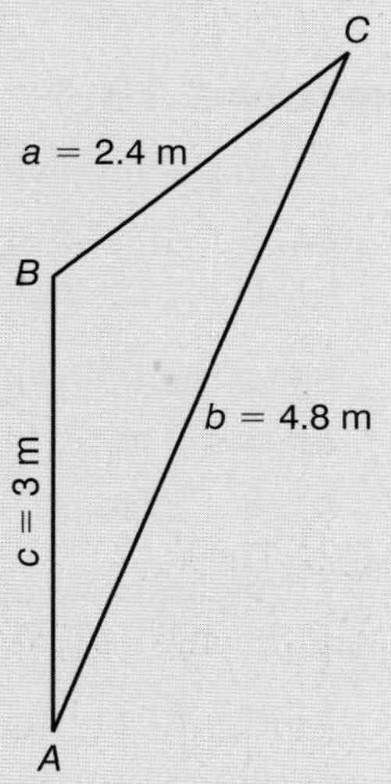

Fig. 13.9

EXAMPLE 13.6

The instantaneous values, i_1 and i_2, of two alternating currents are represented by the two sides of a triangle shown in Fig. 13.10. The resultant current i_R is represented by the third side. Calculate the magnitude of i_R and the angle ϕ between the current i_1 and i_R.

In $\triangle ABC$, Fig. 13.10, we have $b = 10$, $a = 15$ and $\angle C = 120°$.

Using the cosine rule gives

$$c^2 = a^2 + b^2 - 2ab\cos C$$
$$= 15^2 + 10^2 - 2 \times 15 \times 10\cos 120°$$
$$= 225 + 100 + 150$$
$$c = \sqrt{475} = 21.79 = i_R$$

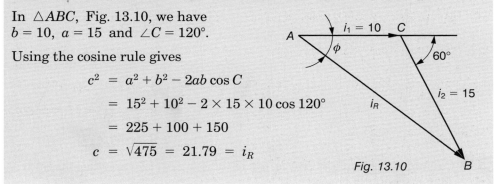

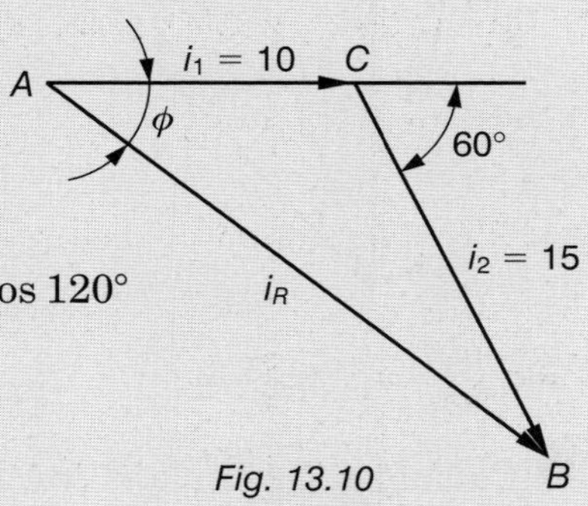

Fig. 13.10

To find $\angle A$ we use the sine rule

$$\frac{a}{\sin A} = \frac{c}{\sin C}$$

$$\therefore \quad \sin A = \frac{a \sin C}{c} = \frac{15 \times \sin 120°}{21.79} = 0.5962$$

$$\therefore \quad A = 36.6° = \phi$$

Hence the magnitude of i_R is 21.8 and the angle ϕ is 36.6°

Exercise 13.1

1) Solve the following triangles using the sine rule:

a) $A = 75°$, $B = 34°$ and $a = 102\,\text{mm}$

b) $C = 61°$, $B = 71°$ and $b = 91\,\text{mm}$

2) Solve the following triangles ABC using the cosine rule:

a) $a = 9\,\text{m}$, $b = 11\,\text{m}$ and $C = 60°$

b) $b = 10\,\text{m}$, $c = 14\,\text{m}$ and $A = 56°$

3) Three holes lie on a pitch circle and their chordal distances are 41.82 mm, 61.37 mm and 58.29 mm. Find their pitch circle diameter.

4) In Fig. 13.11, find the angle BCA given that BC is parallel to AD.

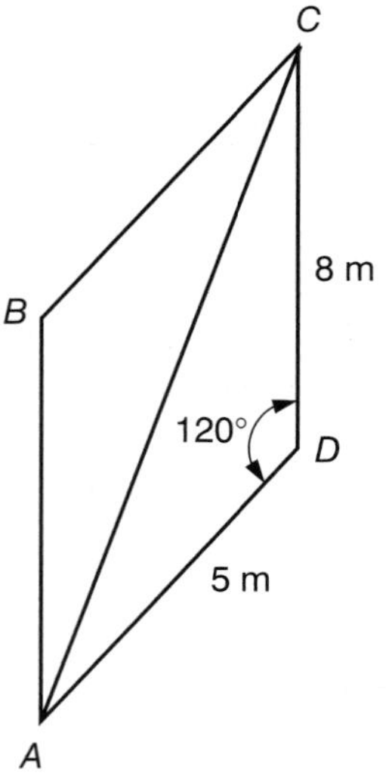

Fig. 13.11

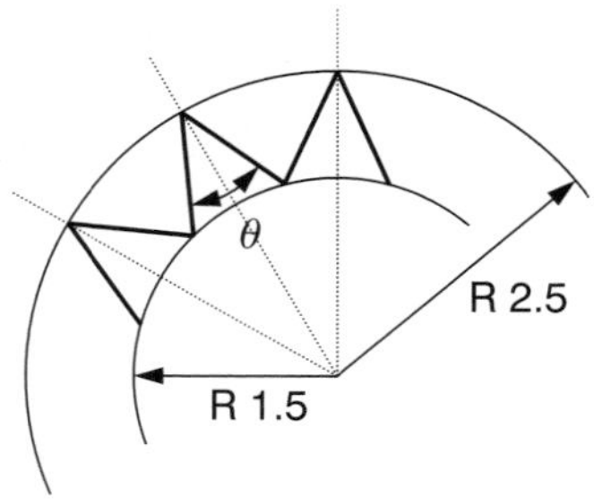

Fig. 13.12

5) Calculate the angle θ in Fig. 13.12. There are 12 castellations and they are equally spaced.

6) Find the smallest angle in a triangle whose sides are 20, 25 and 30 m long.

7) In Fig. 13.13 find:

a) The distance AB **b)** The angle ACB

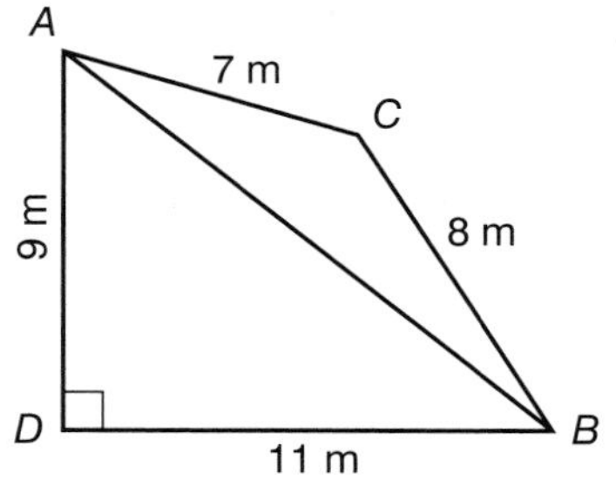

Fig. 13.13

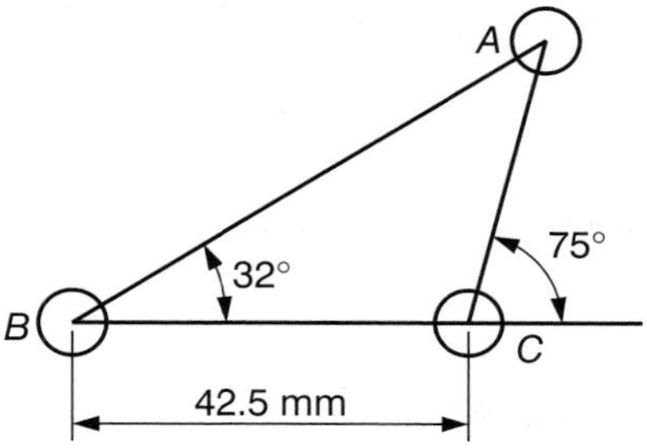

Fig. 13.14

8) Three holes are spaced in a plate detail as shown in Fig. 13.14. Calculate the centre distances from A to B and from A to C.

9) In Fig. 13.15, ab and bc are phasors representing the alternating currents in two branches of a circuit. The line ac represents the resultant current. Find by calculation this resultant current.

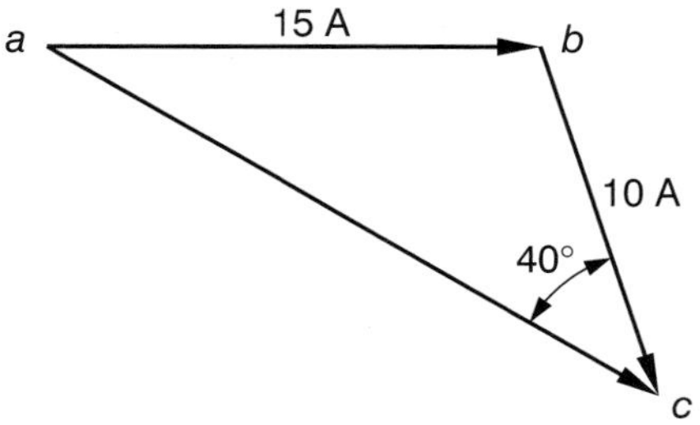

Fig. 13.15

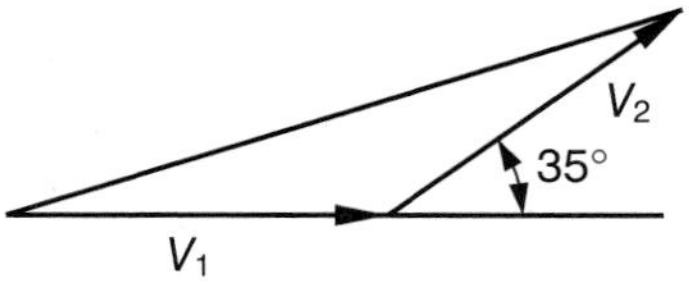

Fig. 13.16

10) Two phasors are shown in Fig. 13.16. If $V_1 = 8$ and $V_2 = 6$ calculate the value of their resultant and the angle it makes with V_1.

11) Calculate the resultant of the two phasors shown in Fig. 13.17.

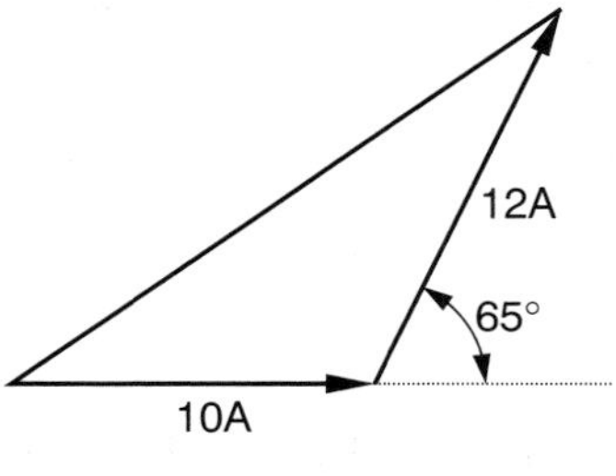

Fig. 13.17

AREA OF A TRIANGLE

The area of a triangle is another important feature needed if we are to know all the facts relating to our basic triangular shape. Areas are needed when calculating the surface of fabricated components – they may be required in order that the mass of a part may be estimated. The costs of plating and also painting are very often based on the surface areas of items.

Three formulae are commonly used for finding the areas of triangles. These are used if we know any one of the following cases:

1) The base and the altitude (i.e. the 'height' perpendicular to the base)
2) Any two sides and the included angle
3) The three sides.

Area Given the Base and the Altitude

$$\text{Area of triangle} = \tfrac{1}{2} \times \text{Base} \times \text{Altitude}$$

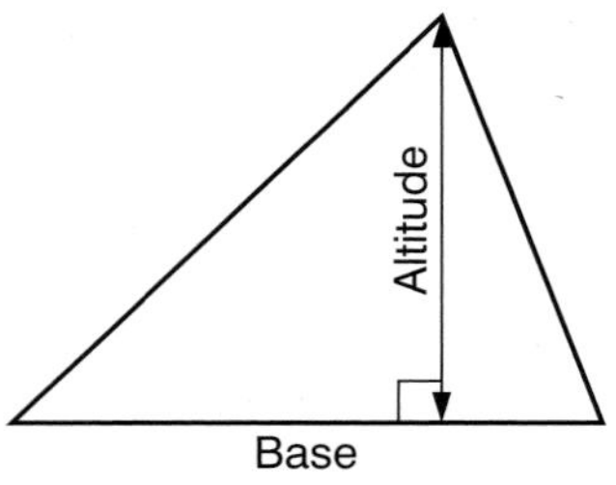

EXAMPLE 13.7

Find the areas of the triangular shaped templates shown in Fig. 13.18. One purpose of this example is for you to appreciate that the 'base' side need not be horizontal. In each case, the 'base' is chosen as the side of known length, and the altitude is measured at right angles to this side.

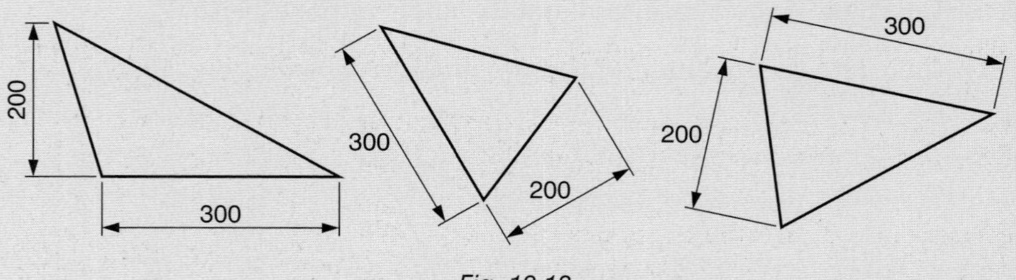

Fig. 13.18

$$\text{Template area} = \tfrac{1}{2} \times \text{base} \times \text{altitude} = \tfrac{1}{2} \times 300 \times 200 = 30\,000\ \text{mm}^2$$

Area Given Any Two Sides and the Included Angle

$$\begin{aligned}\text{Area of triangle} &= \tfrac{1}{2}bc\sin A\\ \text{Area of triangle} &= \tfrac{1}{2}ac\sin B\\ \text{Area of triangle} &= \tfrac{1}{2}ab\sin C\end{aligned}$$

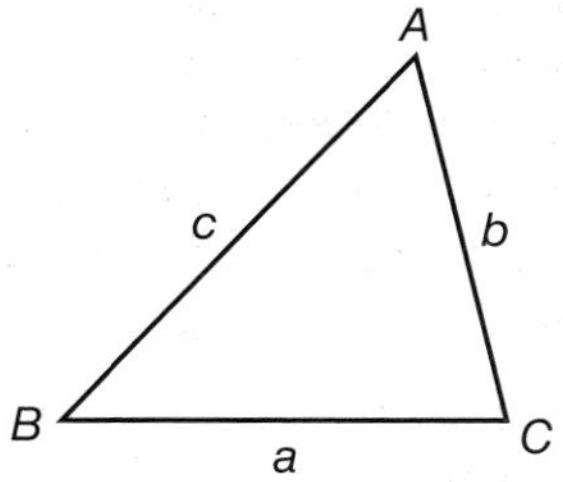

EXAMPLE 13.8

The profile shown in Fig. 13.19 is that of a cutting blade for use in a carpet-making machine. These blades will have to be electroplated when produced in quantity and the cost involved is largely based on the total surface area, neglecting the thickness of the blade.

$$\begin{aligned}\text{Area of triangle} &= \tfrac{1}{2}ab\sin C\\ &= \tfrac{1}{2}\times 105\times 75\times \sin 140^\circ\\ &= 2530\ \text{mm}^2\end{aligned}$$

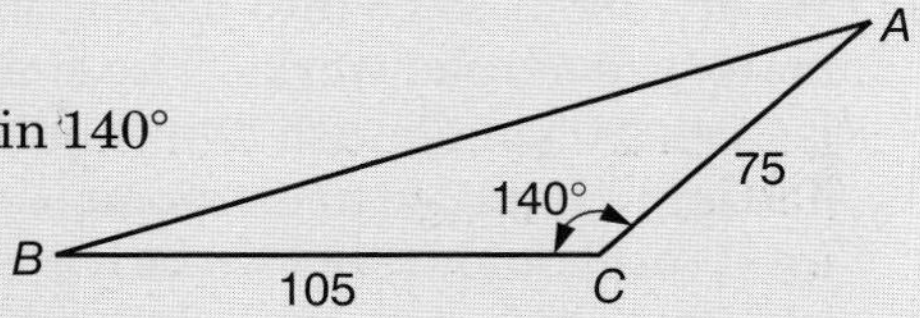

Fig. 13.19

$$\therefore \underset{\text{(two sides)}}{\text{total blade area}} = 2\times 2530 = 5060\ \text{mm}^2$$

Area Given the Three Sides

$$\begin{aligned}\text{Area of triangle} &= \sqrt{s(s-a)(s-b)(s-c)}\\ \text{where } s &= \frac{a+b+c}{2}\end{aligned}$$

EXAMPLE 13.9

The cover for a gearbox on a machine tool is to be formed from the sheet metal blank shown in Fig. 13.20. The production department need to know the mass of the blank if it is cut from material having a mass of 8 kg per square metre of surface area.

Since we need the area in square metres, and also to keep the figures reasonably simple we will work in metre units.

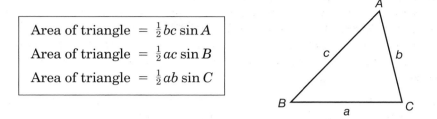

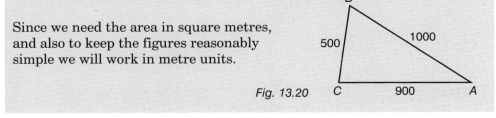

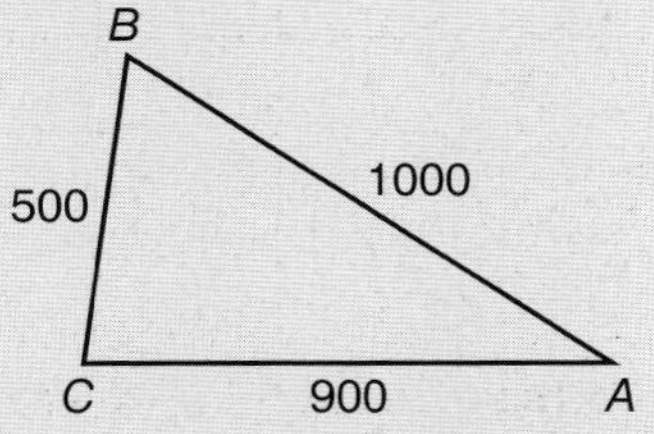

Fig. 13.20

$$\text{Now } s = \frac{a+b+c}{2} = \frac{0.5+0.9+1.0}{2} = 1.2$$

$$\begin{aligned}\text{Area of } \triangle ABC &= \sqrt{s(s-a)(s-b)(s-c)}\\ &= \sqrt{1.2(1.2-0.5)(1.2-0.9)(1.2-1.0)}\\ &= \sqrt{1.2\times 0.7\times 0.3\times 0.2} = 0.2245\ \text{m}^2\\ \text{Mass of blank} &= 0.2245\times 8\\ &= 1.80\ \text{kg correct to 3 s.f.}\end{aligned}$$

Exercise 13.2

1) We are about to go into production of portable notices to alert motorists of road works. The shape will essentially be that of an isosceles triangle with two equal angles of 50° and a base length of 450 mm. In order to estimate the cost of painting we need to know the total (back and front) surface area in square metre units.

2) A plate in the shape of an equilateral triangle has a mass of 12.25 kg. If the material has a mass of 3.7 kg/m^2, find the dimensions of the plate in millimetres.

3) Obtain the area of a triangular plastic sheet whose sides are 39.3 m and 41.5 m if the angle between them is 41° 30′.

4) Find the area of the template shown in Fig. 13.21.

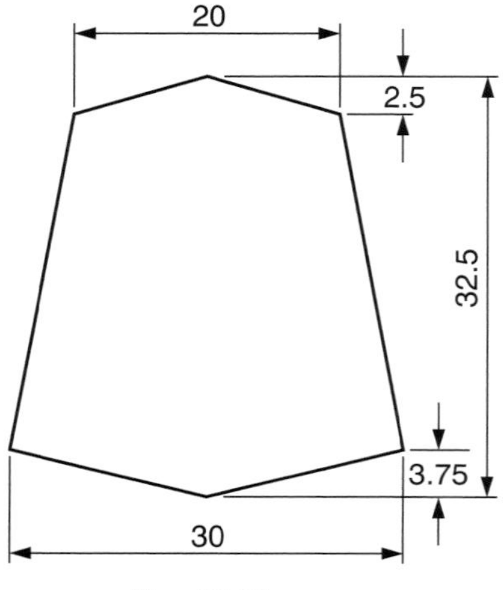

Fig. 13.21

5) A small aluminium wedged shaped component (Fig. 13.22) is used in a patent levelling device for a precision instrument. Since the overall mass is of paramount importance we need to know how much extra mass is added to the instrument if there are four of these wedges per unit. Take the density of aluminium as $2700\ \text{kg/m}^3$.

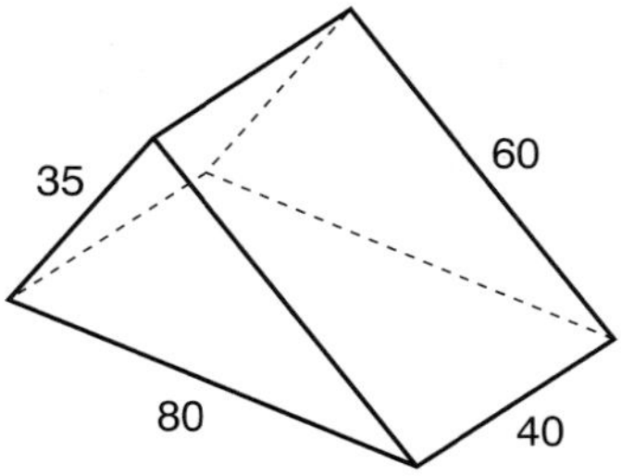

Fig. 13.22

6) We have been informed that the wedges shown in Fig. 13.22 are 30% over the maximum permitted mass. It has therefore been decided that the top apex portion will be removed. This is to be achieved by a cut parallel to the $80\ \text{mm}$ by $40\ \text{mm}$ base. What will be the depth of the final component?

14 Trigonometrical Waveforms

Construction of sine and cosine curves – their properties – the tangent curve and its properties – finding angles from inverse functions – sinusoidal waveforms – amplitude – angular and time base – cycle – period – frequency

WHAT ARE WAVEFORMS?

This is the name given to many trigonometric graphs, or curves as they are usually known, because they may be likened to gentle waves in the sea. They have shapes which keep repeating and 'go on for ever in either direction'.

In electricity, alternating voltage and current are represented by trig. curves. Vibrations, light and sound are other examples. So you will appreciate why it is useful to have a good understanding of this topic.

We will start by finding out all about these graphs, the most common being sine, cosine and tangent curves.

Construction of Sine and Cosine Curve

From right-angled $\triangle OPM$ in Fig. 14.1 we have $\sin\theta = \dfrac{PM}{OP}$.

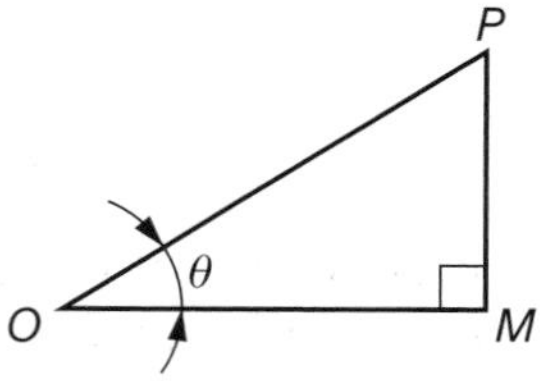

Fig. 14.1

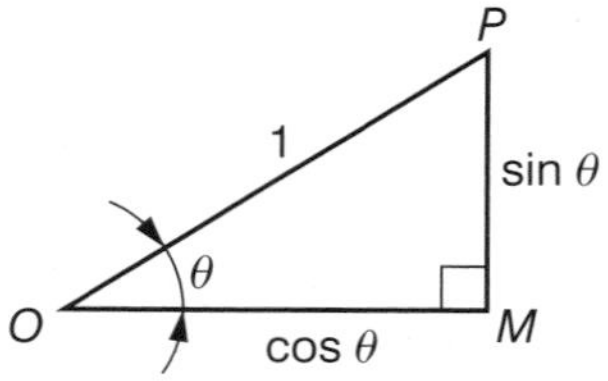

Fig. 14.2

Now if we make the length of OP unity, i.e. $OP = 1$ unit, as shown in Fig. 14.2, then length $PM = \sin\ \theta$. Similarly length $OM = \cos\ \theta$. In Fig. 14.3, the axes Ox and Oy have been drawn at right angles to each other, just like the x and y axes for a graph. This enables us to use the same sign convention (Fig. 14.4) for the horizontal and vertical scales.

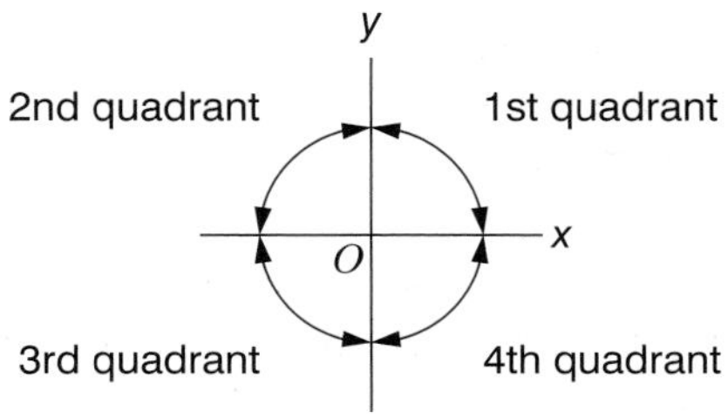

Fig. 14.3

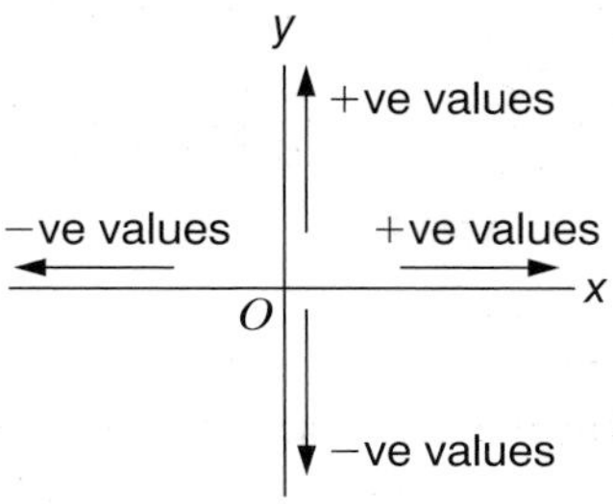

Fig. 14.4

If we now draw a circle, with centre O and a radius of unity (Fig. 14.5), we can easily fit in $\triangle OPM$ for whatever value of angle θ we choose. All angles are measured from Ox as a datum (i.e. starting position). The angles with which we are familiar are positive, and measured in an anti-clockwise direction. Negative angles are not so well-known, and are measured clockwise from Ox, as shown in Fig. 14.6.

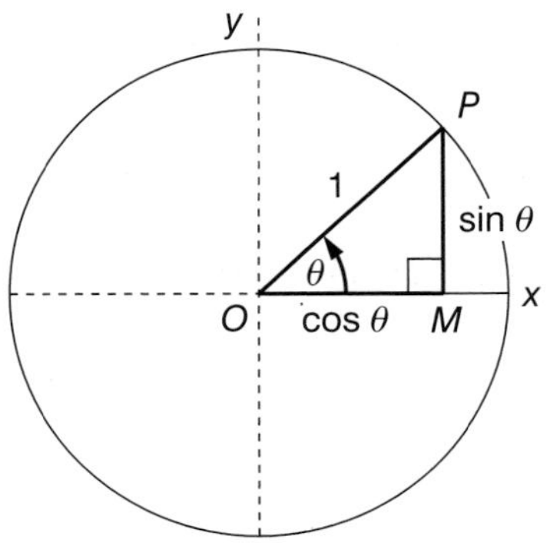

Fig. 14.5

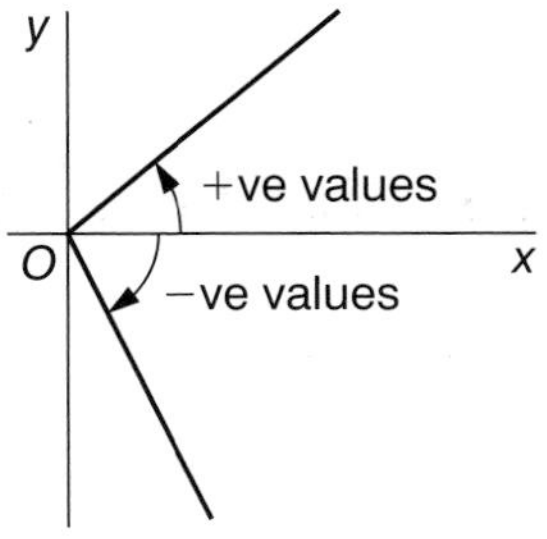

Fig. 14.6

We are now in a position to use these ideas to help with plotting the sine and cosine graphs. If you look at the top portion of Fig. 14.7 you will see the general arrangement.

The cosine curve may also be constructed as shown in Fig. 14.7. However, it is usually drawn with the angle base horizontal (Fig. 14.9) in order that it may be compared with other trigonometrical curves.

It is a good idea for you to actually draw a circle with axes, and the graph scales. A radius of 20 mm and a horizontal scale of 80 mm will fit your notepaper – it doesn't matter if it is not exactly to scale, but you will be surprised how good the result can be! The horizontal angle scale will be from 0° to 360° representing one revolution of the radius OP. The sine curve is obtained by joining up the points where the horizontal projections from P cut the corresponding angle verticals.

You are now able to find the sine value for any particular angle, by simply measuring the vertical height (called the ordinate on a graph). This will give you a direct result only if you started with a circle of radius 1. But if you started with a 20 mm radius circle, and the ordinate measurement is 8.3 mm, then the correct value for the sine of the angle is $\frac{8.3}{20}$ or 0.415

Try this for some values and compare the results with those obtained from your calculator

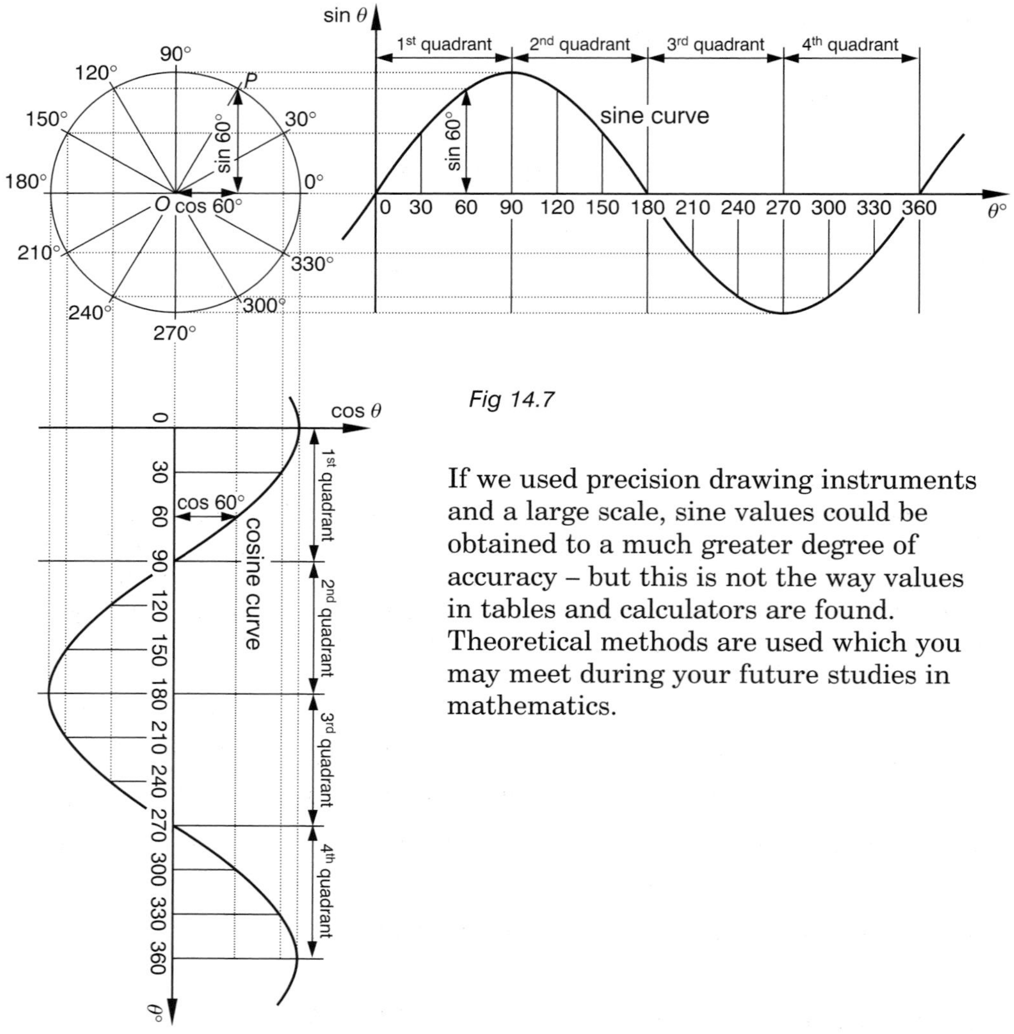

Fig 14.7

If we used precision drawing instruments and a large scale, sine values could be obtained to a much greater degree of accuracy – but this is not the way values in tables and calculators are found. Theoretical methods are used which you may meet during your future studies in mathematics.

A Never-ending Curve

The curve we have drawn is for one anti-clockwise revolution of OP and angles $0°$ to $360°$. But we could do a second revolution giving $360°$ to $720°$ and for each revolution of OP we would get a similarly shaped waveform. In fact, the shape repeats itself and the curve is called **cyclic**. Now if OP rotated clockwise, the angle values would be negative if also measured clockwise from Ox. One revolution would be for angles $0°$ to $-360°$. Another revolution would be for $-360°$ to $-720°$ and so on. Again, the curve shape would be similar.

The waveform is never-ending, being of infinite length in each direction. We should be careful to show we understand this every time we draw, or even sketch, the waveform by putting 'tails' on each end of our plot.

Details of the Sine Curve

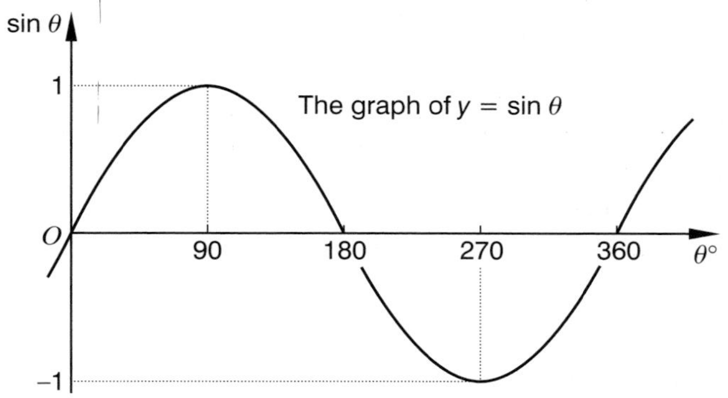

Fig. 14.8

Most of the time, as engineers, we are only interested in the sine curve for angle values $0°$ to $360°$ which is shown in Fig. 14.8. But it is vital that you have full knowledge of this: you should be able to sketch (not draw accurately as it would take too long) the figure with every detail exactly as it is shown here. You should also know the following facts:

Properties of the Sine Curve

1) The curve cuts the horizontal axis at $0°$, $180°$ and $360°$.

   Thus $\sin 0° = 0$, $\sin 180° = 0$, and $\sin 360° = 0$.

2) The maximum value of $\sin\theta$ is $+1$ at $90°$.

   Thus $\sin 90° = 1$.

3) The minimum value of $\sin\theta$ is -1 at $270°$.

   Thus $\sin 270° = -1$.

4) Values of $\sin\theta$ are: $+$ve for angles $0°$ to $180°$

   and $-$ve for angles $180°$ to $360°$.

Details of the Cosine Curve

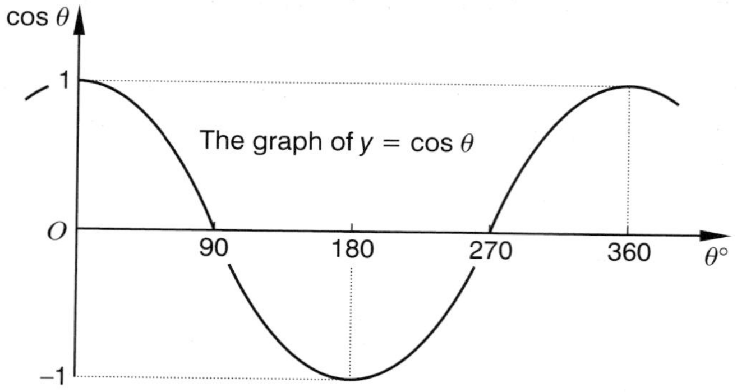

Fig. 14.9

The cosine curve, Fig. 14.9, is similar to the sine curve in all aspects except one. The waveform has been 'shifted bodily horizontally' through $90°$. We say that there is a phase difference of $90°$ between the sine and cosine curves. Again, it is essential that you can sketch the arrangement and know the following facts:

Properties of the Cosine Curve

1) The curve cuts the horizontal axis at $90°$ and $270°$.
   Thus $\cos 90° = 0$ and $\cos 270° = 0$.
2) The maximum value of $\cos\theta$ is $+1$ at $0°$ and $360°$.
   Thus $\cos 0° = 1$ and $\cos 360° = 1$.
3) The minimum value of $\cos\theta$ is -1 at $180°$.
   Thus $\cos 180° = -1$.
4) Values of $\cos\theta$ are: $+$ve for angles $0°$ to $90°$ and $270°$ to $360°$
   and $-$ve for angles $90°$ to $270°$.

Details of the Tangent Curve

Since this is your first meeting with the tangent curve, it is a good idea to plot the graph of $y = \tan\theta$. Values for plotting may be obtained using the identity $\tan\theta = \dfrac{\sin\theta}{\cos\theta}$ and the numerical values of sine and cosine from the curves you have drawn previously. Alternatively, the values of tangent may be found directly from your calculator.

Remember that $\dfrac{1}{\text{very small number}} = \text{very large number}$

Thus $\dfrac{1}{\text{zero}} = \text{infinity (symbol } \infty)$.

Although 'disjointed', this is a **cyclic** waveform and, like the sine and cosine waveforms, extends indefinitely in either direction for +ve and −ve angle values.

Although not used as much as the sine and cosine curves, you should still be able to sketch the arrangement in Fig. 14.10 and know the following important facts:

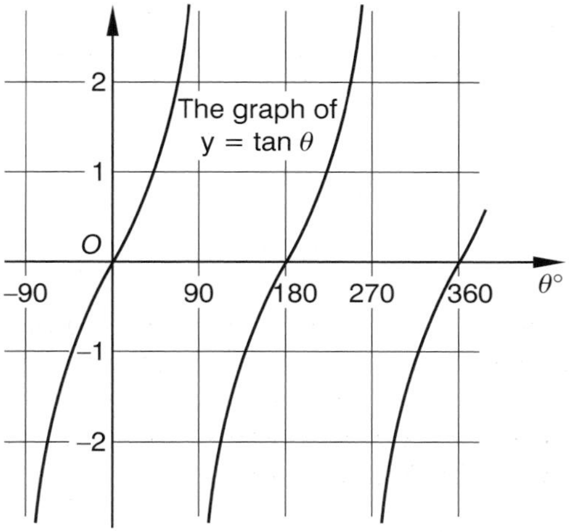

Fig. 14.10

Properties of the Tangent Curve

1) The curve cuts the horizontal axis at 0°, 180° and 360°.

   Thus $\tan 0° = 0$, $\tan 180° = 0$ and $\tan 360° = 0$

2) At the discontinuities:

   $\tan 90° = \infty$ and $\tan 270° = \infty$

3) Values of $\tan\theta$ are: +ve for angles 0° to 90° and 180° to 270°
   −ve for angles 90° to 180° and 270° to 360°.

4) When sketching the curve it is also worth remembering that at the '45° intervals' the tangent values are either +1 or −1.

   Thus $\tan 45° = 1$ $\tan 135° = -1$ $\tan 225° = 1$ and $\tan 315° = -1$

INVERSE TRIGONOMETRIC FUNCTIONS

If we know an angle we can find the value of its sine. The reverse of this is to start with the sine value and find the corresponding angle. Surely this is easy!? Simply enter the sine value and press the correct keys on the calculator and the required angle will appear. But there is a snag because there are many angles which all have the same sine value – the calculator gives us one, but it is our job to sort out any other relevant angles.

This leads us on to inverse trig. functions.

When determining the values of the angles we use the three principal trigonometric waveforms as shown in the three examples which follow.

Inverse Notation

Suppose that $\sin\theta = 0.4771$

This means that θ is the angle whose sine is 0.4771

This may be written as $\theta = \text{inv}\sin 0.4771$

or $\theta = \arcsin 0.4771$

or $\theta = \sin^{-1} 0.4771$

These RHS expressions are known as inverse trigonometrical functions.

Finding Angles over a Specified Range when given the Sine, Cosine or Tangent

EXAMPLE 14.1

Find all the angles, between 0° and 360°, whose sines are 0.4771.

Our first move is to obtain a solution from our calculator using:

AC INV sin 0.4771 = displaying 28.496169

giving an angle 28.5° correct to 1 d.p.

Are there any other solutions? Well, this is where our knowledge of the trigonometrical waveforms will help.

Let us sketch the sine curve for angle values 0° to 360°.

Now in a graph of $y = \sin\theta$ we need to consider when $y = 0.4771$ so we draw a horizontal line for an ordinate height of 0.4771 as shown in Fig. 14.11.

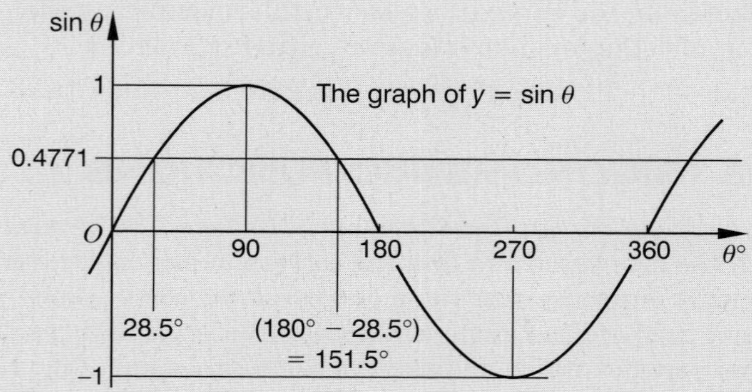

Fig. 14.11

At this stage, you will have no difficulty in identifying the result from the calculator and also another angle whose sine is 0.4771. You can see from the symmetry of the curve how the other result is obtained. Thus, 28.5° and 151.5° are the required angles.

EXAMPLE 14.2

Find all the angles between 0° and 360° whose cosines are −0.6354.

Again using our calculator we have:

AC INV cos − 0.6354 = displaying 129.449 66

giving an angle 129.4° correct to 1 d.p.

We will sketch the curve for angle values 0° to 360°, and then draw the horizontal line at ordinate height −0.6354 as shown in Fig. 14.12.

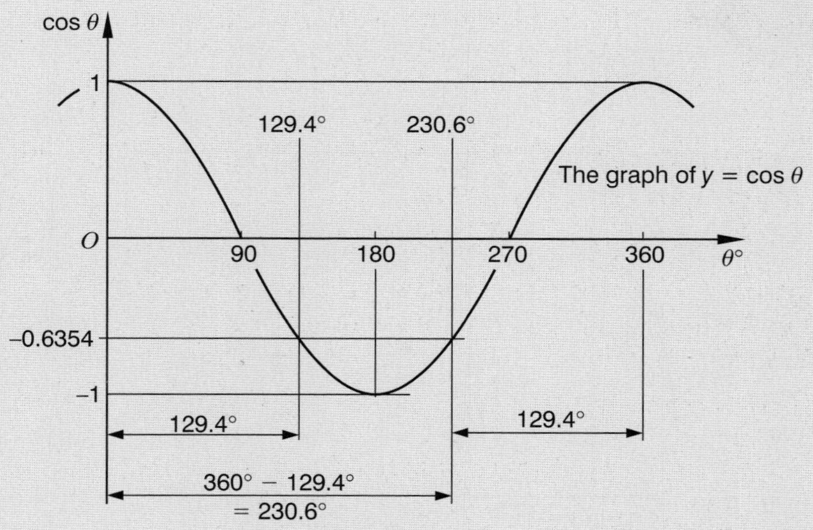

Fig. 14.12

Once again, the diagram will explain how we use the symmetry of the waveform to find the value of the second angle. This is only one of many ideas which you could use.

Thus, the required angles are 129.4° and 230.6°.

EXAMPLE 14.3

Find all the angles between 0° and 360° whose tangents are −1.8972.

Using our calculator, we have:

AC INV tan − 1.8972 =

displays −62.206 619 giving −62.2° correct to 1 d.p.

This is interesting since this result from the calculator is outside the range of 0°–360°. We should not really be surprised since there are an infinite number of angles whose tangents are −1.8972. So that we can fit in this negative angle we will sketch the graph of $y = \tan\theta$ from −90° to 360°, and then draw the horizontal line at ordinate height −1.8972 as shown in Fig. 14.13.

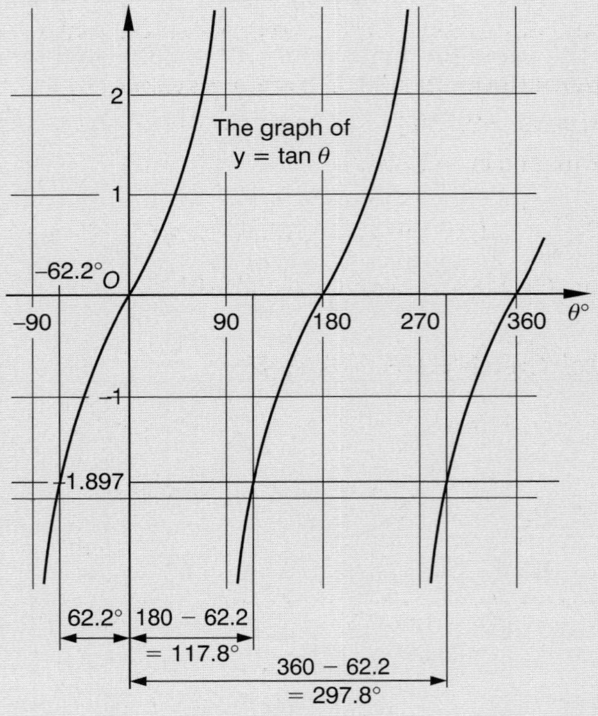

Fig. 14.13

This time it is slightly more difficult to see how the two required results are obtained, but symmetry is still important.

Hence, the required angles are 117.8° and 297.8° correct to 1 d.p.

Exercise 14.1

1) Evaluate: $6 \sin 23° - 2 \cos 47° + 3 \tan 17°$.

2) Evaluate: $5 \sin 142° - 3 \tan 148° + 3 \cos 230°$.

3) Evaluate: $\sin A.\cos B - \cos A.\sin B$ given that $\sin A = \frac{3}{5}$ and $\tan B = \frac{4}{3}$. A and B are both acute angles. (*Hint:* sketch a right-angled triangle and show the given data on it.)

4) An angle A is in the 2nd quadrant. If $\sin A = \frac{3}{5}$ find, without actually finding angle A, the values of $\cos A$ and $\tan A$.

5) If $\sin \theta = 0.1432$ find all the values of θ from $0°$ to $360°$.

6) If $\cos \theta = -0.8927$ find all the values of θ from $0°$ to $360°$.

7) Find the angles in the first and second quadrants:

a) whose sine is 0.7137 **b)** whose cosine is -0.4813

c) whose tangent is 0.9476 **d)** whose tangent is -1.7642.

8) Find the angles in the third or fourth quadrants:

a) whose sine is -0.7880 **b)** whose cosine is 0.5592

c) whose tangent is -2.9042.

9) If $\sin A = \dfrac{a \sin B}{b}$ find the values of A between $0°$ and $360°$ when $a = 7.26$ mm, $b = 9.15$ mm and $B = 18°29'$.

AMPLITUDE OR PEAK VALUE

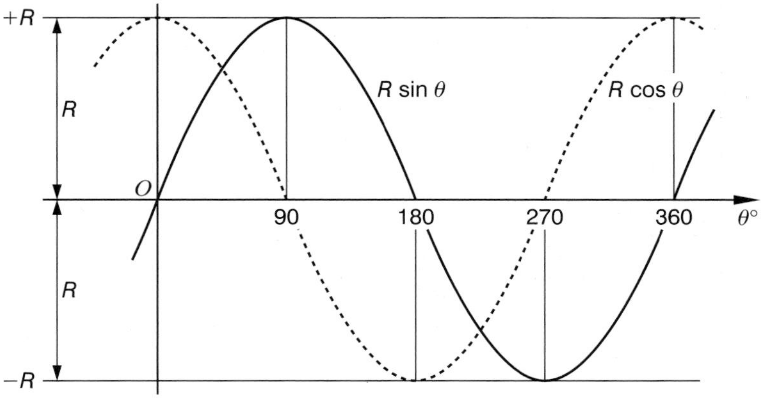

Fig. 14.14

The graphs of $R \sin \theta$ and $R \cos \theta$ shown in Fig. 14.14 each have a maximum value of $+R$ and a minimum value of $-R$. The value of R is known as the **amplitude** or **peak value.**

Graphs of $\sin\theta$, $\sin 2\theta$, $2\sin\theta$ and $\sin\frac{1}{2}\theta$

Curves of the above trigonometrical functions are shown plotted in Fig. 14.15. You may find it useful to construct the curves using values obtained from a calculator.

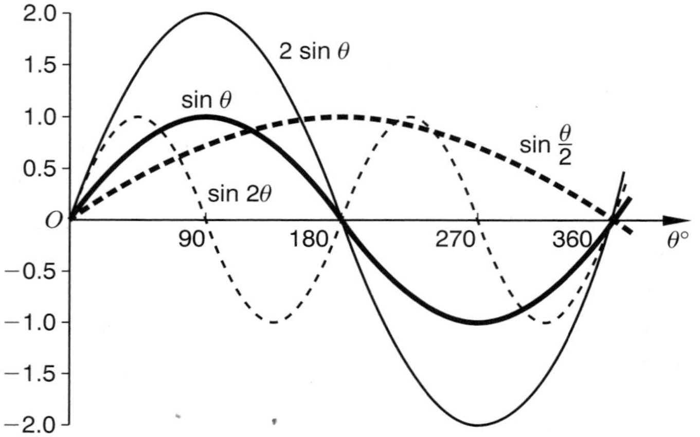

Fig. 14.15

Graphs of $\cos\theta$, $\cos 2\theta$, $2\cos\theta$ and $\cos\frac{1}{2}\theta$

Cosine graphs are similar in shape to sine curves. You should plot graphs of the above functions from $0°$ to $360°$ using values obtained from a calculator.

Graphs of $\sin^2\theta$ and $\cos^2\theta$

It is sometimes necessary in engineering applications, such as when finding the root mean square value of alternating currents and voltages, to be familiar with the curves $\sin^2\theta$ and $\cos^2\theta$.

Values of the functions can be obtained using a calculator and their graphs are shown in Fig. 14.16. We should note that the curves are wholly positive, since squares of negative or positive values are always positive.

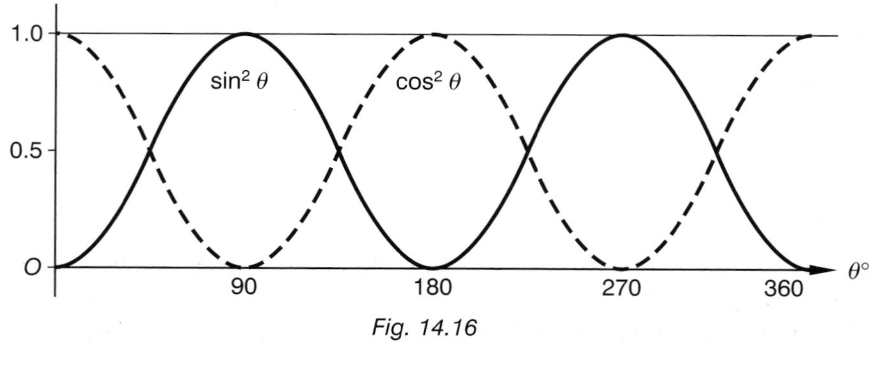

Fig. 14.16

Relation between Angular and Time Scales

In Fig. 14.17 OP represents a radius, of length R, which rotates at a uniform angular velocity ω radians per second about O, the direction of rotation being anticlockwise.

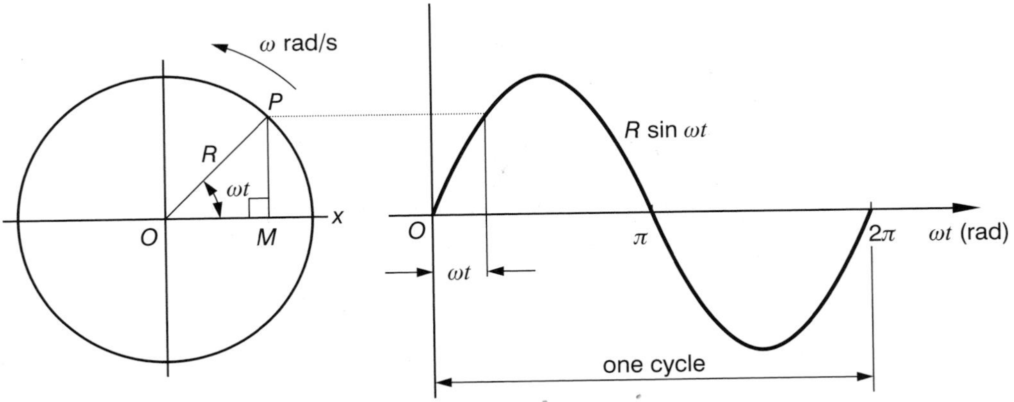

Fig. 14.17

$$\text{Angular velocity} = \frac{\text{Angle turned through}}{\text{Time taken}}$$

$$\therefore \quad \text{Angle turned through} = (\text{Angular velocity}) \times (\text{Time taken})$$

$$= \omega t$$

Also $$\frac{PM}{OP} = \sin P\hat{O}M \quad \text{from right-angled } \triangle OPM$$

$$\therefore \quad PM = OP \sin P\hat{O}M$$

or $$PM = R \sin \omega t$$

If a graph is drawn, as in Fig. 14.17, showing how PM varies with the angle ωt, the sine wave representing $R \sin \omega t$ is obtained. It can be seen that the **peak value** of this sine wave is $\boldsymbol{R}$ (i.e. the magnitude of the rotating radius).

The horizontal scale shows the angle turned through, ωt, and the waveform is said to be plotted on an **angular** or $\boldsymbol{\omega t}$ **base**.

Cycle

A **cycle** is the portion of the waveform which shows its **complete shape without any repetition**. It may be seen from Fig. 14.17 that one cycle is completed whilst the radius OP turns through 360° or 2π radians.

Period

This is the **time** taken for the waveform **to complete one cycle.** It will also be the time taken for OP to complete one revolution or 2π radians.

Now we know that $$\text{Time taken} = \frac{\text{Angle turned through}}{\text{Angular velocity}}$$

Hence

$$\boxed{\text{The period} = \frac{2\pi}{\omega} \text{ seconds}}$$

Frequency

The number of **cycles per second** is called the **frequency**. The unit of frequency representing one cycle per second is the hertz (Hz).

Now if 1 cycle is completed in $\dfrac{2\pi}{\omega}$ seconds (**a period**)

then $1 \div \dfrac{2\pi}{\omega}$ cycles are completed in 1 second

or $\dfrac{\omega}{2\pi}$ cycles are completed in 1 second

Hence $$\boxed{\text{frequency} = \frac{\omega}{2\pi} \text{ Hz}}$$

and since $\text{period} = \dfrac{2\pi}{\omega}$ then $$\boxed{\text{frequency} = \frac{1}{\text{period}}}$$

Graphs of $\sin t$, $\sin 2t$, $2\sin t$ and $\sin \frac{1}{2}t$

Now waveform $\sin \omega t$ has a period of $\dfrac{2\pi}{\omega}$ seconds

Thus waveform $\sin t$ has a period of $\dfrac{2\pi}{1} = 6.26$ seconds

We have seen how a graph may be plotted on an 'angular' or 'ωt' base as in Fig. 13.4. Alternatively, the **units on the horizontal axis** may be those of **time (usually seconds),** and this is called a **'time' base**, as displayed on an oscilloscope.

In order to plot one complete cycle of the waveform it is necessary to take values of t from 0 to 6.28 seconds. We suggest that you plot the curve of $\sin t$, remembering to set your calculator to the 'radian' mode when finding the value of $\sin t$. The curve is shown plotted on a time base in Fig. 14.18.

Similarly,

$$\text{The waveform } \sin 2t \text{ has a period of } \frac{2\pi}{2} = 3.14 \text{ seconds}$$

$$\text{and waveform } \sin \tfrac{1}{2}t \text{ has a period of } \frac{2\pi}{\frac{1}{2}} = 12.56 \text{ seconds}$$

Each of the above waveforms has an amplitude of unity. However, the waveform $2\sin t$ has an amplitude of 2, although its period is the same as that of $\sin t$, namely 6.28 seconds.

All these curves are shown plotted in Fig. 14.18. This enables a visual comparison to be made and it may be seen, for example, that the curve of $\sin 2t$ has a frequency twice that of $\sin t$ (since two cycles of $\sin 2t$ are completed during one cycle of $\sin t$).

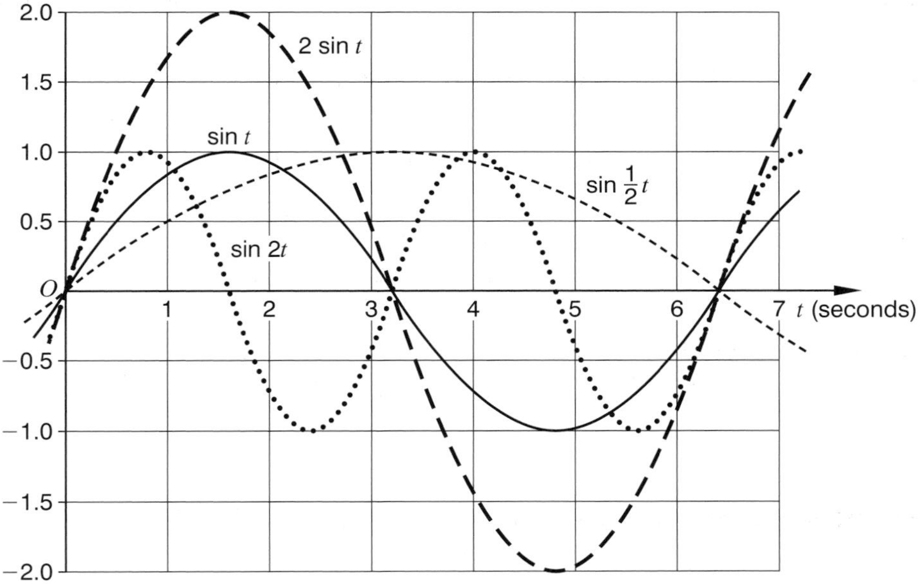

Fig. 14.18

Graphs of $R\cos\omega t$

The waveforms represented by $R\cos\omega t$ are similar to sine waveforms, R being the peak value and $\dfrac{2\pi}{\omega}$ the period. You are left to plot these as instructed in the following exercise.

Exercise 14.2

1) On the same axes, using a time base, plot the waveforms of $\cos t$ and $2\cos t$ for one complete cycle from $t = 0$ to $t = 6.28$ seconds.

2) Using the same axes on which the curves were plotted in Question 1, plot the waveforms of $\cos 2t$ and $\cos\dfrac{t}{2}$.

3) On the same axes, using an angle base from $0°$ to $360°$, sketch the following waveforms:

a) $5\cos\theta$ **(b)** $3\sin 2\theta$ **(c)** $4\cos 3\theta$ **(d)** $2\sin 3\theta$.

Data Collection and Display 15

Information displays – sampling – recording data – histograms – discrete and continuous distributions

INTRODUCTION

Statistics is the name given to the science of collecting and analysing data in the form of groups of numbers. These are often presented by means of tables and diagrams. We shall discuss ideas of analysing the figures and making practical use of the results obtained – for example taking samples of a factory production and hence being able to monitor quality control.

Displaying Information

Suppose that in a certain factory the number of persons employed on various jobs is as given in the following table:

TABLE 15.1

Type of personnel	*Number employed*	*Percentage*
Machinists	140	35
Fitters	120	30
Clerical staff	80	20
Labourers	40	10
Draughtsmen	20	5
Total	400	100

The information in Table 15.1 can be represented pictorially in several ways:

(1) *The pie chart* (Fig. 15.1) displays the proportions as angles (or sector areas), the complete circle representing the total number employed.
Thus for machinists the angle is $\dfrac{140}{400} \times 360 = 126°$ etc.

(2) *The bar chart* (Fig. 15.2) relies on heights (or areas) to convey the proportions; the total height of the diagram represents 100%.

(3) *The horizontal bar chart* (Fig. 15.3), or *the vertical bar chart* (Fig. 15.4), gives a better comparison of the various types of personnel employed but it does not readily display the total number employed in the factory.

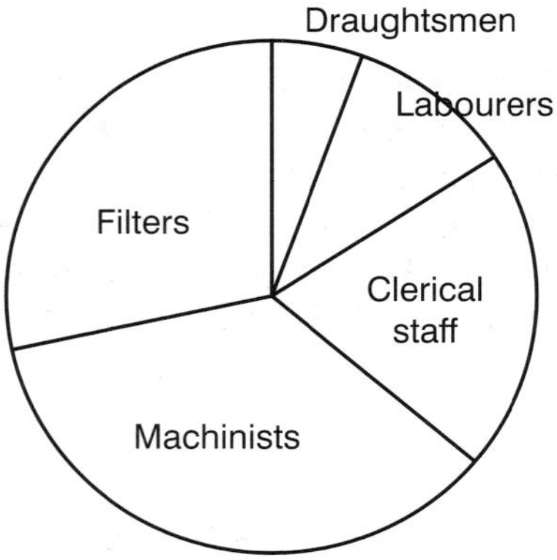

Fig. 15.1 Pie chart

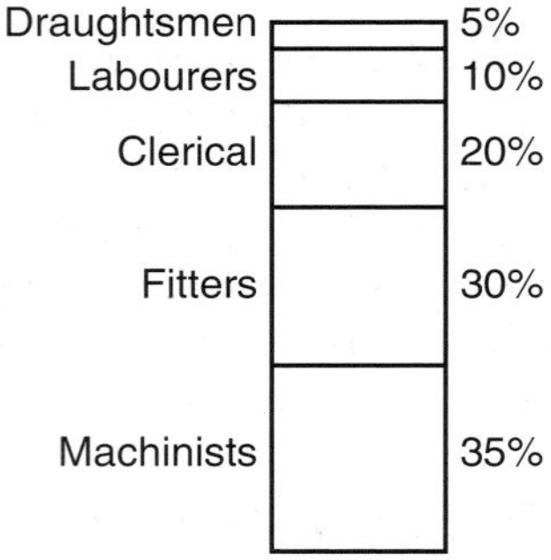

Fig. 15.2 100% bar chart

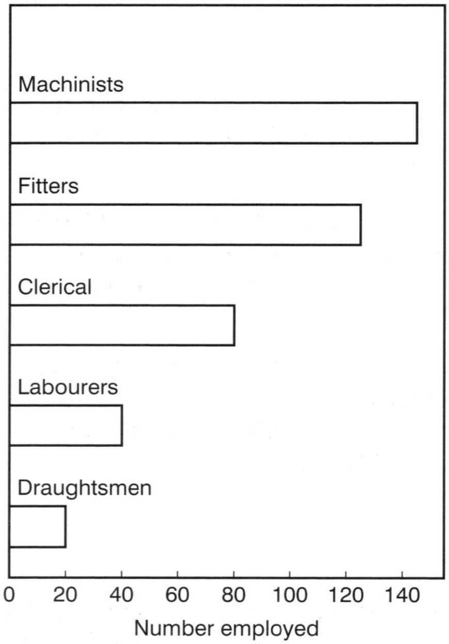

Fig. 15.3 Horizontal bar chart

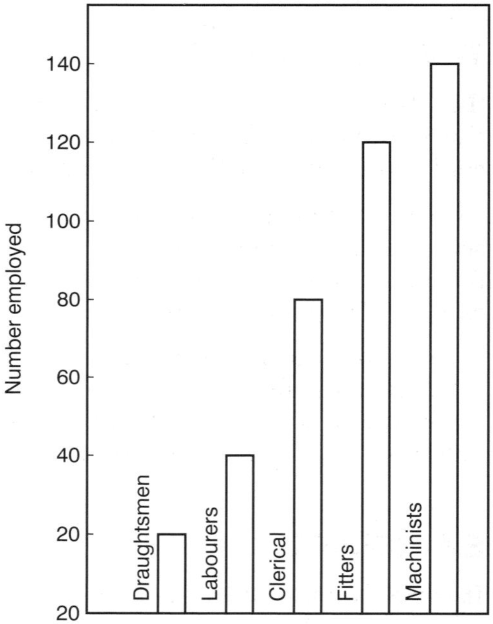

Fig. 15.4 Vertical bar chart

VARIABLES

Variables are measured quantities which can be expressed as numbers as, for instance, the number of cars in a garage or the height of a person. In statistics, a variable is sometimes called a variate, particularly when dealing with histograms and frequency distributions.

Discrete Variables

Some variables can only take certain values and are called discrete. Usually, but not always, these values are whole numbers. Examples are the number of cars in a garage or the number of persons working in an office (you can hardly have parts of people implied by 21.7 say!). Shoe sizes are discrete although they are not all whole numbers since they include half sizes in their range: for example 5, $5\frac{1}{2}$, 6, $6\frac{1}{2}$, 7, $7\frac{1}{2}$, etc. But a size of 7.19 is not available.

Continuous Variables

These are all other non-exact numbers usually in a range between two given end values. A continuous variable is a resistance of 125 ± 0.2 ohm which may be anywhere between end values 124.8 ohm and 125.2 ohm. Most measurements in technology are continuous and thus occupy most of our attention.

THE POPULATION

'In 1978, 14 million people watched the Cup Final on BBC television.' Statements like this are made every day but how could the BBC be so confident that their figure is correct?

Clearly, they cannot send researchers to every household in the country to see how many people are watching. What they do is to select a *sample* from the total population and then use the results of this sample to estimate the number watching.

In this case, the *parent* population is the population of the country. But in the case of the data of Table 15.1, the parent population is the total workforce in the factory. Again, suppose a factory produces one million ball bearings. This is the parent population of ball bearings.

SAMPLING

It is rarely possible to examine every item making up a parent population and recourse has to be made to sampling. For the information obtained to be of value the sample must be representative of the population as a whole. We might take a sample of 100 ball bearings and measure their diameters. The results obtained would then be regarded as being representative of the population as a whole.

FREQUENCY DISTRIBUTIONS

Suppose we measure the diameters of a sample of 100 ball bearings. We might get the following readings in millimetres:

TABLE 15.2

6.2	6.3	5.8	5.8	6.0	6.1	6.0	6.1	5.9	6.2
5.9	6.3	6.2	6.1	6.1	6.2	6.4	5.8	6.1	6.2
5.8	6.1	6.1	6.1	5.9	6.0	6.0	6.0	6.1	6.1
6.1	6.3	5.8	5.9	5.9	5.8	6.0	5.7	6.0	6.2
6.0	6.1	6.0	5.9	6.0	6.0	6.2	5.6	6.1	5.8
6.1	6.0	6.1	6.0	6.1	5.9	6.1	6.0	5.9	6.2
5.9	6.1	6.0	6.1	6.0	5.9	5.8	5.7	5.9	6.0
5.8	5.7	6.0	5.9	5.8	6.3	5.9	6.3	6.0	5.9
5.7	6.2	6.3	6.3	5.9	6.0	5.9	5.9	5.6	6.4
5.9	6.1	6.0	6.0	6.0	6.3	5.8	5.9	6.1	5.9

These figures do not mean very much as they stand and so we rearrange them into what is called a frequency distribution. To do this we collect all the 5.6 mm readings together, all the 5.7 mm readings and so on. A tally chart (Table 15.3) is the best way of doing this. Each time a measurement arises a tally mark is placed opposite the appropriate measurement. The fifth tally mark is usually made in an oblique direction thus tying the tally marks into bundles of five to make counting easier. When the tally marks are complete the marks are counted and the numerical value recorded in the column headed 'frequency'. The frequency is the number of times each measurement occurs. From Table 15.3 it will be seen that the measurement 5.6 occurs twice (that is, it has a frequency of 2). The measurement 5.7 occurs four times (a frequency of 4) and so on.

TABLE 15.3

Measurement (mm)	*Number of bars with this measurement*	*Frequency*
5.6	‖	2
5.7	‖‖	4
5.8	~~‖‖~~ ~~‖‖~~ |	11
5.9	~~‖‖~~ ~~‖‖~~ ~~‖‖~~ ~~‖‖~~	20
6.0	~~‖‖~~ ~~‖‖~~ ~~‖‖~~ ~~‖‖~~ |||	23
6.1	~~‖‖~~ ~~‖‖~~ ~~‖‖~~ ~~‖‖~~ |	21
6.2	~~‖‖~~ ‖‖	9
6.3	~~‖‖~~ |||	8
6.4	‖	2

Class Boundaries and Width

In Fig. 15.5 the measurement 5.8 mm represents a group of figures from the halfway point between 5.7 and 5.8, to the halfway point between 5.8 and 5.9 – this is between 5.75 and 5.85 mm.

This represents a class having a lower class boundary of 5.75 mm and an upper class boundary of 5.85 mm.

$$\begin{aligned} \text{The class width} &= \text{upper class boundary} - \text{lower class boundary} \\ &= 5.85 - 5.75 = 0.1\,\text{mm} \end{aligned}$$

The next class would have lower and upper boundaries of 5.85 mm and 5.95 mm and a class width also of 0.1 mm.

THE HISTOGRAM

The frequency distribution of Table 15.3 becomes even more understandable if we draw a diagram to represent it. A good type of diagram is the histogram (Fig. 15.5), which consists of a set of rectangles whose areas represent the frequencies.

If all the class widths are the same, which is usually the case, then the heights of the rectangles represent the frequencies. Note also that the left hand edge of each rectangle represents the lower boundary and the right hand edge represents the upper class boundary.

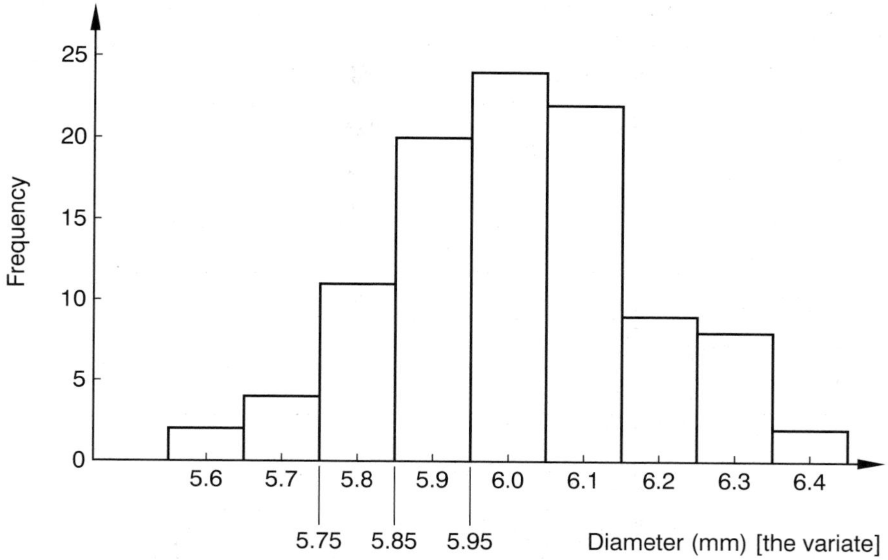

Fig. 15.5

On studying the histogram the pattern of the variation becomes clear, most of the measurements being grouped near the centre of the diagram with a few values more widely dispersed.

Grouped Data

When dealing with a large number of observations it is often useful to group them into classes or categories. We can then determine the number of items which belong to each class thus obtaining the class frequency.

EXAMPLE 15.1

The following table gives the heights, in centimetres, of 100 small coniferous trees:

TABLE 15.4

53	62	68	54	51	68	62	53	61	67
57	54	65	56	63	65	60	71	70	73
64	58	63	55	67	62	68	53	61	66
63	62	63	63	63	64	65	63	62	62
63	61	62	62	58	62	67	58	69	68
68	56	60	58	69	56	58	57	68	63
64	62	64	63	62	61	69	64	61	56
67	68	67	59	64	74	68	65	59	65
68	59	62	65	68	54	63	62	57	50
65	69	64	63	63	63	69	60	64	67

Draw up a tally chart for the classes 50–54, 55–59, etc.

The tally chart is shown in Table 15.5.

TABLE 15.5

Class (cm)	*Tally*	*Frequency*
50 – 54	~~IIII~~ III	8
55 – 59	~~IIII~~ ~~IIII~~ ~~IIII~~ I	16
60 – 64	~~IIII~~ ~~IIII~~ ~~IIII~~ ~~IIII~~ ~~IIII~~ ~~IIII~~ ~~IIII~~ ~~IIII~~ III	43
65 – 69	~~IIII~~ ~~IIII~~ ~~IIII~~ ~~IIII~~ ~~IIII~~ IIII	29
70 – 74	IIII	4
	Total	100

The main advantage of grouping is that it produces a clear overall picture of the distribution.

The number of classes chosen depends upon the amount of original data. However, it should be borne in mind that too many groups will destroy the pattern of the data, whilst too few will destroy much of the detail contained in the original data.

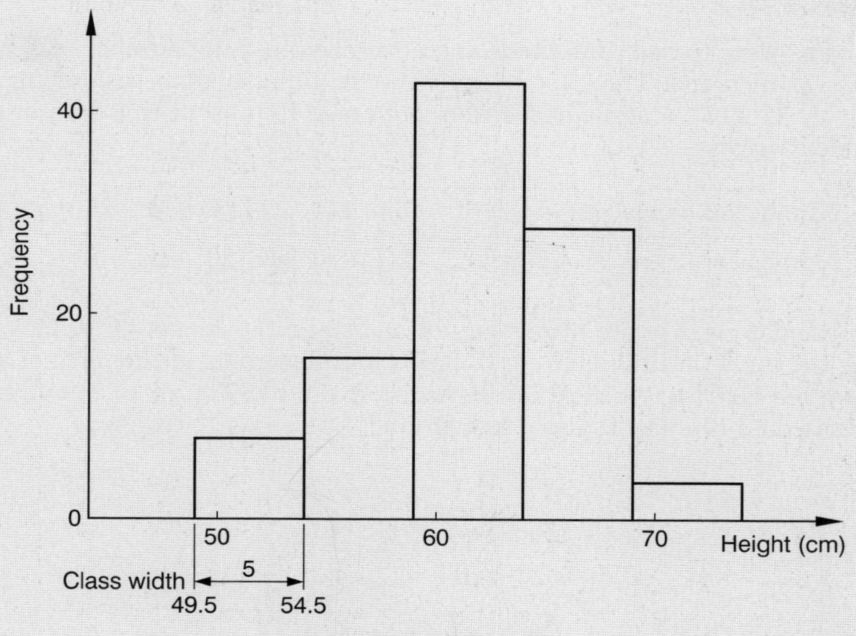

Fig. 15.6

Note that for the first class (50 – 54) the lower boundary is 49.5 cm and the upper boundary is 54.5, the class width being 5 cm. For the fourth class (65 – 69) the lower and upper boundaries are 64.5 and 69.5 cm respectively. The width of each class is the same and hence the frequencies of the various classes are represented by the heights of the rectangles in Fig. 15.6.

Discrete Distributions

The histogram shown in Fig. 15.6 represents a distribution in which the variable is continuous. The data in Example 15.2 is discrete and we shall see how a discrete distribution is represented.

EXAMPLE 15.2

Five coins were tossed 100 times and after each toss the number of heads was recorded. The table below gives the number of tosses during which 0, 1, 2, 3, 4 and 5 heads were obtained. Represent this data in a suitable diagram.

Number of heads	0	1	2	3	4	5
Number of tosses (frequency)	4	15	34	29	16	2

Since the data is discrete (there cannot be 2.3 or 3.6 heads), Fig. 15.7 seems the most natural diagram to use. This diagram is in the form of a vertical bar chart in which the bars have zero width. Figure 15.8 shows the same data represented as a histogram.

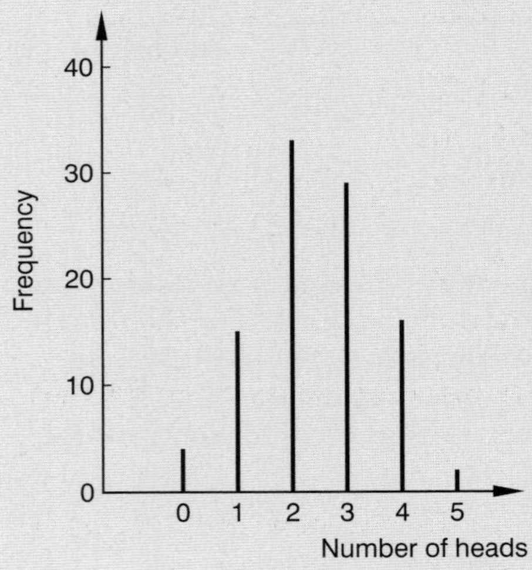

Fig. 15.7

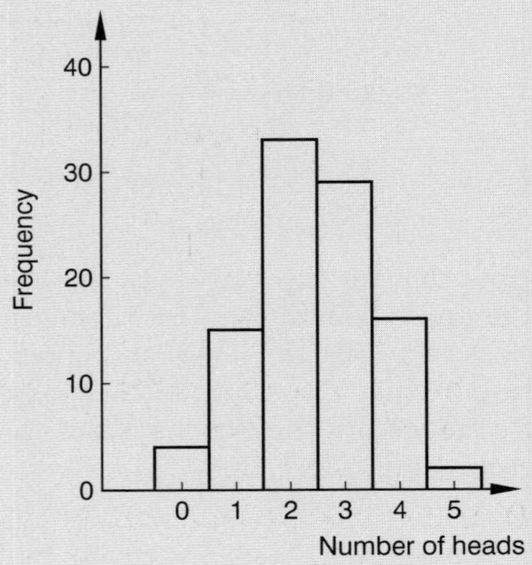

Fig. 15.8

Note that the area under the diagram gives the total frequency of 100 which is as it should be. Discrete data is often represented as a histogram as was done in Fig. 15.8, despite the fact that in doing this we are treating the data as though it were continuous.

Exercise 15.1

1) Which of the following are discrete variables and which are continuous variables:

(a) The size of men's shirts.

(b) The length of plastic rod being produced in quantity.

(c) The masses of castings being produced in a foundry.

(d) The temperature of a furnace.

(e) The number of electric motors produced per day in a factory.

2) The following figures are the hottest daily temperatures (°C) during June at a particular coastal resort:

20	21	19	22	22	23	23	23	24	25	25	26	27	28	25
24	24	23	22	21	22	23	23	24	25	24	25	26	27	26

With the aid of a frequency table draw a histogram for these temperatures.

3) During trials of one variety of broad bean plant a seed merchant noted the number of beans in each pod as listed below:

7,	10,	6,	7,	10,	7,	8,	9,	7,	7,	6,	5,	7,	7,	3,
6,	9,	5,	11,	4,	7,	5,	4,	10,	7,	7,	6,	8,	5,	6,
9,	9,	8,	8,	7,	4,	8,	6,	5,	8,	7,	7,	4,	6,	2,
8,	5,	7,	9,	5,	5,	8,	5,	6,	6,	6,	8,	8,	9,	5,
8,	6,	6,	9,	9,	6,	9,	8,	9,	6,	7,	6,	8,	6,	8,
6,	8,	6,	8,	7,	7,	7,	7,	7,	9,	7,	6,	7,	6,	7,
7,	10,	10,	7,	7,	9,	6,	8,	11,	8					

Draw up a frequency table and hence construct a histogram for the number of beans per pod.

4) Group the distribution in Question 3 into 5 classes. Hence construct an amended frequency table and histogram.

5) For the grouped frequency distribution given below, draw a histogram and state the class width for each of the classes.

Resistance (ohms)	110–112	113–115	116–118	119–121	122–124
Frequency	2	8	15	9	3

6) The data below was obtained by measuring the frequencies (in kilohertz) of 60 tuned circuits. Construct a frequency distribution and hence draw a histogram to represent the distribution.

12.37	12.29	12.40	12.41	12.31	12.35	12.37	12.35
12.33	12.36	12.32	12.36	12.40	12.38	12.33	12.35
12.30	12.30	12.34	12.39	12.44	12.32	12.27	12.32
12.41	12.40	12.37	12.46	12.35	12.34	12.38	12.43
12.36	12.35	12.26	12.28	12.36	12.24	12.42	12.39
12.45	12.42	12.28	12.25	12.34	12.33	12.32	12.39
12.38	12.27	12.35	12.35	12.34	12.36	12.36	12.32
12.31	12.35	12.29	12.30				

7) The table below gives a grouped frequency distribution for the compressive strength of a certain type of load-carrying brick.

Strength (N/mm^2)	59.4–59.6	59.7–59.9	60.0–60.2	60.3–60.5	60.6–60.8
Frequency	8	37	90	52	13

Determine the class width and draw a histogram for this distribution.

Frequency Analysis 16

Frequency distribution curves – average – mean – median – mode – normal distribution curve – mean and standard deviation – variance – range – probability from the normal curve

FREQUENCY DISTRIBUTIONS

In the last chapter we saw how frequency distributions could be exhibited graphically by histograms. However it is often necessary to compare mathematically different sets of data. This is achieved by showing the frequency distributions as curves rather than 'block' diagrams – from these we can find the central tendency position and the spread, or dispersion, of the distribution about this position.

Frequency Curves

In a grouped frequency distribution represented by a histogram we could make the class intervals smaller and smaller. The widths of the rectangles would also become smaller and smaller and the jumps in frequency between one class and another would become very tiny. Eventually the outline of the histogram would have the appearance of a smooth curve. This frequency curve is obtained by plotting frequency against the corresponding class mid-point, as shown in Fig. 16.1 for the data in Table 16.1.

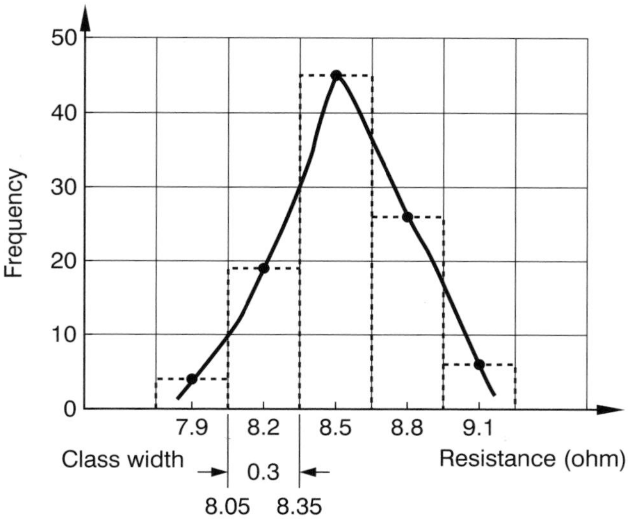

Fig. 16.1

TABLE 16.1

Resistance (ohm)	*Frequency*
7.8–8.0	4
8.1–8.3	19
8.4–8.6	45
8.7–8.9	26
9.0–9.2	6

Cumulative Frequency Distribution

An alternative display may be obtained by using cumulative (or running total) frequencies, as shown in the next example.

EXAMPLE 16.1

The results of 80 compression tests on cube specimens were:

Crushing strength (N/mm^2)	8.7	8.8	8.9	9.0	9.1	9.2
Frequency	5	9	19	25	18	4

Plot a cumulative frequency distribution diagram and use it to estimate:

a) the number of cubes having crushing strength below 8.9 N/mm^2,
b) the median crushing strength,
c) the upper and lower quartiles.

Table 16.2 shows the cumulative frequencies corresponding to the appropriate class boundaries.

TABLE 16.2

Crushing strength (N/mm^2)	*Cumulative frequency*
Not more than 8.75	5
Not more than 8.85	$5 + 9 = 14$
Not more than 8.95	$14 + 19 = 33$
Not more than 9.05	$33 + 25 = 58$
Not more than 9.15	$58 + 18 = 76$
Not more than 9.25	$76 + 4 = 80$

A smooth curve, called an ogive, is drawn (Fig. 16.2) through the plotted points.

a) Reading off from 8.9 N/mm^2 we see that the cumulative frequency is 22, and this indicates the number of cubes of strength below 8.9 N/mm^2.
b) The median is the strength which corresponds to half the total frequency – here 40. This gives the median as 8.98 N/mm^2.
c) Quartiles divide the frequency into four – they are values of the variate, here crushing strength, which occur at $\frac{1}{4}$, $\frac{1}{2}$ and $\frac{3}{4}$ of the total frequency.

The second quartile coincides with the median, and reading off from the curve the lower (or first) quartile is 8.89 N/mm^2 at a frequency of $\frac{1}{4} \times 80$ or 20. Also, the higher (or third) quartile is 9.06 N/mm^2 at a frequency of $\frac{3}{4} \times 80$ or 60.

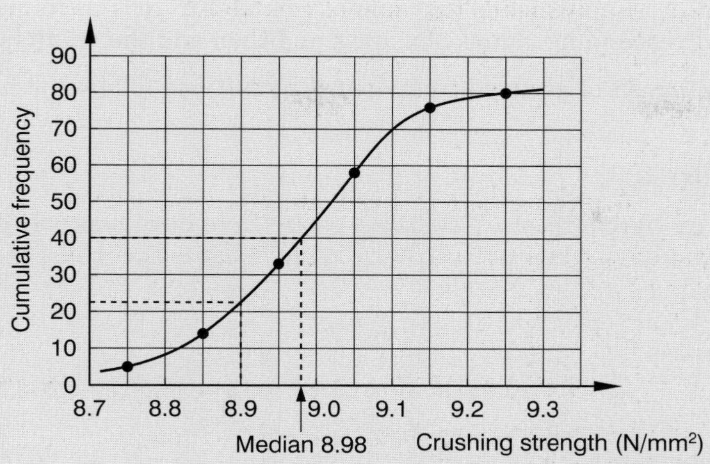

Fig. 16.2

THE AVERAGE

Mean, median and mode are the more common types of average.

The Mean (or Arithmetic Mean)

The arithmetic mean is found by adding up all the observations in a set and dividing the result by the number of observations. That is,

$$\text{Arithmetic mean} = \frac{\text{Sum of observations}}{\text{Number of observations}}$$

EXAMPLE 16.2

Five turned bars are measured and their diameters were found to be: 15.03, 15.02, 15.02, 15.00 and 15.03 mm. What is their mean diameter?

$$\text{Mean diameter} = \frac{15.03 + 15.02 + 15.02 + 15.00 + 15.03}{5} = \frac{75.10}{5}$$

$$= 15.02\,\text{mm}$$

The Mean of a Frequency Distribution

The mean of a frequency distribution must take into account the frequencies as well as the measured observations.

If $x_1, x_2, x_3 \ldots x_n$, are measured observations which have frequencies $f_1, f_2, f_3 \ldots f_n$, then the mean of the distribution is

$$\bar{x} = \frac{x_1 f_1 + x_2 f_2 + x_3 f_3 + \ldots\ldots\ldots + x_n f_n}{f_1 + f_2 + f_3 + \ldots + f_n} = \frac{\Sigma x f}{\Sigma f}$$

The symbol Σ simply means the 'sum of'. Thus Σxf tells us to multiply together corresponding values of x and f and then add the results together.

Finding the mean of grouped frequency distributions follows later in the chapter.

EXAMPLE 16.3

Five castings have a mass of 20.01 kg each, three have mass of 19.98 kg each and two have a mass of 20.03 kg each. What is the mean mass of the ten castings?

The total mass is

$$(5 \times 20.01) + (3 \times 19.98) + (2 \times 20.03) = 200.05\,\text{kg}$$

$$\text{Mean mass} = \frac{\text{Total mass of the castings}}{\text{Number of castings}} = \frac{200.05}{10} = 20.005\,\text{kg}$$

The Median

If a set of numbers is arranged in ascending (or descending) order of size, the median is the value which lies half-way along the set. Thus for the set

3, 4, 4, 5, 6, 7, 7, 9, 10 the median is 6

If there is an even number of values, the median is found by taking the average of the two middle values. Thus for the set

3, 3, 5, 7, 9, 10, 13, 15 the median is $\frac{1}{2}(7 + 9) = 8$

EXAMPLE 16.4

The hourly wages of five employees in an office are £4.04, £6.92, £5.56, £17.40 and £6.50. Find the median.

Arranging the amounts in ascending order we have

£4.04, £5.56, £6.50, £6.92, £17.40

The median is therefore £6.50

The Median of a Frequency Distribution

This is shown in Example 16.1.

The Mode

The mode of a set of numbers is the number which occurs most frequently. Thus the mode of

2 3 3 4 4 4 5 5 6 6 7 8

is 4, since this number occurs three times which is more than any of the other numbers in the set.

For a set of numbers, the mode may not exist. Thus the set of numbers

4 5 6 8 9 10 12

has no mode.

It is possible for there to be more than one mode. The set of numbers

2 3 3 5 5 5 6 6 7 8 8 8 9 10

has two modes, 5 and 8. The set of numbers is said to be *bimodal*. If there is only one mode, then the set of numbers is said to be *unimodal*.

The Mode from a Histogram

Using the tallest rectangle the construction is as shown in Fig. 16.3 for a typical histogram representation of a frequency distribution.

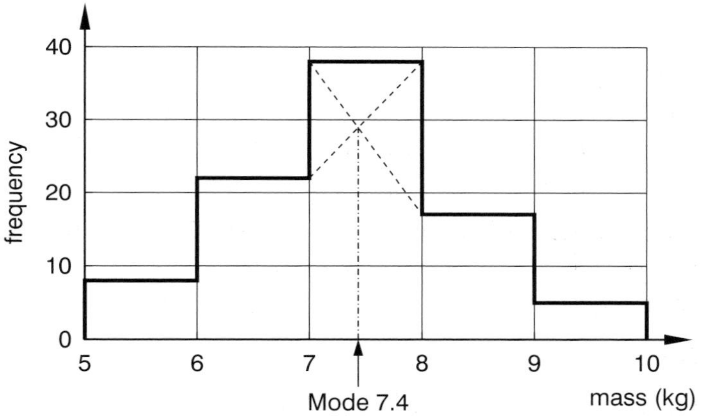

Fig. 16.3

Discussion on the Mean, Median and Mode

Which of the above averages to use will depend upon the particular application.

The arithmetic mean is the most familiar kind of average and it is used extensively in statistical work. However, it can be misleading especially if it is affected by extreme values. Again, the mean size of screws is not of much use to a purchasing officer, because it might be at some point between stock sizes – better here to use the mode.

The median is the value half-way along a set of numbers and simple to find. Not often favoured in scientific work.

The mode will indicate the most popular item(s) and so will help the stock-purchasing officer, and is useful in applications of this nature.

Exercise 16.1

1) Find the mode of the following set of numbers:

3, 5, 2, 7, 5, 8, 5, 2, 7, 6

2) Find the mode of:

38.7, 29.6, 32.1, 35.8, 43.2

3) Find the modes of:

8, 4, 9, 3, 5, 3, 8, 5, 3, 8, 9, 5, 6, 7

4) The data below relates to the resistance in ohms of an electrical part. Find the mode of this distribution, by drawing a histogram.

Resistance (ohms)	119	120	121	122	123	124
Frequency	5	9	19	25	18	4

5) The information below shows the distribution of the diameters of rivet heads for rivets manufactured by a certain company.

Diameter (mm)	18.407–18.412	18.413–18.418	18.419–18.424
Frequency	2	6	8

Diameter (mm)	18.425–18.430	18.431–18.436	18.437–18.442
Frequency	12	7	3

Find the mode of this distribution.

6) Find the median of the following set of numbers:

9, 2, 7, 3, 8, 5, 4

7) A student receives the following marks in an examination in five subjects: 84, 77, 95, 80 and 97. What is the median mark?

8) The following are the weekly wages earned by six people working in a small factory: £164, £263, £227, £239, £224 and £254. What is the median wage?

9) Find the mean and the median for the following set of observations: 15.63, 14.95, 16.00, 12.04, 15.88 and 16.04 ohms. Which of these do you think is the better to use for these observations?

10) Draw up a cumulative frequency distribution for the distribution given in Table 16.3. Hence, find the median and the 1st and 3rd quartiles for the distribution.

TABLE 16.3

Resistance (ohm)	*Frequency*
115	3
116	7
117	12
118	20
119	15
120	8
121	2

TABLE 16.4

Diameter (mm)	*Frequency*
20.00–20.03	4
20.04–20.07	12
20.08–20.11	23
20.12–20.15	11
20.16–20.19	2

11) By drawing an ogive for the distribution of Table 16.4 determine the values of the quartiles.

12) The diameters of eight pipes were measured with the following results: 109.23, 109.21, 108.98, 109.03, 108.98, 109.22, 109.20, 108.91 mm. What is the mean diameter of the pipes ?

13) 22 bricks have a mean mass of 24 kg and 18 similar bricks have a mean mass of 23.7 kg. What is the mean mass of the 40 bricks?

14) A sample of 100 lengths of timber was measured with the following results:

Length (m)	9.61	9.62	9.63	9.64	9.65	9.66	9.67	9.68	9.69
Frequency	2	4	12	18	31	22	8	2	1

Calculate the mean length of the timber.

15) The table below shows the distribution of the maximum loads supported by certain cables.

Max. load (kN)	19.2–19.5	19.6–19.9	20.0–20.3	20.4–20.7
Frequency	4	12	18	3

Calculate the mean load which the cables will support.

The Normal Distribution

It will be recalled that a frequency distribution may be represented by a frequency curve (Fig. 16.1). Where the data has been obtained by actual measurement this approximates to a symmetrical bell-shaped curve. This will only be so if sufficient measurements are made – usually 100 will suffice. This curve is called a normal distribution curve and it may be defined in terms of total frequency, the arithmetic mean and the standard deviation.

Since the normal curve is symmetrical about its vertical centre-line, then this centre-line represents the mean of the distribution. This mean locates the position of the curve from the reference axis as shown in Fig. 16.4 which displays similar distributions with different means.

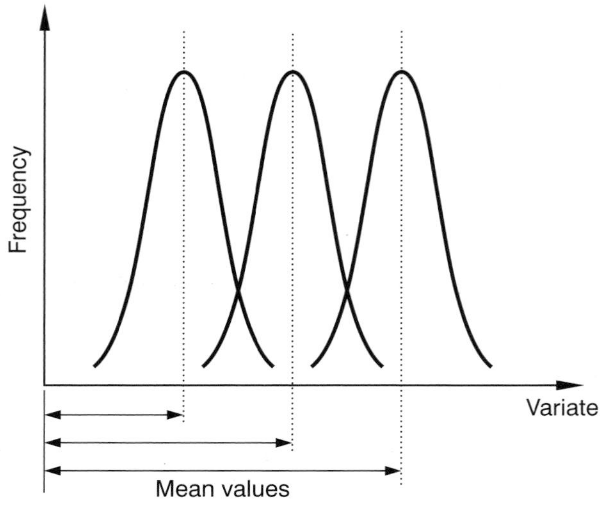

Fig. 16.4

Spread or Dispersion

Dispersion is how a distribution is spread out on either side of its central position. Tall and closely packed distributions such as in Fig. 16.4 will have a small dispersion value whilst a low broader figure such as Fig. 16.6 will have a larger value.

The range is the difference between the largest value and the smallest value of a set. It gives some idea of the spread but it depends solely on end values – it has the advantage of being easily obtained, but gives no idea of the distribution of data and is never used as a measure for calculation purposes.

The standard deviation is the most valuable and widely used measure and gives an idea of dispersion about the mean. It is always represented by the Greek letter σ (sigma).

The variance is the square of the standard deviation (σ^2) and this value also helps to describe the spread mathematically.

Although the normal curve extends to infinity on either side of the mean, for most practical purposes it may be assumed to terminate at three standard deviations on either side of the mean (Fig. 16.6).

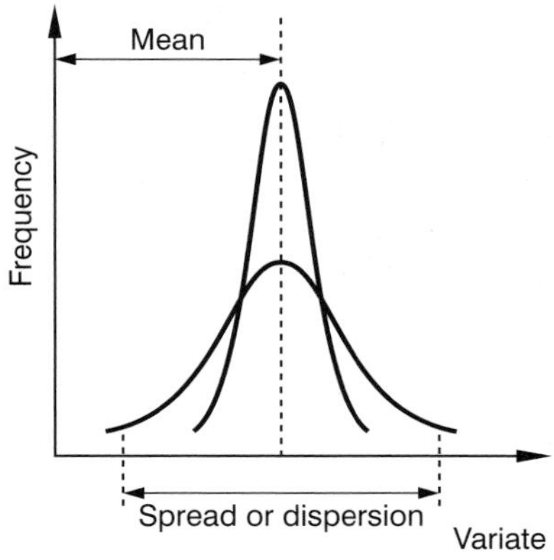

Fig. 16.5

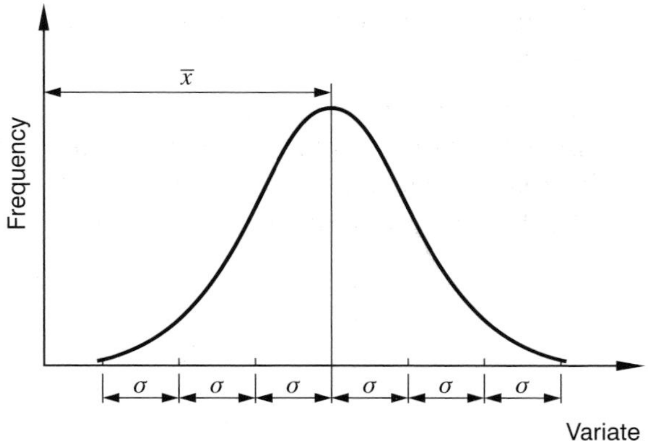

Fig. 16.6

Calculation of the Mean and the Standard Deviation

The formulae used are

$$\text{Mean } \overline{x} = \frac{\Sigma xf}{\Sigma f}$$

$$\text{Standard deviation } \sigma = \sqrt{\frac{\Sigma x^2 f}{\Sigma f} - (\overline{x})^2}$$

A calculator will generally have the facilities for you to enter the values of the variate x and the corresponding values of frequency f. The results may then be found from the keys labelled $\overline{x}$ and σ.

Some machines also have another standard deviation labelled $\sigma_n - 1$ which is based on a slightly different formula – this is **not** the one we shall use.

Each make of calculator will require a different procedure, which will be given in the instruction booklet that accompanies the machine.

However you should be warned that, from experience, it is not easy to enter two sets of numbers accurately. Often the whole procedure has to be gone through **at least** twice to guarantee a correct answer.

Alternatively, the two examples which follow show a tabulation method. This is called the coded method and this uses the idea of choosing a mean value and then working out by how much the true mean value varies.

EXAMPLE 16.5

Calculate the mean and standard deviation for the following frequency distribution.

Resistance (ohms)	5.37	5.38	5.39	5.40	5.41	5.42	5.43	5.44
Frequency	4	10	14	24	34	18	10	6

Our chosen mean value of $x = 5.40$ and unit size = 0.01 ohm

A unit size of 0.01 ohm has been chosen because each value of x differs from its preceding value by 0.01. Making the unit size as large as possible simplifies the calculations.

x	x_c	f	x_cf	x_c^2f
5.37	−3	4	−12	36
5.38	−2	10	−20	40
5.39	−1	14	−14	14
5.40	0	24	0	0
5.41	1	34	34	34
5.42	2	18	36	72
5.43	3	10	30	90
5.44	4	6	24	96
	Totals =	120	78	382

Now $\bar{x}_c = \dfrac{\Sigma x_cf}{\Sigma f} = \dfrac{78}{120} = 0.65$

$\therefore$ mean $\bar{x} = 5.40 + 0.65 \times 0.01 = 5.4065$ ohm

and $\sigma_c = \sqrt{\dfrac{\Sigma x_c^2f}{\Sigma f} - (\bar{x}_c)^2} = \sqrt{\dfrac{382}{120} - (0.65)^2} = 1.662$ ohm

$\therefore$ std. dev. $\sigma = \sigma_c \times \text{unit size} = 1.662 \times 0.01 = 0.016\,62$ ohm

Rough Check on Standard Deviation using the Range

In the last example: Range $= 5.44 - 5.37 = 0.07$

Hence: approximately $\sigma = \dfrac{0.07}{6} = 0.012$ ohm

This does not verify the accuracy of the calculated value 0.016 62 but it does show it is of the right order (i.e. not wildly incorrect).

EXAMPLE 16.6

The table indicates experimental results from a sample of resistors.

Resistance (ohm)	24.92–24.94	24.95–24.97	24.98–25.00
Frequency	2	3	9

Resistance (ohm)	25.01–25.03	25.04–25.06	25.07–25.09
Frequency	23	18	5

Calculate the standard deviation and the variance.

The resistance data has been grouped into classes. Here we use the centre of each class for the x value.

Our chosen mean value of $x = 25.02$ ohm and unit size $= 0.03$ ohm.

A unit size of 0.03 ohm has been chosen because each value of x differs from its preceding value by 0.03.

Class	x	x_c	f	$x_c f$	$x_c^2 f$
24.92–24.94	24.93	−3	2	−6	18
24.95–24.97	24.96	−2	3	−6	12
24.98–25.00	24.99	−1	9	−9	9
25.01–25.03	25.02	0	23	0	0
25.04–25.06	25.05	1	18	18	18
25.07–25.09	25.08	2	5	10	20
		Totals =	60	7	77

Now $\qquad \bar{x}_c = \dfrac{\Sigma x_c f}{\Sigma f} = \dfrac{+7}{60} = +0.116$

$\therefore$ mean $\qquad \bar{x} = 25.02 + (0.03)(0.116) = 25.0235$ ohm

Also $\qquad \sigma_c = \sqrt{\dfrac{\Sigma x_c^2 f}{\Sigma f} - (\bar{x}_c)^2} = \sqrt{\dfrac{77}{60} - (0.116)^2} = 1.1268$ ohm

$\therefore$ std. dev. $\qquad \sigma = 1.1268 \times 0.03 = 0.0338$ ohm

A rough check gives $\sigma = \dfrac{\text{range}}{6} = \dfrac{25.09 - 24.92}{6} = 0.0283$ ohm

which is of the same order as the value calculated above.

Thus $\qquad$ the variance $= \sigma^2 = 0.0338^2 = 0.001\,14$

CHANCE (OR PROBABILITY) FROM THE NORMAL CURVE

If a sample – the bigger the better but at least 100 measurements – has been taken from a production line, the results will generally follow the profile of a normal curve. Figure 16.7 shows the area of each vertical strip as a percentage of the total area under the normal curve. As you will see, these areas may be used to estimate the chances of something happening, which is extremely useful, for example, in quality control.

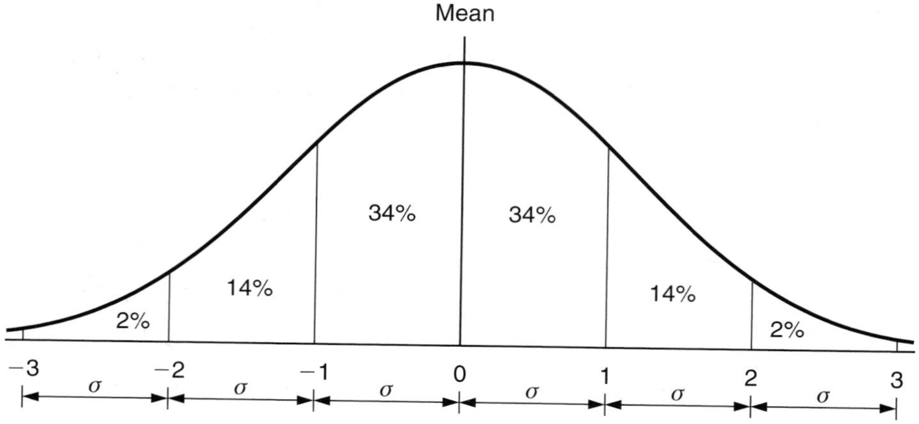

Fig. 16.7

For instance, there is a 34% chance of something happening between the mean and one standard deviation from the mean. Tables are available for the areas of any width of strip, but those shown in Fig. 16.7 will suffice to give you the general idea.

On the base scale of -3 to $+3$ the value corresponding to a particular value of variate x is given by $\dfrac{(x - \bar{x})}{\sigma}$.

The following example will show you how this works.

EXAMPLE 16.7

By measuring a large number of components produced on an automatic lathe it was found that the mean length was 20.10 mm with a standard deviation of 0.03 mm. Find:

a) Within what limits would you expect the lengths for the whole of the components to lie.

b) The chance that one component taken at random would have
   (i) a length greater than 20.16 mm,
   (ii) a length less than 20.07 mm,
   (iii) a length between 20.04 mm and 20.13 mm.

a) For most practical purposes, the normal curve may be regarded as terminating at three standard deviations either side of the mean. Thus, we would expect the lengths for the whole of the components to lie between

$$\text{Mean} \pm 3\sigma = 20.10 \pm 3 \times 0.03 = 20.10 \pm 0.09$$
$$= \text{between } 20.01 \text{ and } 20.19\,\text{mm}$$

b) (i) For $x = 20.16$ Scale value $= \dfrac{20.16 - 20.10}{0.03} = 2$

Now the area is 2% between 2 and the upper limit, so we would expect 2% of all components to have lengths greater than 20.16 mm.

(ii) For $x = 20.07$ Scale value $= \dfrac{20.07 - 20.10}{0.03} = -1$

Now the area between -1 and the lower limit is $2\% + 14\% = 16\%$. Thus we would expect 16% of all components to have lengths less than 20.07 mm.

(iii) For $x = 20.04$ Scale value $= \dfrac{20.04 - 20.10}{0.03} = -2$

and $x = 20.13$ Scale value $= \dfrac{20.13 - 20.10}{0.03} = 1$

Now the area between -2 and 1 is $14\% + 34\% + 34\% = 82\%$ so we would expect 82% of all components to have lengths between 20.04 and 20.13 mm.

Exercise 16.2

1) In a water absorption test on 100 bricks the following results were obtained:

% absorption	7	8	9	10	11	12	13	14
Frequency	1	4	9	24	30	26	5	1

Calculate the mean and standard deviation.

2) Find the mean and standard deviation for the following distribution which relates to the strength of load carrying bricks:

Strength (N/mm^2)	11.46	11.47	11.48	11.49	11.50	11.51	11.52	11.53
Frequency	1	4	12	15	11	6	3	1

3) 100 watt is the nominal value of the sample of electric light bulbs given below. Calculate the mean and standard deviation from the sample.

Power (watt)	99.6	99.7	99.8	99.9	100.0	100.1	100.2	100.3
Frequency	3	8	13	18	15	9	6	3

4) A brand of washing powder tested prior to marketing revealed its capacity to launder woollen garments of equivalent sizes.

Laundered garments	5–7	8–10	11–13	14–16	17–19
Frequency	1	5	11	7	3

From the data above, calculate the mean and standard deviation.

5) It is considered that a person uses, on average, 40 gallons of water daily. Using the following data calculate the mean water consumption and the standard deviation.

Daily consumption (gallons)	30–34	35–39	40–44	45–49	50–54	55–59
Number of users	3	19	43	26	7	2

6) Measurement from a large batch of mass produced components showed a mean diameter of 18.60 mm, with a standard deviation of 0.02 mm. Find:

(a) Within what limits the diameters of the whole of the components would be expected to lie,

(b) The chance that one component taken at random would have:
(i) a diameter greater than 18.62 mm
(ii) a diameter less than 18.56 mm.

7) In mass production of bushes it was found that the average bore was 12.5 mm with a standard deviation of 0.015 mm. If 2000 bushes are produced find the number of bushes that are expected to have dimensions between 12.47 and 12.53 mm.

8) 70 000 components for a motor vehicle are being produced. A batch of 300 was picked at random and lengths were checked to the nearest 0.01 mm with the following results:

Length (mm)	9.96	9.97	9.98	9.99	10.00	10.01	10.02	10.03	10.04
Frequency	1	6	25	72	93	69	27	6	1

Using results correct to four decimal places, find how many components of the 70 000 produced will be expected to have:

(a) lengths less than 9.9744 mm

(b) lengths between 10.0128 and 10.0256 mm.

Differentiation

17

Deduce graphically the limit of $\frac{\delta y}{\delta x}$, and define it as $\frac{dy}{dx}$, as δy tends to zero – find the derivative of $y = x^n$ from first principles – differentiate polynomial, trigonometrical, logarithmic and exponential functions – rates of change – distance, time, velocity and acceleration

RATES OF CHANGE AND DIFFERENTIATION

It is unfortunate that the word 'differentiation' has to be used before you have any inkling of what it is all about. However, being resolute (as you must be to have reached this part of the book!), we think you will have a pleasant surprise – most of us are happy when drawing a simple graph and taking measurements from it. Well this is exactly how you will begin and you will soon get the 'feel' of what it is all about. Notice how important the word 'feel' is to us as engineers. As this is your first meeting with the vast topic of calculus, and the time that can be spent is limited, you will not appreciate at this stage how useful it can be. However, this serves as a useful introduction and, with the extra knowledge from the final chapter, you will be well prepared when meeting calculus in your future studies.

Differentiation

Here we start by drawing a graph and finding a gradient by measurement. We then move to the idea of small quantities, and what happens to them as they become very tiny. This gives us another way of finding a gradient and we are soon on the way to using differentiation as another 'tool' in problem solving.

Gradient of a Curve – Graphical Method

In mathematics and technology, we often need to know the rate of change of one variable with respect to another. For instance, velocity is the rate of change of distance with respect to time, and acceleration is the rate of change of velocity with respect to time.

Consider the graph of $y = x^2$, part of which is shown in Fig. 17.1. As the values of x increase so do the values of y, but they do not increase at the same rate. A glance at the portion of the curve shown shows that the values of y increase faster when x is large, because the gradient of the curve is increasing.

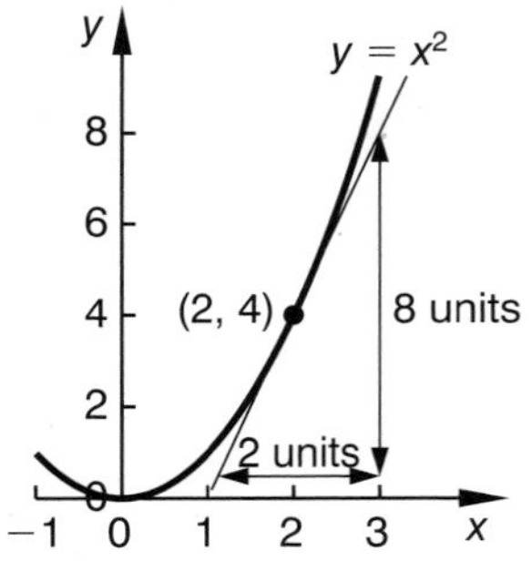

Fig. 17.1

To find the rate of change of y with respect to x at a particular point we need to find the gradient of the curve at that point.

If we draw a tangent to the curve at the point, the gradient of the tangent will be the same as the gradient of the curve.

EXAMPLE 17.1

Find the gradient of the curve $y = x^2$ at the point where $x = 2$.

The point where $x = 2$ is the point $(2, 4)$. We draw a tangent at this point, as shown in Fig. 17.1. Then by constructing a right-angled triangle the gradient is found to be $\frac{8}{2} = 4$. This gradient is positive, in accordance with our previous work, since the tangent slopes upwards from left to right.

EXAMPLE 17.2

Draw the graph of $y = x^2 - 3x + 7$ between $x = -4$ and $x = 3$ and hence find the gradient at a) the point $x = -3$ b) the point $x = 2$.

a) At the point where $x = -3$ then $y = (-3)^2 - 3(-3) + 7 = 25$

At the point $(-3, 25)$, draw a tangent as shown in Fig. 17.2. The gradient is found by drawing a right-angled triangle (which should be as large as conveniently possible for accuracy) as shown, and measuring its height and base.

Hence: at point $(-3, 25)$ gradient $= -\dfrac{28.8}{3.2} = -9$

The negative sign indicating a downward slope from left to right.

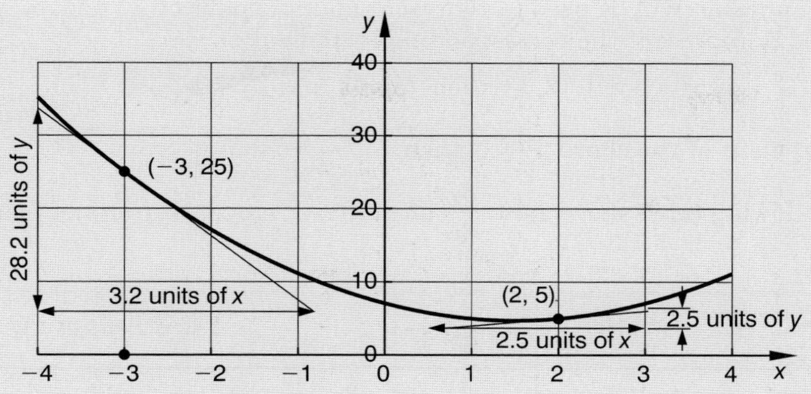

Fig. 17.2

b) At the point where $x = 2$ then $y = 2^2 - 3(2) + 7 = 5$

Hence by drawing a tangent and a right-angled triangle at the point (2, 5) in a similar manner to above

then at point (2, 5) gradient $= \dfrac{2.5}{2.5} = 1$

being positive as the tangent slopes upwards from left to right.

Exercise 17.1

1) Draw the graph of $y = 2x^2 - 5$ for values of x between -2 and $+3$. Draw, as accurately as possible, the tangents to the curve at the points where $x = -1$ and $x = +2$ and hence find the gradient of the curve at these points.

2) Draw the curve $y = x^2 - 3x + 2$ from $x = 2.5$ to $x = 3.5$ and find its gradient at the point where $x = 3$.

3) Draw the curve $y = x - \dfrac{1}{x}$ from $x = 0.8$ to 1.2

Find its gradient at $x = 1$.

Gradient of a Curve – Numerical Method

The gradient of a curve may always be found by graphical means but this method is often inconvenient. A numerical method will now be developed.

Consider the curve $y = x^2$, part of which is shown in Fig. 17.3. Let P be the point on the curve at which $x = 1$ and $y = 1$. Q is a variable point on the curve, which will be considered to start at the point (2, 4) and move down the curve towards P, rather like a bead slides down a wire.

The symbol δx will be used to represent an increment of x, and δy will be used to represent the corresponding increment of y.

When Q is at the point (2, 4) then $\delta x = 1$ and $\delta y = 3$

The gradient of the chord PQ is then $\dfrac{\delta y}{\delta x} = \dfrac{3}{1} = 3$

The following table shows how $\dfrac{\delta y}{\delta x}$ alters as Q moves nearer and nearer to P.

Co-ordinates of Q x	y	δx	δy	*Gradient of PQ* $= \dfrac{\delta y}{\delta x}$
2	4	1	3	3
1.5	2.25	0.5	1.25	2.5
1.4	1.96	0.4	0.96	2.4
1.3	1.69	0.3	0.69	2.3
1.2	1.44	0.2	0.44	2.2
1.1	1.21	0.1	0.21	2.1
1.01	1.0201	0.01	0.0201	2.01
1.001	1.002 001	0.001	0.002 001	2.001

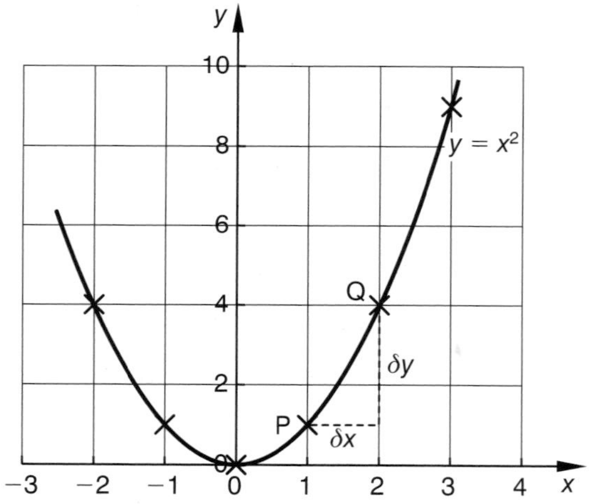

Fig. 17.3

It will be seen that as Q approaches nearer and nearer to P, the value of $\dfrac{\delta y}{\delta x}$ approaches 2. It is reasonable to suppose that eventually when Q coincides with P (that is, when the chord PQ becomes a tangent to the curve at P) the gradient of the tangent will be exactly equal to 2.

The gradient of the tangent will give us the gradient of the curve at P.

Now as Q approaches P, δx tends to zero and the gradient of the chord $\frac{\delta y}{\delta x}$ tends, in the limit (as we say), to the gradient of the tangent.

We denote the gradient of the tangent as $\frac{dy}{dx}$. We can write all this as

$$\operatorname*{Limit}_{\delta x \to 0} \frac{\delta y}{\delta x} = \frac{dy}{dx}$$

Differentiation from First Principles

Instead of selecting special values for δy and δx let us now consider the general case, so that P has the coordinates (x, y) and Q has the coordinates $(x + \delta x, y + \delta y)$, as in Fig. 17.4. Q is taken very close to P, so that δx is a very small quantity.

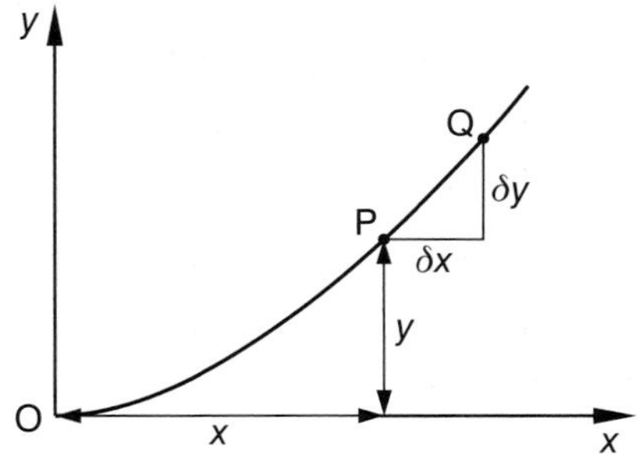

Fig. 17.4

Now $$y = x^2$$

and as $Q(x + \delta x, y + \delta y)$ lies on the curve, then

$$y + \delta y = (x + \delta x)^2$$

$$y + \delta y = x^2 + 2x\,\delta x + (\delta x)^2$$

But $y = x^2$, so $$\delta y = 2x\,\delta x + (\delta x)^2$$

and, by dividing both sides by δx the gradient of chord PQ is

$$\frac{\delta y}{\delta x} = 2x + \delta x$$

As Q approaches P, δx tends to zero. Also $\frac{\delta y}{\delta x}$ tends, in the limit, to the gradient of the tangent of the curve at P.

Thus $$\operatorname*{Limit}_{\delta x \to 0} \frac{\delta y}{\delta x} = \frac{dy}{dx} = 2x$$

The process of finding $\frac{dy}{dx}$ is called **differentiation.**

The symbol $\dfrac{dy}{dx}$ means the differential coefficient of y with respect to x.

We can now check our assumption regarding the gradient of the curve at P. Since at P the value of $x = 1$, then substituting in the expression

$$\frac{dy}{dx} = 2x \quad \text{we get} \quad \frac{dy}{dx} = 2 \times 1 = 2$$

and we see that our assumption was correct.

Differential Coefficient of x^n

It can be shown, by a method similar to that used for finding the differential coefficient of x^2, that

$$\text{if} \quad \boldsymbol{y = x^n} \quad \text{then} \quad \boldsymbol{\frac{dy}{dx} = nx^{n-1}}$$

Remember **'Multiply by the old index, and then reduce the index by one'**

This is true for all values of n including negative and fractional indices. When we use it as a formula, it enables us to avoid having to differentiate each time from first principles.

EXAMPLE 17.3

$y = x^3$ $\therefore \quad \dfrac{dy}{dx} = 3x^2$	$y = \sqrt{x} = x^{\frac{1}{2}}$ $\therefore \quad \dfrac{dy}{dx} = \dfrac{1}{2}x^{-\frac{1}{2}} = \dfrac{1}{2} \times \dfrac{1}{x^{\frac{1}{2}}} = \dfrac{1}{2\sqrt{x}}$
$y = \dfrac{1}{x} = x^{-1}$ $\therefore \quad \dfrac{dy}{dx} = -x^{-2} = -\dfrac{1}{x^2}$	$y = \sqrt[5]{x^2} = x^{\frac{2}{5}}$ $\therefore \quad \dfrac{dy}{dx} = \dfrac{2}{5}x^{\frac{2}{5}-1} = \dfrac{2}{5}x^{-\frac{3}{5}} = \dfrac{2}{5(\sqrt[5]{x^3})}$

When a power of x is multiplied by a constant, that constant remains unchanged by the process of differentiation.

Hence

$$\text{if} \quad \boldsymbol{y = ax^n} \quad \text{then} \quad \boldsymbol{\frac{dy}{dx} = anx^{n-1}}$$

EXAMPLE 17.4

$y = 2x^{1.3}$ $\therefore \quad \dfrac{dy}{dx} = 2(1.3)x^{1.3-1} = 2.6x^{0.3}$	$y = \dfrac{1}{5}x^7$ $\therefore \quad \dfrac{dy}{dx} = \dfrac{1}{5} \times 7x^{7-1} = \dfrac{7}{5}x^6$
$y = \dfrac{3}{4}\sqrt[3]{x} = \dfrac{3}{4}x^{\frac{1}{3}}$ $\therefore \quad \dfrac{dy}{dx} = \dfrac{3}{4} \times \dfrac{1}{3}x^{\frac{1}{3}-1} = \dfrac{1}{4}x^{-\frac{2}{3}}$	$y = \dfrac{4}{x^2} = 4x^{-2}$ $\therefore \quad \dfrac{dy}{dx} = 4(-2)x^{-2-1} = -8x^{-3}$

When a numerical constant is differentiated, the result is zero.

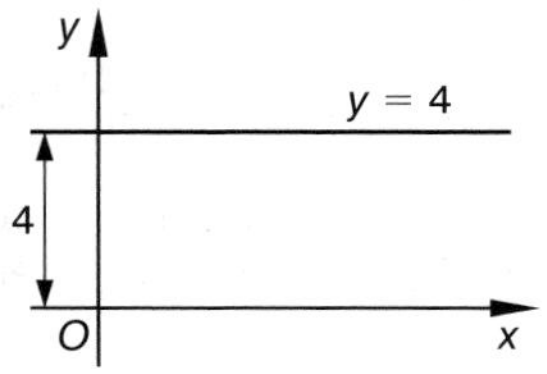

Fig. 17.5

This can be seen since $x^0 = 1$ and we can write, for example, constant 4 as $4x^0$, then differentiating with respect to x we, get $4(0)x^{-1} = 0$.

If, as an alternative method, we plot the graph of $y = 4$ we get a straight line parallel with the x-axis as shown in Fig. 17.5.

The gradient of the horizontal line is zero: that is $\dfrac{dy}{dx} = 0$

To differentiate an expression containing the sum of several terms, differentiate each individual term separately.

EXAMPLE 17.5

a)
$$y = 3x^2 + 2x + 3$$
$$\therefore \quad \frac{dy}{dx} = 3(2)x + 2(1)x^0 + 0 = 6x + 2$$

b)
$$y = ax^3 + bx^2 + cx + d \quad \text{where } a,\ b,\ c \text{ and } d \text{ are constants}$$
$$\therefore \quad \frac{dy}{dx} = 3ax^2 + 2bx + c$$

So far our differentiation has been in terms of x and y only. But they are only letters representing variables and we may choose other letters.

c) $$s = \sqrt{t} + \frac{1}{\sqrt{t}} = t^{\frac{1}{2}} + t^{-\frac{1}{2}}$$

$$\therefore \quad \frac{ds}{dt} = \frac{1}{2}t^{-\frac{1}{2}} + \left(-\frac{1}{2}\right)t^{-\frac{3}{2}} = \frac{1}{2\sqrt{t}} - \frac{1}{2\sqrt{t^3}}$$

d) $$v = 3.1u^{1.4} - \frac{3}{u} + 5 = 3.1u^{1.4} - 3u^{-1} + 5$$

$$\therefore \quad \frac{dv}{du} = (3.1)(1.4)u^{0.4} - 3(-1)u^{-2} = 4.34u^{0.4} + \frac{3}{u^2}$$

Finding the Gradient of a Curve by Differentiation

EXAMPLE 17.6

Find the gradient of the graph $y = 3x^2 - 3x + 4$ a) when $x = 3$ b) when $x = -2$

The gradient at a point is expressed by $\dfrac{dy}{dx}$

So when $$y = 3x^2 - 3x + 4$$

then the gradient $$\frac{dy}{dx} = 6x - 3$$

a) When $x = 3$

gradient $\dfrac{dy}{dx} = 6(3) - 3 = 15$

b) When $x = -2$

gradient $\dfrac{dy}{dx} = 6(-2) - 3 = -15$

You may find this summary of the laws of indices useful when working through Exercise 17.2

$$a^m \times a^n = a^{m+n}$$

$$\frac{a^m}{a^n} = a^{m-n}$$

$$(a^m)^n = a^{m \times n}$$

$$a^0 = 1$$

$$a^{-n} = \frac{1}{a^n}$$

$$\sqrt[n]{a} = a^{1/n}$$

Exercise 17.2

Differentiate the following:

1) $y = x^2$ 2) $y = x^7$ 3) $y = 4x^3$

4) $y = 6x^5$ 5) $s = 0.5t^3$ 6) $A = \pi R^2$

7) $y = x^{1/2}$ 8) $y = 4x^{3/2}$ 9) $y = 2 \times \sqrt{x}$

10) $y = 3 \times \sqrt[3]{x^2}$ 11) $y = \dfrac{1}{x^2}$ 12) $y = \dfrac{1}{x}$

13) $y = \dfrac{3}{5x}$ 14) $y = \dfrac{2}{x^3}$ 15) $y = \dfrac{1}{\sqrt{x}}$

16) $y = \dfrac{2}{3 \times \sqrt{x}}$ 17) $y = \dfrac{5}{x \times \sqrt{x}}$ 18) $s = \dfrac{3 \times \sqrt{t}}{5}$

19) $K = \dfrac{0.01}{h}$ 20) $y = \dfrac{5}{x^7}$ 21) $y = 4x^2 - 3x$

22) $s = 3t^3 - 2t^2 + 5t - 3$ 23) $q = 2u^2 - u + 7$

24) $y = 5x^4 - 7x^3 + 3x^2 - 2x + 5$ 25) $s = 7t^5 - 3t^2 + 7$

26) $y = \dfrac{x + x^3}{\sqrt{x}}$ 27) $y = \dfrac{3 + x^2}{x}$

28) $y = \sqrt{x} + \dfrac{1}{\sqrt{x}}$ 29) $y = x^3 + \dfrac{3}{\sqrt{x}}$

30) $s = t^{1.3} - \dfrac{1}{4t^{2.3}}$ 31) $y = \dfrac{3x^3}{5} - \dfrac{2x^2}{7} + \sqrt{x}$

32) $y = 0.08 + \dfrac{0.01}{x}$ 33) $y = 3.1x^{1.5} - 2.4x^{0.6}$

34) $y = \dfrac{x^3}{2} - \dfrac{5}{x} + 3$ 35) $s = 10 - 6t + 7t^2 - 2t^3$

36) Find the gradient of the curve $y = 3x^2 + 7x + 3$ at the points where $x = -2$ and $x = 2$.

37) Find the gradient of the curve $y = 2x^3 - 7x^2 + 5x - 3$ at the points where $x = -1.5$, $x = 0$ and $x = 3$.

38) Find the values of x for which the gradient of the curve $y = 3 + 4x - x^2$ is equal to: **a)** -1 **b)** 0 **c)** 2

Differentiation of Trigonometric Functions

It can be shown that, for the standard forms of trigonometric expressions, where ω and α are constants:

$$\frac{d}{dt}\sin(\omega t+\alpha) = \omega\cos(\omega t+\alpha)$$
$$\frac{d}{dt}\cos(\omega t+\alpha) = -\omega\sin(\omega t+\alpha)$$

EXAMPLE 17.7

Find $\frac{dy}{dt}$ if $y=\cos\left(2t+\frac{\pi}{2}\right)$

If we compare this with the standard form, then $\omega=2$ and $\alpha=\frac{\pi}{2}$

Thus if $\quad y = \cos\left(2t+\frac{\pi}{2}\right)$

then $\quad \frac{dy}{dt} = -2\sin\left(2t+\frac{\pi}{2}\right)$

Differentiation of Logarithmic Functions

It can be shown that:

$$\frac{d}{dx}(\log_e x) = \frac{1}{x}$$

EXAMPLE 17.8

Find $\frac{d}{dx}(\log_e 2x)$

Let $\quad y = \log_e 2x$

$\quad = \log_e 2 + \log_e x \quad$ using law 1 of logs for numbers multiplied

Now $\log_e 2$ is simply a constant, so it will disappear on differentiation

Thus if $\quad y = \log_e 2 + \log_e x$

then $\quad \frac{dy}{dx} = \frac{1}{x}$

Differentiation of Exponent Functions

It can be shown, where a is a constant, that

$$\frac{d}{dx}(e^{ax}) = ae^{ax}$$

EXAMPLE 17.9

Find $\frac{d}{dx}(e^{5t} + e^{-2t})$.

As usual, when dealing with terms added together, we deal with each term individually.

Thus if we let $\quad y = e^{5t} + e^{-2t}$

then $\quad \frac{dy}{dx} = 5e^{5t} + (-2)e^{-2t} = 5e^{5t} - 2e^{-2t}$

EXAMPLE 17.10

Find $\frac{d}{dx}(e^{x})$.

Here we have the simple exponent function e^x where constant $a = 1$

Thus $\quad \frac{d}{dx}(e^{x}) = e^{x}$

This verifies the important property of the exponent function, namely:

The exponent function e^x has a differential coefficient of e^x, which is therefore equal to itself.

We may now summarise differential coefficients of the more common functions:

y	$\frac{dy}{dx}$
ax^n	anx^{n-1}
$\sin(\omega t + \alpha)$	$\omega \cos(\omega t + \alpha)$
$\cos(\omega t + \alpha)$	$-\omega \sin(\omega t + \alpha)$
$\log_e x$	$\frac{1}{x}$
e^{ax}	$a e^{ax}$

Exercise 17.3

1) Find $\dfrac{d}{d\theta}(\sin 2\theta + \cos 5\theta)$

2) Find $\dfrac{d}{dt}\{\sin(4t + \pi)\}$

3) Find $\dfrac{d}{dt}\left\{\cos\left(7t - \dfrac{3\pi}{2}\right)\right\}$

4) Find $\dfrac{dy}{dx}$ if $y = \log_e 9x$ with the aid of law 1 of logs.

5) Find $\dfrac{dy}{dx}$ if $y = \log_e\left(\dfrac{10}{x}\right)$ with the aid of law 2 of logs.

6) Find $\dfrac{dy}{dx}$ if $y = \log_e(x^2)$ with the aid of law 3 of logs.

7) Find $\dfrac{d}{du}(e^{3u} - e^{-3u})$

8) Find $\dfrac{d}{dv}(6e^{-5v})$

APPLICATION OF CALCULUS TO PROBLEMS

Here is a typical application of differentiation.

Distance, time, velocity and acceleration, either linear or angular, crop up all the time in engineering.

Distance, Time, Velocity and Acceleration

Linear and angular motion

Suppose that a vehicle starts from rest and travels 60 metres in 12 seconds. The average velocity may be found by dividing the total distance travelled by the total time taken, that is $\frac{60}{12} = 5$ m/s. This is **not** the *instantaneous* velocity at any instant but is the *average velocity* over the distance travelled in 12 seconds.

Figure 17.6 shows a graph of distance s against time t. The average velocity over a period is given by the gradient of the chord which meets the curve at the extremes of the period. Thus in the diagram the gradient of the dotted chord QR gives the average velocity between $t = 2$ s and $t = 6$ s. It is found to be $\frac{13}{4} = 3.25$ m/s.

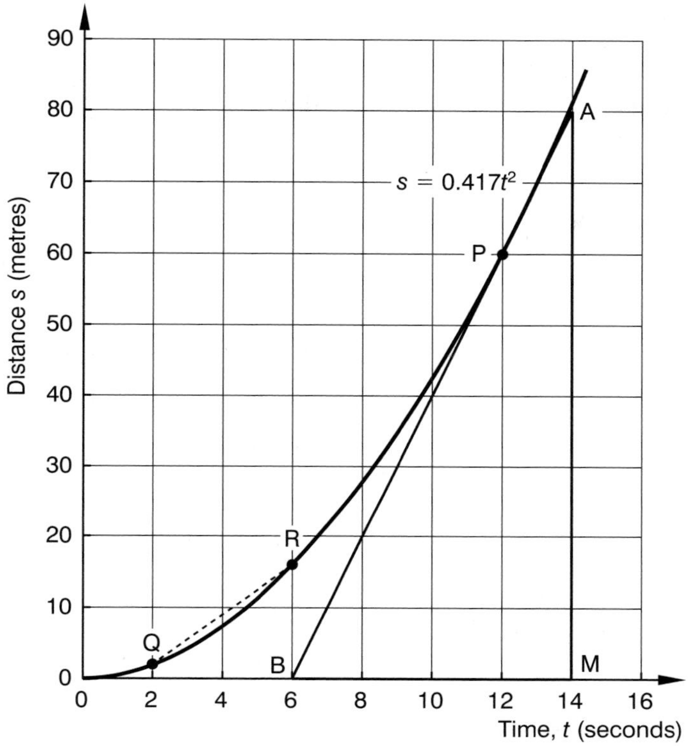

Fig. 17.6

The velocity, at any point, is the rate of change of s with respect to t and may be found by finding the gradient of the curve at that point. In other words

The rate of change of distance with respect to time is called **velocity** and is given by the **gradient of the distance–time graph** at any point.

In mathematical notation that is given by $\dfrac{ds}{dt}$. Thus: velocity $v = \dfrac{ds}{dt}$

Suppose we know that the relationship between s and t is

$$s = 0.417\,t^2$$

Then velocity $$v = \frac{ds}{dt} = 0.834\,t$$

thus when $t = 12$ seconds, $$v = 0.834 \times 12 = 10\text{ m/s}.$$

This result may be found graphically, Fig. 17.6, by drawing the tangent to the curve of s against t at point P and constructing a suitable right-angled $\triangle$ABM.

$$\therefore \quad \text{velocity at P} = \frac{\text{AM}}{\text{BM}} = \frac{80}{8} = 10\,\text{m/s} \text{ verifying the theoretical result.}$$

Similarly, rate of change of velocity with respect to time is called **acceleration** and is given by the **gradient of the velocity–time graph** at any point. In mathematical notation $\frac{dv}{dt}$. Thus acceleration $a = \frac{dv}{dt}$.

The above reasoning was applied to linear motion, but it could also have been used for angular motion. The essential difference is that distance s is replaced by angle turned through θ rad.

Both sets of results are summarised in Fig. 17.7.

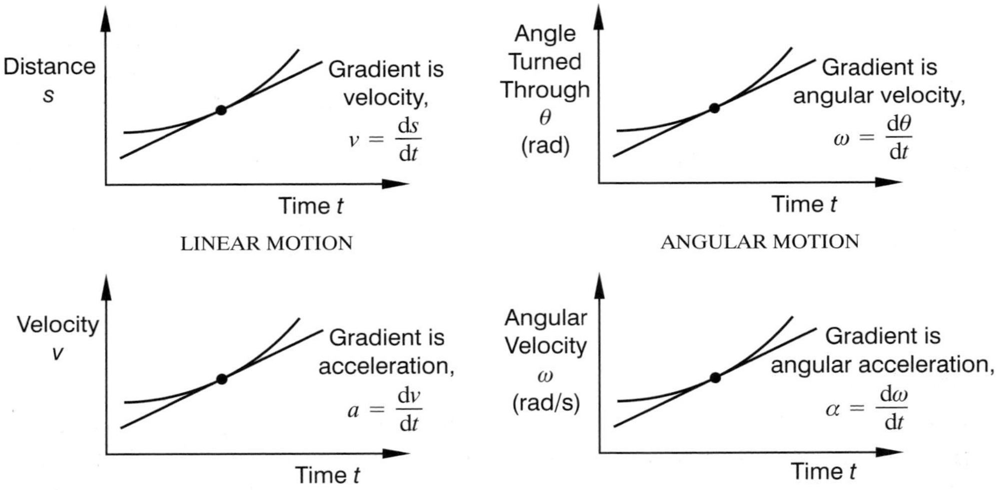

Fig. 17.7

EXAMPLE 17.11

The research and development department of a company is developing a test rig to verify a theory for advanced dimensional analysis. A remotely controlled model has been programmed to move according to the equation $s = 2t^3 - 9t^2 + 12t + 6$ where s metres is the distance moved by the model at a time t seconds. We have been asked to find:

a) its velocity after 3 s

b) its acceleration after 3 s

c) when the velocity is zero

We have the displacement $s = 2t^3 - 9t^2 + 12t + 6$

$\therefore$ the velocity $v = \frac{ds}{dt} = 6t^2 - 18t + 12$

and the acceleration $a = \frac{dv}{dt} = 12t - 18$

a) When $t = 3$ the velocity $v = \frac{ds}{dt} = 6(3)^2 - 18(3) + 12 = 12\,\text{m/s}$

b) When $t = 3$ the acceleration $a = \frac{dv}{dt} = 12(3) - 18 = 18\,\text{m/s}^2$

c) When velocity is zero, that is when $v = \frac{ds}{dt} = 0$

Then $6t^2 - 18t + 12 = 0$

$\therefore$ $t^2 - 3t + 2 = 0$ by dividing through by 6

$\therefore$ $(t-1)(t-2) = 0$ by factorising

$\therefore$ either $t - 1 = 0$ or $t - 2 = 0$

$\therefore$ either $t = 1\,\text{s}$ or $t = 2\,\text{s}$

EXAMPLE 17.12

A displacement transducer has been fitted to a disc attached to a spindle, in order to measure the angle through which the spindle turns. After a period of observation of the machine tool being investigated, it has been established that the angular motion is governed by the relationship $\theta = 20 + 5t^2 - t^3$ where θ radians is the angle turned through at a time t seconds. We have been asked to find

a) the angular velocity when $t = 2$ seconds

b) the value of t when angular deceleration is $4\,\text{rad/s}^2$.

Now the angular displacement $\theta = 20 + 5t^2 - t^3$

$\therefore$ the angular velocity $\omega = \frac{d\theta}{dt} = 10t - 3t^2$

and the angular acceleration $\alpha = \frac{d\omega}{dt} = 10 - 6t$

a) When $t = 2$ then the angular velocity

$$\omega = \frac{d\theta}{dt} = 10(2) - 3(2)^2 = 8 \text{ rad/s}$$

b) An angular deceleration of 4 rad/s^2 may be called an angular acceleration of -4 rad/s^2

$$\therefore \text{ when } \quad \alpha = \frac{d\omega}{dt} = -4 \quad \text{then} \quad -4 = 10 - 6t$$

$$\text{or} \quad t = 2.33 \text{ seconds}$$

Exercise 17.4

1) If $s = 10 + 50t - 2t^2$, where s metres is the distance travelled in t seconds by a body, what is the velocity of the body after 2 seconds?

2) If $v = 5 + 24t - 3t^2$ where v m/s is the velocity of a body at a time t seconds, what is the acceleration when $t = 3$?

3) A body moves s metres in t seconds where $s = t^3 - 3t^2 - 3t + 8$. Find:

(a) its velocity at the end of 3 seconds,

(b) when its velocity is zero,

(c) its acceleration at the end of 2 seconds,

(d) when its acceleration is zero.

4) A body moves s metres in t seconds, where $s = \frac{1}{t^2}$. Find the velocity and acceleration after 3 seconds.

5) The distance s metres travelled by a falling body starting from rest after a time t seconds is given by $s = 5t^2$. Find its velocity after 1 second and after 3 seconds.

6) The distance s metres moved by the end of a lever after a time t seconds is given by the formula $s = 6t^2$. Find the velocity of the end of the lever when it has moved a distance $\frac{1}{2}$ metre.

7) The angular displacement θ radians of the spoke of a wheel is given by the expression $\theta = \frac{1}{2}t^4 - t^3$ where t seconds is the time. Find:

(a) the angular velocity after 2 seconds,

(b) the angular acceleration after 3 seconds,

(c) when the angular acceleration is zero.

8) An angular displacement θ radians in time t seconds is given by the equation $\theta = \sin 3t$. Find:

(a) the angular velocity when $t = 1$ second,

(b) the smallest positive value of t for which the angular velocity is 2 rad/s,

(c) the angular acceleration when $t = 0.5$ seconds,

(d) the smallest positive value of t for which the angular acceleration is $9\ \text{rad/s}^2$.

9) A mass of 5000 kg moves along a straight line so that the distance s metres travelled in a time t seconds is given by $s = 3t^2 + 2t + 3$. If v m/s is its velocity and m kg is its mass, then its kinetic energy is given by the formula $\frac{1}{2}mv^2$. Find its kinetic energy at a time $t = 0.5$ seconds, remembering that the joule (J) is the unit of energy.

18 Integration

The reverse of differentiation – indefinite integration and constants – definite integration and limits – determination of areas under graphs

INTEGRATION

One way to approach integration is to think of it as the reverse of differentiation – the rules we develop will be 'backwards' versions of those we used for differentiation. However, the basic idea comes from areas, whereas for differentiation it came from gradients.

If we draw a graph of force against distance moved, then the area under the curve gives work done – as, for instance, from indicator diagrams when testing engines. Another application is the area under a graph of torque against angle turned through for a spring – this could give us the energy stored.

There are a number of numerical methods for finding areas – the simplest maybe, but one of the best, is by counting the squares on the graph paper. But sometimes we are lucky enough to know the equation of the graph and then integration gives a speedy and accurate value of the area under the curve.

Integration as the Inverse of Differentiation

We have previously discovered how to obtain the differential coefficients of various functions. Our objective in this section is to find out how to reverse the process. That is, being given the differential coefficient of a function we try to discover the original function.

If $$y = \frac{x^4}{4}$$

then $$\frac{dy}{dx} = x^3$$

or we may write $$dy = x^3\,dx$$

The expression $x^3\,dx$ is called the differential of $\frac{x^4}{4}$.

Reversing the process of differentiation is called *integration*. It is indicated by using the integration sign $\int$ in front of the differential.

Thus if $\quad \mathrm{d}y = x^3\,\mathrm{d}x$

then reversing the process $\quad y = \int x^3\,\mathrm{d}x = \frac{x^4}{4}$

Similarly if $\quad y = \frac{x^5}{5}$

then $\quad \frac{\mathrm{d}y}{\mathrm{d}x} = x^4$

or $\quad \mathrm{d}y = x^4\,\mathrm{d}x$

and reversing the process $\quad y = \int x^4\,\mathrm{d}x = \frac{x^5}{5}$

Also, if $\quad y = \frac{x^{n+1}}{n+1}$

then $\quad \frac{\mathrm{d}y}{\mathrm{d}x} = x^n$

or $\quad \mathrm{d}y = x^n\,\mathrm{d}x$

from which $\quad y = \int x^n\,\mathrm{d}x = \frac{x^{n+1}}{n+1}$

Now $\quad \frac{x^{n+1}}{n} + 1$ is called the integral of $x^n\,\mathrm{d}x$

$$\boxed{\int x^n\,\mathrm{d}x = \frac{x^{n+1}}{n+1}}$$

Remember **'increase the index by one, and then divide by the new index'**

This rule applies to all indices whether positive, negative or fractional except for $\int x^{-1}\,\mathrm{d}x = \int \frac{1}{x}\,\mathrm{d}x$ because since $\frac{\mathrm{d}}{\mathrm{d}x}(\log_e x) = \frac{1}{x}$ the reverse of this gives:

$$\boxed{\int \frac{1}{x}\,\mathrm{d}x = \log_e x}$$

Since $\frac{\mathrm{d}}{\mathrm{d}t}\sin(\omega t + \alpha) = \omega\cos(\omega t + \alpha)$ the reverse of this gives:

$$\boxed{\int \cos(\omega t + \alpha)\,\mathrm{d}t = \frac{1}{\omega}\sin(\omega t + \alpha)}$$

Similarly

$$\boxed{\int \sin(\omega t + \alpha)\,\mathrm{d}t = -\frac{1}{\omega}\cos(\omega t + \alpha)}$$

Since $\dfrac{d}{dx} e^{ax} = ae^{ax}$ the reverse of this gives:

$$\int e^{ax}\,dx = \frac{1}{a}e^{ax}$$

Summarising:

$$\int x^n\,dx = \frac{x^{n+1}}{n+1}$$

$$\int \cos(\omega t + \alpha)\,dt = \frac{1}{\omega}\sin(\omega t + \alpha)$$

$$\int \sin(\omega t + \alpha)\,dt = -\frac{1}{\omega}\cos(\omega t + \alpha)$$

$$\int \frac{1}{x}\,dx = \log_e x$$

$$\int e^{ax}\,dx = \frac{1}{a}e^{ax}$$

The Constant of Integration

We know that the differential of $\frac{1}{2}x^2$ is $x\,dx$. Therefore if we are asked to integrate $x\,dx$, $\frac{1}{2}x^2$ is one answer; but it is not the only possible answer because $\frac{1}{2}x^2 + 2$, $\frac{1}{2}x^2 + 5$, $\frac{1}{2}x^2 + 19$ etc. are all expressions whose differential is $x\,dx$. The general expression for $\int x\,dx$ is therefore $\frac{1}{2}x^2 + c$, where c is a constant, known as the constant of integration. Each time we integrate, the constant of integration must be added.

EXAMPLE 18.1

a) $\displaystyle\int x^5\,dx = \frac{x^{5+1}}{5+1} + c = \frac{x^6}{6} + c$

b) $\displaystyle\int \sqrt{x}\,dx = x^{\frac{1}{2}}\,dx = \frac{x^{3/2}}{3/2} + c = \frac{2x^{3/2}}{3/2} + c$

c) $\displaystyle\int \frac{dx}{x^3} = \int x^{-3}\,dx = \frac{x^{-2}}{-2} + c = -\frac{1}{2x^2} + c$

d) $\displaystyle\int \cos 3\theta\,d\theta = \tfrac{1}{3}(\sin 3\theta) + c$

A constant coefficient may be taken outside the integral sign

EXAMPLE 18.2

a) $\int 6e^{2x}\,dx = 6\int e^{2x}\,dx = 6(\tfrac{1}{2}e^{2x}) + c = 3e^{2x} + c$

b) $\int 4\sin\theta\,d\theta = 4\int \sin\theta\,d\theta = 4(-\cos\theta) + c = -4\cos\theta + c$

The integral of a sum is the sum of their separate integrals

EXAMPLE 18.3

Integrate each term separately. One constant suffices for all terms.

a) $\int (x^2 + x)\,dx = \int x^2\,dx + \int x\,dx = \dfrac{x^3}{3} + \dfrac{x^2}{2} + c$

b) $\int \left(\dfrac{1}{x} + 7\right)dx = (\log_e x) + 7x + c$

c) $\int (3\sin t - 5\cos t)\,dt = -3\cos t - 5\sin t + c$

d) $\int (e^{4u} + e^{-4u})\,du = \dfrac{1}{4}e^{4u} + \dfrac{1}{(-4)}e^{-4u} + c = \dfrac{1}{4}e^{4u} - \dfrac{1}{4}e^{-4u} + c$

Exercise 18.1

Integrate with respect to the variable in each example.

1) x^2

2) $\sin\theta$

3) $\sqrt{x}$

4) $\dfrac{1}{x^2}$

5) $\dfrac{1}{x}$

6) e^{8t}

7) $3\cos 2\theta$

8) $5x^8 + e^x$

9) $\dfrac{1}{x} + x + 3$

10) $2\cos\theta - \sin 3\theta$

11) $6 + 5x + \dfrac{1}{\sqrt{x}} + \dfrac{2}{x^2}$

12) $10 + \tfrac{1}{2}(e^{5u} + e^{-5u})$

Evaluating the Constant of Integration

The value of the constant of integration may be found provided a corresponding pair of values of x and y are known, as shown in the following example.

EXAMPLE 18.4

The gradient of the curve which passes through the point $(2, 3)$ is given by x^2. Find the equation of the curve.

We are given $\dfrac{dy}{dx} = x^2$

$\therefore$ $y = \int x^2\,dx$

From which $y = \dfrac{x^3}{3} + c$

Substituting $x = 2$ when $y = 3$ then $3 = \dfrac{2^3}{3} + c \quad \therefore \quad c = \dfrac{1}{3}$

Hence the equation of the curve is $y = \dfrac{x^3}{3} + \dfrac{1}{3}$

or $y = \frac{1}{3}(x^3 + 1)$

Exercise 18.2

1) The gradient of the curve which passes through the point $(2, 3)$ is given by x. Find the equation of the curve.

2) The gradient of the curve which passes through the point $(3, 8)$ is given by $(x^2 + 3)$. Find the value of y when $x = 5$.

3) It is known that for a certain curve $\dfrac{dy}{dx} = 3 - 2x$ and the curve cuts the x-axis where $x = 5$. Express y in terms of x. State the length of the intercept on the y-axis.

4) Find the equation of the curve which passes through the point $(1, 4)$ and is such that $\dfrac{ds}{dt} = e^{3t}$.

5) If $\dfrac{dp}{dt} = \dfrac{1}{t}$ find p in terms of t given that $p = 3$ when $t = 2$.

6) The gradient of a curve is $ax + b$ at all points, where a and b are constants. Find the equation of the curve given that it passes through the points $(0, 4)$ and $(1, 3)$ and that the tangent at $(1, 3)$ is parallel to the x-axis.

7) Find the equation of the curve which passes through the point $(1, 2)$ and has the property of $\dfrac{dy}{dx} = \cos x$.

8) A curve is such that $\dfrac{dy}{d\theta} = \cos\theta$. Find the equation of the curve if we know that $y = 1$ when $\theta = \dfrac{\pi}{2}$ radians.

9) At any point on a curve $\dfrac{dy}{d\theta} = 3\sin\theta$. Find the equation of the curve given that $y = 2$ when θ has a value equivalent to 25 degrees.

The Definite Integral

It has been shown that $\displaystyle\int x^n\,dx = \frac{x^{n+1}}{n+1} + c$.

Since the expression contains an arbitrary constant c, the value of which is not known, it is called an indefinite integral.

A definite integral has a specific numerical answer without an unknown constant. The notation for this definite integral is $\displaystyle\int_a^b x^n\,dx$.

a and b are called limits, a being the lower limit and b the upper limit.

The method of evaluating a definite integral is shown in the following examples.

EXAMPLE 18.5

Find the value of $\displaystyle\int_2^3 x^2\,dx$

$$\int_2^3 x^2\,dx = \left[\frac{x^3}{3} + c\right]_2^3$$

$$= \left(\text{value of } \frac{x^3}{3} + c \text{ when } x \text{ is put equal to } 3\right)$$

$$- \left(\text{value of } \frac{x^3}{3} + c \text{ when } x \text{ is put equal to } 2\right)$$

$$= \left(\frac{3^3}{3} + c\right) - \left(\frac{2^3}{3} + c\right) = \frac{27}{3} + c - \frac{8}{3} - c$$

$$= \frac{19}{3} = 6.33$$

Square Brackets in Integration

In integration, the use of the square brackets, as in the above solution has a specific meaning. That is **'the integration of each term has been completed and the next step is to substitute the values of the limits for x'.** The square brackets must *not* be used again when finding the value of the integral.

We should also note that the constant c cancelled out. This will always happen and in solving definite integrals it is usual to omit c as shown in the next example.

EXAMPLE 18.6

Find the value of $\int_1^2 (3x^2 - 2x + 5)\,dx$

$$\begin{aligned}\int_1^2 (3x^2 - 2x + 5)\,dx &= [x^3 - x^2 + 5x]_1^2 \\ &= (2^3 - 2^2 + 5 \times 2) - (1^3 - 1^2 + 5 \times 1) \\ &= 14 - 5 = 9\end{aligned}$$

EXAMPLE 18.7

Find the value of $\int_0^{\pi/2} \sin\theta\,d\theta$

$$\begin{aligned}\int_0^{\pi/2} \sin\theta\,d\theta &= [-\cos\theta]_0^{\pi/2} \\ &= \left(-\cos\frac{\pi}{2}\right) - (-\cos 0) \\ &= 0 - (-1) = 1\end{aligned}$$

Exercise 18.3

1) $\int_1^2 x^2\,dx$

2) $\int_2^3 (2x + 3)\,dx$

3) $\int_3^5 \frac{1}{v}\,dv$

4) $\int_0^{\pi} (3\cos\theta)\,d\theta$

5) $\int_1^2 (7 + e^{2t})\,dt$

6) $\int_0^2 \sqrt{x}\,dx$

AREA UNDER A GRAPH

The application of integration to the finding of areas under graphs is extremely important in technology.

You may have already met some instances in engineering where it was necessary to calculate areas under graphs, and we had to use area rules which gave approximate results.

Now, providing we have the equation of a graph, we may find the area underneath the graph using integration and obtain a much more accurate value, and in a much shorter time.

Suppose that we wish to find the shaded area shown in Fig. 18.1. P is a point on the curve whose coordinates are (x, y).

Let us now draw, below P, a vertical strip whose width δx is very small. Since the width of the strip is very small we may consider the strip to be a rectangle with height y. Hence the area of the strip is approximately $(y \times \delta x)$. Such a strip is called an elementary strip and we will consider that the shaded area is made up from many elementary strips. Hence the required area is the sum of all the elementary strip areas between the values $x = a$ and $x = b$. In mathematical notation this may be stated as

$$\text{Area} = \sum_{x=a}^{x=b} y\,\delta x \quad \text{approximately}$$

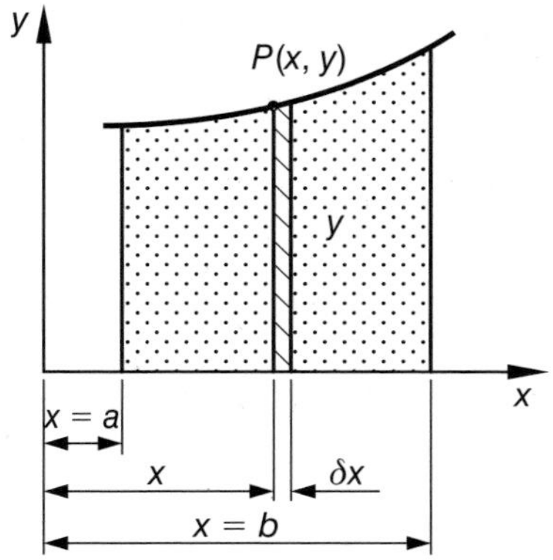

Fig. 18.1

The process of integration may be considered to sum up an infinite number of elementary strips and hence gives an exact result.

$$\text{Area} = \int_a^b y\,dx \quad \text{exactly}$$

EXAMPLE 18.8

Find the area bounded by the curve $y = x^3 + 3$, the x-axis and the lines $x = 1$ and $x = 3$.

It is always wise to sketch the graph of a given curve and show the area required together with an elementary strip, as shown in Fig. 18.2.

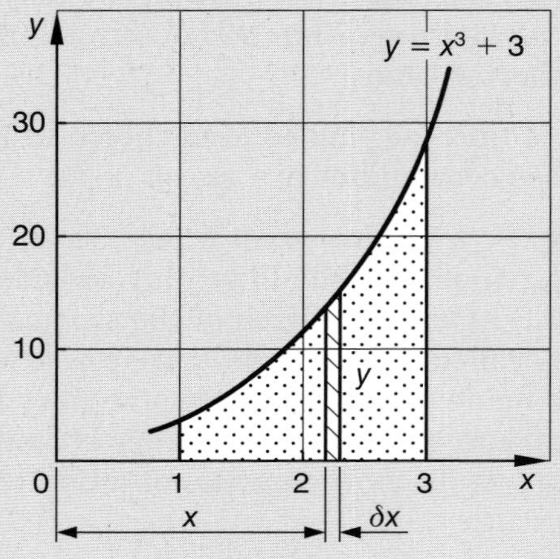

Fig. 18.2

$$\text{Required area} = \sum_{x=1}^{x=3} y\,\delta x \quad \text{approx.}$$

$$= \int_1^3 y\,\mathrm{d}x \quad \text{exactly}$$

$$= \int_1^3 (x^3 + 3)\,\mathrm{d}x$$

$$= \left[\frac{x^4}{4} + 3x\right]_1^3$$

$$= \left\{\frac{3^4}{4} + 3 \times 3\right\} - \left\{\frac{1^4}{4} + 3 \times 1\right\}$$

$$= 26 \text{ square units}$$

We may get a rough check of the result by looking at the graph. The area approximates to a right angled triangle of base length 2 units and height 30 units which has an area $= \frac{1}{2} \times 2 \times 30 = 30$ square units. This shows the result is of the right order.

EXAMPLE 18.9

A voltage is given by $v = R \sin \theta$. What will be its mean value over a half wave?

The mean value is given by the area under a graph divided by the length of the base of the area.

Now a complete cycle, or full wave as it is sometimes called, of a sine waveform occurs over a range of 0° to 360° (or 0 to 2π radians), so a half wave goes from $\theta = 0$ rad to $\theta = \pi$ rad. If you sketch the graph it will be as shown in Fig. 18.3.

Area of elementary strip

$$= v\,\delta\theta$$

Total area under curve

$$= \sum_{\theta=0}^{\theta=\pi} v\,\delta\theta \quad \text{approx.}$$

$$= \int_0^{\pi} v\,\mathrm{d}\theta \quad \text{exactly}$$

$$= \int_0^{\pi} R \sin\theta\,\mathrm{d}\theta$$

$$= R\int_0^{\pi} \sin\theta\,\mathrm{d}\theta$$

$$= R[-\cos\theta]_0^{\pi}$$

$$= R\{(-\cos\pi) - (-\cos 0)\}$$

$$= R\{-(-1) - (-1)\}$$

$$= 2R \text{ square units}$$

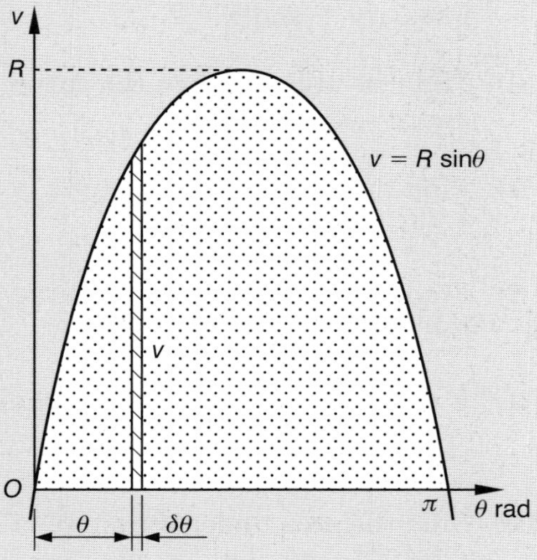

Fig. 18.3

$$\left.\begin{array}{l}\text{Mean}\\ \text{value}\end{array}\right\} = \frac{\text{Area under curve}}{\text{Length of base}}$$

$$= \frac{2R}{\pi} = 0.637R$$

So the mean value of a sine waveform over half a cycle is 0.637 times the amplitude – an important result.

Again for a rough check of the area value we may look at the graph. The area seems to occupy about $\frac{2}{3}$ of the 'surrounding rectangle' which has base length π and height R giving a result $\frac{2}{3} \times \pi \times R$ or $2.1R$ square units.

Exercise 18.4

Don't forget to sketch the graph in each case so that you will have some idea of the required area.

1) Find the area between the curve $y = x^3$, the x-axis and the lines $x = 5$ and $x = 3$.

2) Find the area between the curve $z = 3 + 2x + 3x^2$, the x-axis and the lines $x = 1$ and $x = 4$.

3) Find the area between the curve $y = x^2(2x - 1)$, the x-axis and the lines $x = 1$ and $x = 2$.

4) Find the area between the curve $y = \dfrac{1}{x^2}$, the x-axis and the lines $x = 1$ and $x = 3$.

5) Find the area between the curve $y = 5x - x^3$, the x-axis and the lines $x = 1$ and $x = 2$.

6) Find the area between the curve $y = \dfrac{1}{x}$, the x-axis and lines $x = 1$ and $x = 4$.

7) Find the area under the curve $y = e^x$ between the co-ordinates $x = 0$ and $x = 2$.

8) Find the area between the curve $y = 3e^{-2x}$, the x- and y-axes and the line $x = -1$.

9) Evaluate the integral and explain the result with reference to a sketched $\int_0^{2\pi} \sin\theta \, d\theta$ graph.

10) Find the area under the curve of $2\cos\theta$ between $\theta = 20°$ and $\theta = 60°$.

11) Find the area under the curve $2\sin\theta + 3\cos\theta$ between $\theta = 0$ and $\theta = \pi$ radians.

12) The velocity of an automatic chuck for moving the wire through a nail-making machine may be found from the expression $v = 0.1t(1 - t)$ where v is the velocity in m s^{-1} and t is the time in seconds. You have been asked to calculate the distance moved by the chuck between the two times when the velocity is zero.

Information: the area under a velocity–time graph gives the distance travelled. Sketch the graph, set up an integral and you are on your way!

Answers to Exercises

Exercise 1.1

1) 24.865 8, 24.87, 25
2) 0.008 357, 0.00 836, 0.0084
3) 4.978 5, 4.98, 5
4) 22
5) 35.60
6) 28.388 000, 28.000 000
7) 4.1498, 4.150, 4.15
8) 9.2
9) **(a)** 2.138 9
(b) 2.139
(c) 2.14
10) **(a)** 25.17 **(b)** 25.2
11) **(a)** 0.003 99 **(b)** 0.004 0
(c) 0.004
12) **(a)** 7.204 **(b)** 7.20 **(c)** 7.2
13) **(a)** 0.726 **(b)** 0.73

Exercise 1.2

1) 64.5, 63.5, 0.781%
2) 2474, 2464, 0.203%
3) 3.075, 3.065, 0.163%
4) 0.65, 0.55, 8.33%
5) 29.95, 28.85, 0.55
6) 1.315, 1.205, 0.055
7) 2.80, 2.60, 0.1
8) 0.7515, 0.7405, 0.0055
9) 39.07 ± 0.005,
0.005, 0.013%
10) 0.372 ± 0.0005,
1.238 ± 0.0005,
3.222, 3.218,
0.002, 0.0621%
11) 0.553, 0.844%
12) 7.00 ± 0.005,
0.005, 0.0714%
13) 12.015, 11.985,
0.015, 0.125%

Exercise 2.1

1) 13.1
2) −11.35
3) 27.4
4) 0.001 49
5) 1.94
6) −4.26
7) 1.28
8) 18.7
9) −2.52
10) 527
11) −22.8
12) −22.8
13) 0.007 6
14) −0.348
15) 0.66
16) 0.55
17) −4.1
18) 4.0
19) 6.6
20) 0.001 30

Exercise 2.2

1) 470
2) 3.22
3) 20
4) 150
5) $337\,000\ \text{mm}^2$
6) 63
7) 1.92×10^8
8) 1.2
9) 9.2
10) 70.3
11) 55.8°
12) 74
13) 50
14) 2.11×10^{-3}
15) 6.54×10^{-6}
16) 4.24 A
17) 2.37
18) **(a)** 72.4 **(b)** 3.22
(c) 244 **(d)** 10.7

Exercise 3.1

1) 8 km
2) 15 Mg
3) 3.8 Mm
4) 1.8 Gg
5) 7 mm
6) 1.3 μm
7) 28 g
8) 360 mm
9) 64 mg
10) 3.6 mA

Exercise 3.2

1) 0.45 V
2) (a) 2 kN (b) 4 ms^{-2}
3) 30 kJ
4) 60 kW
5) 2 kW
6) 0.111 MJ
7) 147 kJ, 4.9 kW

Exercise 3.3

1) 805
2) 54.9
3) 0.391
4) 0.227
5) 44.0
6) 1270
7) 49.2
8) 23.01 ± 0.03 mm
9) 0.110, 0.020 9, 0.000 492
10) (a) 24.1 (b) 683 (c) 0.683
11) 0.011
12) (a) 88.0 (b) 26.8 (c) 96.6
13) 42.5

Exercise 4.1

1) $9x + 6y$
2) $10p - 15q$
3) $-a + 2b$
4) $-4x - 12$
5) $2k^2 - 10k$
6) $-9xy - 12y$
7) $ap - aq - ar$
8) $4abxy - 4acxy + 4dxy$
9) $3x^4 - 6x^3y + 3x^2y^2$
10) $-14P^3 + 7P^2 - 7P$
11) $2m - 6m^2 + 4mm$
12) $x + 7$
13) $16 - 17x$
14) $7x - 11y$
15) $\frac{7y}{6} - \frac{3}{2}$
16) $-8a - 11b + 11c$
17) $3a - 9b$
18) $-x^3 + 18x^2 - 9x - 15$

Exercise 4.2

1) $x^2 + 9x + 20$
2) $2x^2 + 11x + 15$
3) $6x^2 + 16x + 8$
4) $10x^2 + 17x + 3$
5) $21x^2 + 41x + 10$
6) $x^2 - 4x + 3$
7) $x^2 + 2x - 3$
8) $x^2 + 5x - 14$
9) $x^2 - 2x - 15$
10) $2x^2 + x - 10$
11) $6x^2 + x - 15$
12) $12x^2 + 4x - 21$
13) $2p^2 - 7pq + 3q^2$
14) $6v^2 - 5uv - 6u^2$
15) $6a^2 + ab - b^2$
16) $x^2 + 2x + 1$
17) $4x^2 + 12x + 9$
18) $9x^2 + 42x + 49$
19) $x^2 - 2x + 1$
20) $4x^2 - 12x + 9$
21) $x^2 + 2xy + y^2$
22) $P^2 + 6PQ + 9Q^2$
23) $9x^2 - 24xy + 16y^2$
24) $4x^2 - y^2$
25) $4m^2 - 9n^2$
26) $x^4 - y^2$
27) $x^3 + 2x^2 - 5x - 6$
28) $2x^3 - 3x^2 - 11x + 6$
29) $x^3 - 3x - 2$
30) $x^4 - 1$
31) $x^3 + (a + b + c)x^2 + (ab + bc + ca)x + abc$

Exercise 4.3

1) p^2q
2) ab^2
3) $3mn$
4) b
5) $3xyz$
6) $2(x + 3)$
7) $4(x - y)$
8) $5(x - 1)$
9) $4x(1 - 2y)$
10) $m(x - y)$
11) $x(a + b + c)$
12) $\frac{1}{2}\left(x - \frac{y}{4}\right)$
13) $5(a - 2b + 3c)$
14) $ax(x + 1)$
15) $\pi r(2r + h)$
16) $3y(1 - 3y)$
17) $ab(b^2 - a)$
18) $xy(xy - a + by)$
19) $5x(x^2 - 2xy + 3y^2)$

20) $3xy(3x^2 - 2xy + y^4)$
21) $I_0(1 + at)$
22) $\frac{1}{3}\left(x - \frac{y}{2} + \frac{z}{3}\right)$
23) $a(2a - 3b) + b^2$
24) $x(x^2 - x + 7)$
25) $\frac{m^2}{pn}\left(1 - \frac{m}{n} + \frac{m^2}{pn}\right)$

Exercise 4.4

1) $(x + y)(a + b)$
2) $(p - q)(m + n)$
3) $(ac + d)^2$
4) $(2p + q)(r - 2s)$
5) $2(a - b)(2x + 3y)$
6) $(x^2 + y^2)(ab - cd)$
7) $(mn - pq)(3x - 1)$
8) $(k^2l - mn)(l - 1)$

Exercise 4.5

1) $(x + 1)(x + 3)$
2) $(x + 2)(x + 4)$
3) $(x - 1)(x - 2)$
4) $(x + 5)(x - 3)$
5) $(x + 7)(x - 1)$
6) $(x + 2)(x - 7)$
7) $(x + y)(x - 3y)$
8) $(2x + 3)(x + 5)$
9) $(p + 1)(3p - 2)$
10) $(2x + 1)(2x - 6)$
11) $(m + 2)(3m - 14)$
12) $(3x + 1)(7x + 10)$
13) $(2a + 5)(5a - 3)$
14) $(2x + 5)(3x - 7)$
15) $(2p + 3q)(3q - p)$
16) $(4x + y)(3x - 2y)$
17) $(x + y)^2$
18) $(2x + 3)^2$
19) $(p + 2q)^2$
20) $(3x + 1)^2$
21) $(m - n)^2$
22) $(5x - 2)^2$
23) $(x - 2)^2$
24) $(m + n)(m - n)$
25) $(2x + y)(2x - y)$
26) $(3p + 2q)(3p - 2q)$
27) $(x + 1/3)(x - 1/3)$
28) $(1 + b)(1 - b)$
29) $(1/x + 1/y)(1/x - 1/y)$
30) $(11p + 8q)(11p - 8q)$

Exercise 4.6

1) $6a^2$
2) $2x^2y$
3) m^2n^2
4) $2abc^2$
5) $2(x + 1)$
6) $x^2(a + b)^2$
7) $(a + b)(a - b)$
8) $x(1 - x)(x + 1)$

Exercise 4.7

1) $\frac{1}{ab}$
2) $\frac{a}{b}$
3) $\frac{x^2}{y^2}$
4) $\frac{xy}{2}$
5) $\frac{1}{ab}$
6) $c(a + b)$
7) $1 - x^2$
8) $\frac{c}{(a - b)^2}$
9) $\frac{x + y}{xy}$
10) $\frac{a + 1}{a}$
11) $\frac{m - n}{n}$
12) $\frac{b - c^2}{c}$
13) $\frac{ad - bc}{bd}$
14) $\frac{ac - 1}{bc}$
15) $\frac{1 + y + xy}{xy}$
16) $\frac{12 + x^2}{4x}$
17) $\frac{3de + 2ce - 5cd}{cde}$
18) $\frac{ad + cb + bd}{bd}$

19) $\dfrac{2h - 5f - 3g}{6fgh}$

20) $\dfrac{4 - 2x}{x(x + 2)}$

21) $\dfrac{2}{2 - x}$

Exercise 4.8

1) $1 + \dfrac{b}{a}$

2) $\dfrac{1}{b} - \dfrac{1}{a}$

3) $\dfrac{1}{c} + 1$

4) $\dfrac{x}{2} + \dfrac{y}{2x}$

5) $\dfrac{a}{bc} - \dfrac{1}{c} + \dfrac{1}{b}$

6) $\dfrac{1}{(x - y)} + \dfrac{1}{x}$

Exercise 4.9

1) $\dfrac{x}{x + 1}$

2) $(x^2 - 1)$

3) $\dfrac{1}{a^2 - 1}$

4) $\dfrac{u}{1 - u}$

5) $x + y$

6) $\dfrac{R_1 R_2}{R_1 + R_2}$

Exercise 5.1

1) $m = 2$
2) $x = 5$
3) $m = 5$
4) $x = -29/5$
5) $x = -2$
6) $x = 45/8$
7) $x = -15$
8) $m = 15/28$
9) $t = 6$
10) $y = -70$
11) $x = 5/3$
12) $x = 13$
13) $u = 9/7$
14) $x = 3.5$
15) $v = 20$
16) $x = 4$
17) $i_1 = 9/7A$
18) $l = 48.75$ mm
19) $d = 300$ mm
20) $R_2 = 6\ \Omega$
21) $x = 4$
22) $R_1 = 2.85\ \Omega$

Exercise 5.2

1) 1, 2
2) 4, 5
3) 4, 1
4) 7, 3
5) $\frac{1}{2}$, $\frac{3}{4}$
6) 10, 7
7) 3, 2
8) 5, 2

Exercise 5.3

1) 0.2, 1.3, 3.7
2) £224, £168
3) £1.60, £0.80
4) 0.3, 0.2, 4.7
5) £0.50, £1.50
6) 9 and 7 g/cm^3
7) 19.0 m s^{-1}, 3.11 m s^{-2}
8) $i_1 = 7.16$, $i_2 = 5.23$
9) 24 Ω, 0.004 17

Exercise 6.1

1) $T = \dfrac{pV}{nR}$

2) $h = \dfrac{Hr}{R}$

3) $u = v - at$

4) $t = \dfrac{v - u}{a}$

5) $C = \frac{5}{9}(F - 32)$

6) $x = \dfrac{y - c}{m}$

7) $r = 1 - \dfrac{a}{S}$

8) $R = \dfrac{V}{I} - r$

9) $h = \dfrac{S}{\pi r} - r$

10) $T = \dfrac{H}{ws} + t$

11) $t = \dfrac{l - l_o}{\alpha l_o}$

12) (*a*) $S = \dfrac{n}{2}[2a + (n - 1)d]$

(*b*) $a = \dfrac{S}{n} - \dfrac{d}{2}(n - 1)$

13) $R_1 = \dfrac{R_2 R}{R_2 - R}$

14) $R_2 = \dfrac{R_1 R}{R_1 - R}$

Exercise 6.2

1) $h = \dfrac{v^2}{2g}$

2) $r = \sqrt{\dfrac{A}{\pi}}$

3) $v = \sqrt{\dfrac{2E}{m}}$

4) $A = \dfrac{\pi d^2}{4}$

5) $f = \sqrt{\dfrac{2EU}{V}}$

6) $c = \sqrt{a^2 - b^2}$

7) $l = \dfrac{g}{4f^2\pi^2}$

8) $M = \sqrt{T_e^2 - T^2}$

9) $C = \dfrac{\pi}{L}\sqrt{\dfrac{EI}{P}}$

10) $v = \sqrt{\dfrac{2}{m}(E_t - mgh)}$

11) $b = \sqrt{12k^2 - a^2}$

12) $L = \sqrt{12k^2 - 3R^2}$

13) $f = \dfrac{(D^2 + d^2)p}{D^2 - d^2}$

14) $P = \sqrt{4Q_e^2 - Q^2}$

15) $Q = \sqrt{P_e^2 - PP_e}$

Exercise 7.1

1) $x^2 - 4x + 3 = 0$
2) $x^2 + 2x - 8 = 0$
3) $x^2 + 3x + 2 = 0$
4) $x^2 - 2.3x + 1.12 = 0$
5) $x^2 - 1.07x - 4.53 = 0$
6) $x^2 + 7.32x + 12.19 = 0$
7) $x^2 - 1.4x = 0$
8) $x^2 + 4.36x = 0$
9) $x^2 - 12.25 = 0$
10) $x^2 - 8x + 16 = 0$

Exercise 7.2

1) ± 6
2) ± 1.25
3) ± 1.33
4) -4 or -5
5) 8 or -9
6) 2 or $\frac{1}{3}$
7) 3 repeated
8) 4 or -8
9) $\frac{4}{7}$ or $\frac{3}{2}$
10) $\frac{7}{3}$ or $-\frac{4}{3}$
11) 1.175 or -0.425
12) $\frac{5}{6}$ or $\frac{1}{6}$
13) 0.573 or -2.907
14) 0.211 or -1.354
15) 1 or -0.2
16) 3.886 or -0.386
17) 0.956 or -1.256
18) 2.388 or 0.262
19) 0.44 or -3.775
20) 8.385 or -2.385
21) -0.225 or -1.775
22) 11.14 or -3.14
23) 1.303 or -2.303
24) ± 53.67
25) 5.24 or 0.76
26) -3.064 or -0.935

Exercise 7.3

1) 149.6
2) 92.4 mm
3) 65 mm × 95 mm
4) 40 mm
5) 0.685 or 23.3 mm
6) 30 or 72 mm
7) 54.6 mm
8) 50
9) 2.88 m
10) 94.6 × 94.6 mm
11) 2.41 and -0.41 s

Exercise 8.1

1) 2^{11}
2) a^8
3) n^3
4) 3^{11}
5) b^{-3}
6) 10^4
7) z^3
8) 3^{-4}
9) m^4
10) x^{-3}
11) 9^{12}
12) y^{-6}
13) t^8
14) c^{14}
15) a^{-9}
16) 7^{-12}
17) b^{10}
18) s^{-9}
19) 8
20) 1
21) 0.5
22) 8
23) 0.25
24) 100
25) 0.25
26) 1/7
27) 0.04
28) 3
29) 7
30) 25
31) 7
32) 3.375
33) 1/256

Exercise 8.2

1) 5
2) 2
3) 2
4) 2
5) 4
6) 125
7) 8
8) 27
9) 2
10) 4
11) 1/6
12) 0.125
13) 1/32
14) 64
15) 3

Exercise 8.3

1) $x^{1\backslash 2}$
2) $x^{4\backslash 5}$
3) $x^{-1/2}$
4) $x^{-1/3}$
5) $x^{-4/3}$
6) $x^{-3/2}$
7) $x^{2/3}$
8) $x^{0.075}$
9) $-x^{2/3}$
10) $x^{1/3}$
11) $x^{1/3}$
12) x
13) $a^{-13/6}$
14) $a^{-11/13}$
15) $x^{3.75}$
16) $b^{1/2}$
17) $m^{7/4}$
18) $z^{2.3}$
19) 1
20) $u^{-5/2}$
21) $y^{1/4}$
22) $n^{1/4}$
23) $x^{11/14}$
24) $t^{-2/3}$

Exercise 9.1

1) $\log_a n = x$
2) $\log_2 8 = 3$
3) $\log_5 0.04 = -2$
4) $\log_{10} 0.001 = -3$
5) $\log_x 1 = 0$
6) $\log_{10} 10 = 1$
7) $\log_a a = 1$
8) $\log_e 7.39 = 2$
9) $\log_{10} 1 = 0$
10) 3
11) 3
12) 4
13) 3
14) 9
15) 64
16) 100
17) 1
18) 2
19) 3
20) $\frac{1}{2}$
21) 1

Exercise 9.2

1) **(a)** $2 \log a + \log b$
(b) $\log a + 3 \log c - 4 \log b$
(c) $\log a + \log b - \log c - \log d$
2) **(a)** 1.324 **(b)** −1.079
(c) 1.544 **(d)** −1.108
3) **(a)** 15.80 **(b)** 1.094
(c) 0.031 43 **(d)** 0.5810
4) **(a)** 85.1 **(b)** 1.98
(c) 0.987 **(d)** 0.265
5) 2.485
6) 0.096 91
7) 3.466

Exercise 9.3

1) 2.08
2) 350
3) 0.795
4) 0.000 179
5) 0.267
6) 1.77
7) −7.38
8) −0.322
9) 4.63
10) 2.35
11) −2.28
12) −36.5
13) 22.2

Exercise 9.4

1) **(a)** 853 **(b)** 39.3 **(c)** 2.18
2) 0.003 57
3) 0.0164
4) 0.590
5) 25.7
6) 132
7) 4.44
8) 44.2
9) 0.005 49
10) 0.769

Exercise 10.1

1) $m = 1, c = 3, y = x + 3$
2) **(a)** $m = 1, c = 3$
(b) $m = -3, c = 4$
(c) $m = -3.1, c = -1.7$
(d) $m = 4.3, c = -2.5$
(e) infinite , none
(f) zero , 2.9
(g) $m = 1 , c = -4$
(h) $m = -0.5 , c = 1.5$
(j) $m = 0.556 , c = 0$

Exercise 10.2

1) $m = 2 , c = 1$
2) $a = 0.25 , b = 1.25$
3) $a = 0.29 , b = -1.0$
4) 529 N

Exercise 10.3

1) 524 N/m
2) 51 ohms
3) $P = 0.27d + 0.76$, 1.63 mm
4) $a = 0.03, b = 0$
5) $E = 0.0984\,W + 0.72$

Exercise 10.4

1) circle, centre at O, radius 3
2) rectangular hyperbola
3) logarithmic graph
4) typical cubic curve, a graph of an equation of the 3rd degree
5) ellipse or oval

Exercise 11.1

1) 8.8 mm
2) 0.0128 m^2
3) **(a)** 1200 mm^2
(b) 275 mm^2 **(c)** 260 mm^2
(d) 774 mm^2 **(e)** 1050 mm^2
4) **(a)** 892 mm^2 **(b)** 3060 mm^2
5) **(a)** 1380 mm^2 **(b)** 6500 mm^2
(c) 331 mm^2 **(d)** 1930 mm^2
6) 29.9 mm
7) 302 mm^2
8) 34.1 mm
9) 2592 mm^2
10) 909
11) 1910 mm

Exercise 11.2

1) 335 mm
2) 0.00875 m^3
3) 477 mm
4) 1.51 m^2
5) 19.9 ℓ
6) 75.4 mm
7) 5.33 m^3, 20.5 m^2
8) 0.437 m^3
9) **(a)** 0.366 m^3, **(b)** 0.583 m
10) 2.09 ℓ
11) 14 m^3, 22.9 m^2
12) 150 mm

Exercise 12.1

1) 38.39 mm
2) 32.5 mm
3) 20.4 mm
4) 37.9 mm

Exercise 12.2

1) 24.3
2) 58.2
3) 23.1
4) 121
5) 39.7
6) 255
7) 30.55°
8) 21.55°
9) 64.74°
10) 177 mm

Exercise 12.3

1) **(a)** 0.6109 **(b)** 1.457
(c) 0.3367 **(d)** 0.7620
2) **(a)** 9°55′25″
(b) 89°33′53″
(c) 4°29′11″
3) **(a)** 1.05 m
(b) 22.9 m
4) **(a)** 120° **(b)** 10.2°
5) 89.1 mm, 3120 mm
6) 866 mm^2
7) **(a)** 29.3 mm, 80.7 mm
(b) 104 mm^2
8) 163 mm^2
9) 369 mm, 20 600 mm^2

Exercise 13.1

1) **(a)** C = 71°,
b = 59.0 mm,
c = 99.8 mm
(b) A = 48°,
a = 71.5 mm
c = 84.2 mm
2) **(a)** c = 10.1 mm,
A = 50.2°
B = 69.8°
(b) a = 11.8 mm.
B = 44.7°,
C = 79.3°
3) 64.00 mm
4) 37.6°
5) 40.5°
6) 41.4°
7) **(a)** 14.2 m **(b)** 142.6°
8) AB = 60.2, AC = 33.0
9) 21.2 A
10) 13.4, 14.9°
11) 18.6 A

Exercise 13.2

1) 0.121 m^2
2) 2765 mm each side
3) 540 m^2
4) 738 mm^2
5) 0.420 kg
6) 12.6 mm

Exercise 14.1

1) 1.897
2) 3.025
3) −0.28
4) $-\frac{4}{5}, -\frac{3}{4}$
5) 8.23, 171.77°
6) 153.21°, 206.79°
7) **(a)** 45.54°, 134.46°
(b) 118.77°
(c) 43.46° **(d)** 119.55°
8) **(a)** 232.00° and 308.00°
(b) 304.00°
(c) 289.00°
9) 14.57°, 165.43°

Exercise 14.2

No answers

Exercise 15.1

1) Discrete (a), (e)
5) 3 Ω
7) 0.3 N/mm^2

Exercise 16.1

1) 5
2) no mode
3) 3, 5 and 8
4) 121.96 Ω
5) 18.4272 mm
6) 5
7) 84
8) £233
9) Mean = 15.09 Ω
Median = 15.76 Ω
10) 118.1, 117.2, 119.1 Ω
11) 20.063, 20.095, 20.115 mm

12) 109.095 mm
13) 23.87 kg
14) 9.65 m
15) 19.97 kN

Exercise 16.2

1) 10.81%, 1.2782%
2) 11.4925 N/mm^2
0.01452 N/mm^2
3) 99.93 W, 0.17 W
4) 12.67, 2.98
5) 43.05, 4.965 gallons
6) (a) 18.54 mm and 18.66 mm
(b) (i) 16% (ii) 2%
7) 1920
8) $\bar{x} = 10.0000$, $\sigma = 0.0128$ mm
(a) 1400 (b) 9800

Exercise 17.1

1) −4, 8
2) 3
3) 2

Exercise 17.2

1) $2x$
2) $7x^6$
3) $12x^2$
4) $30x^4$
5) $1.5t^2$
6) $2\pi R$
7) $\frac{1}{2}x^{-1/2}$
8) $6x^{1/2}$
9) $x^{-1/2}$
10) $2x^{-1/3}$
11) $-2x^{-3}$
12) $-x^{-2}$
13) $-\frac{3}{5}x^{-2}$
14) $-6x^{-4}$
15) $-\frac{1}{2}x^{-3/2}$
16) $-\frac{1}{3}x^{-3/2}$
17) $-\frac{15}{2}x^{-5/2}$
18) $\frac{3}{10}t^{-1/2}$
19) $-0.01h^{-2}$
20) $-35x^{-8}$
21) $8x - 3$
22) $9t^2 - 4t + 5$
23) $4u - 1$
24) $20x^3 - 21x^2 + 6x - 2$
25) $35t^4 - 6t$
26) $\frac{1}{2}x^{-1/2} + \frac{5}{2}x^{3/2}$
27) $-3x^{-2} + 1$
28) $\frac{1}{2}x^{-1/2} - \frac{1}{2}x^{-3/2}$
29) $3x^2 - \frac{3}{2}x^{-3/2}$
30) $1.3t^{0.3} + 0.575t^{-3.3}$
31) $\frac{9}{5}x^2 - \frac{4}{7}x + \frac{1}{2}x^{-1/2}$
32) $-0.01x^{-2}$
33) $4.65x^{0.5} - 1.44x^{-0.4}$
34) $\frac{3}{2}x^2 + 5x^{-2}$
35) $-6 + 14t - 6t^2$
36) −5, 19
37) 39.5, 5, 17
38) 2.5, 2, 1

Exercise 17.3

1) $2\cos 2\theta - 5\sin 5\theta$
2) $4\cos(4t + \pi)$
3) $-7\sin\left(7t - \dfrac{3\pi}{2}\right)$
4) $\dfrac{1}{x}$
5) $-\dfrac{1}{x}$
6) $\dfrac{2}{x}$
7) $3e^{3u} + 3e^{-3u}$
8) $-30e^{5v}$

Exercise 17.4

1) 42 m/s
2) 6 m/s^2
3) (a) 6 m/s
(b) 2.41 or −0.41 s
(c) 6 m/s^2 (d) 1 s
4) −0.074 m/s, 0.074 m/s^2
5) 10 m/s, 30 m/s
6) 3.46 m/s
7) (a) 4 rad/s (b) 36 rad/s^2
(c) 0 s or 1 s
8) (a) −2.97 rad/s
(b) 0.280 s
(c) −8.98 rad/s^2
(d) 1.57 s
9) 62.5 kJ

Exercise 18.1

1) $\frac{1}{3}x^3 + c$
2) $-\cos\theta + c$
3) $\frac{2}{3}x^{3/2} + c$

4) $-\dfrac{1}{x}+c$
5) $(\log_e x)+c$
6) $\frac{1}{8}e^{8t}+c$
7) $\frac{3}{2}(\sin 2\theta)+c$
8) $\frac{5}{9}x^9+e^x+c$
9) $(\log_e x)+\frac{1}{2}x^2+3x+c$
10) $2\sin\theta+\frac{1}{3}\cos 3\theta+c$
11) $6x+\dfrac{5}{2}x^2+2x^{1/2}-\dfrac{2}{x}+c$
12) $10u+\frac{1}{10}(e^{5u}-e^{-5u})+c$

Exercise 18.2

1) $y=\dfrac{x^2}{2}+1$
2) 46.7
3) $y=10+3x-x^2$, 10
4) $y=\frac{1}{3}e^{3t}-2.70$
5) $p=\log_e t+2.31$
6) $y=x^2-2x+4$
7) $y=\sin x+1.16$
8) $y=\sin\theta$
9) $y=4.72-3\cos\theta$

Exercise 18.3

1) 2.33
2) 8
3) 0.511
4) 0
5) 30.6
6) 1.89

Exercise 18.4

1) 136
2) 87
3) 5.167
4) 0.667
5) 3.75
6) 1.386
7) 6.389
8) 9.584
9) zero
10) 1.048
11) 4
12) 16.7 mm

Index